The Sandemanian Story

The Social and Religious Context of a Scottish Non-Presbyterian Dissenting Community

Derek B. Murray

Foreword by David W. Bebbington

☙PICKWICK *Publications* · Eugene, Oregon

THE SANDEMANIAN STORY
The Social and Religious Context of a Scottish Non-Presbyterian Dissenting Community

Pickwick Publications
An Imprint of Wipf and Stock Publishers
199 W. 8th Ave., Suite 3
Eugene, OR 97401

www.wipfandstock.com

PAPERBACK ISBN: 978-1-5326-1781-2
HARDCOVER ISBN: 978-1-4982-4280-6
EBOOK ISBN: 978-1-4982-4279-0

Cataloguing-in-Publication data:

Names: Murray, Derek Boyd [author]. | Bebbington, D. W. (David William), 1949– [foreword writer]

Title: The Sandemanian story : the social and religious context of a Scottish non-Presbyterian community / Derek B. Murray ; with a foreword by David W. Bebbington.

Description: Eugene, OR: Pickwick Publications, 2024 | Includes bibliographical references and index.

Identifiers: ISBN 978-1-5326-1781-2 (paperback) | ISBN 978-1-4982-4280-6 (hardcover) | ISBN 978-1-4982-4279-0 (ebook)

Subjects: LCSH: Sandemanianism. | Sandemanianism—History. | Glas, John, 1695–1773 | Faraday, Michael, 1791–1867 | Church history. | Scotland—Church history. | United States—Church history.

Classification: BX9747 M87 2024 (paperback) | BX9747 (ebook)

VERSION NUMBER 04/10/24

With thanksgiving to God for the gift of life, and
the ability to communicate in diverse ways.

And for all those whose love has made it possible for me
to say, with Joseph (according to Tyndale's translation)
'Truly, I am a lucky fellow'.

The Sandemanian Story

Contents

Foreword

THE SANDEMANIANS—OR GLASITES, FOR the names are interchangeable—
were a strange Christian body. Spreading from Scotland to England and
New England during the eighteenth century, they became extinct at the end
of the twentieth century. They insisted on distinctive practices that they
drew from the Bible. The Lord's Supper, presided over by more than one
elder, was observed every Sunday because there is a single reference in the
book of Acts to that being done by one of the earliest churches. In morning
worship congregations heard around six chapters of the Old Testament read
in their totality. In afternoon worship they heard three from the New Testament. In between the services there was a lovefeast, confined to members, at
which lunch was eaten and items from their own *Christian Songs* were sung.
Each congregation, which was responsible for its own affairs, had to reach
unanimity in decision making. There were times when members washed
each other's feet. Sandemanians had to refrain from eating blood, to avoid
any games of chance and to greet each other with a holy kiss—so that in
America they were nicknamed 'the Kissites'. They never attended worship of
other denominations for they believed they alone had succeeded in repro-
ducing the church pattern of the New Testament.

Likewise they adopted a doctrinal position that set them apart from
most other Christians. Although much of their theology consisted of the
Calvinism inherited from the Reformation, they maintained a specific understanding of the nature of faith. It consisted, according to their founder,
John Glas, of 'a persuasion of a thing upon a testimony'.[1] Faith, that is to
say, was no different from any other form of belief, not requiring the type
of anxious self-examination that Calvinists had normally required to discover if they were truly trusting in Christ. Faith was simple acceptance of
God's message in Scripture that he had raised his Son from the dead. The
affections had nothing to do with it. This Sandemanianism, as it came to be

---

1. Glas, *Works of Mr John Glas*, 142.

called, showed the influence of the age of reason in which it emerged. It was a rational account of the nature of faith, casting aside the elaborate analyses of feeling that had been so popular in the past. Although many believed it to be an inadequate representation of biblical teaching, Sandemanians claimed that it was the correct way to safeguard the Reformation principle that salvation is by faith alone.

The alternative names 'Glasite' and 'Sandemanian' reflect the two figures whose convictions remained normative for the movement over the years. John Glas (1695–1771) was originally a minister of the Church of Scotland who was troubled by the seventeenth-century covenants committing Scotland to the enforcement of Reformed religion by the civil power. In 1725 he published *The Testimony of the King of Martyrs*, which declared that Christ's kingdom was purely spiritual. Those submitting to his kingship should form gathered churches separate from any national church. Glas set up his own independent congregation, working out from the study of Scripture how it should be organised, and through extensive writing encouraged the creation of other local churches operating on the same lines. Glas's son-in-law Robert Sandeman (1718–1771) was the author of *Letters on Theron and Aspasio* (1757), a trenchant critique of a book of that title written by the Anglican clergyman James Hervey. Glas took Hervey and his fellow evangelicals to task for expecting assurance of salvation to accompany the embracing of true faith. Such 'popular preachers' obscured the true path of simple belief that led to heaven. Sandeman took his fierce polemic across the Atlantic, so launching his movement in New England. There and in England the term 'Sandemanian' was preferred whereas in Scotland 'Glasite' remained the normal designation. The movement included significant figures such as the scientist Michael Faraday in its ranks, but steadily declined during the nineteenth and twentieth centuries. Its last meeting house closed in Edinburgh in 1989.

The author of this study of the Sandemanians, Derek Murray (1936–2022), was a Scottish Baptist minister who served in several congregations, became a pioneer of hospice chaplaincy and taught church history at the denomination's college. He published several books and articles on Scottish Baptist history, was the long-term chairman of the Scottish Baptist History Project and from 2008 to 2011 acted as president of the Scottish Church History Society. As he explains towards the end of the book, Derek came to know a fellow student in Edinburgh who was a Sandemanian and discovered that even as a boy he had been loyal to the principles of his faith. The poor Sandemanian could not join in as his friends played Monopoly, believing that a game using dice was an affront to the Almighty's treatment of the lot as sacred. Later Derek found as he explored the history of Baptists in Scotland that Sandemanian principles had swayed the early members of the denomination, which explained why Scottish Baptists, by contrast with almost all other Baptists throughout the world, still normally observed the Lord's Supper every Sunday. He became enthralled by eighteenth-century Scottish Dissent, completing a St Andrews PhD dissertation on that subject in 1977. This volume is a further expression of his abiding fascination with the subject.

In this book there are the fruits of Derek's long-term exploration of the history of the Sandemanians. It is very much the result of his personal quest. He several times attended the final meeting house of the movement to remain open, sustaining friendship with the last of the elders at a time when, since he had no colleague in the eldership, the church could no longer hold the Lord's Supper. There is a certain poignancy in the experience, but Derek has been able to weave what he witnessed of the expiring days into the story. He has examined the writings of Glas and Sandeman in detail and tracked down many other primary sources that illuminate the various phases of the movement. Often he chooses to quote from the sources so as to bring out features of Sandemanian practice. Consequently he has been able to expound the theology of the movement and identify the full geographical range of its congregations, tracing their rise and fall over the centuries. He demonstrates that, although small in numbers, the Sandemanians included many capable individuals, especially in business and education. Derek also brings out the significance of the controversies that split congregations from one another and recounts the process of decline. He shows that growth did not come to the Sandemanians since they rejected evangelism outside the doors of their meeting houses, holding that the Almighty would bring in the elect without any activism on their part. Nevertheless he can point to their influence over other groups—Old Scots Independents, Bereans, Scotch Baptists, Haldaneites and Churches of Christ, who remain numerous in the United States—as an enduring contribution to the universal church. The Sandemanians may have ceased to meet, but something of their legacy lives on.

David W. Bebbington
University of Stirling
January 2023

Preface

I WAS IN MY early teens when my father took me to the place he kept disappearing to on a Sunday afternoon; the—to me—strange congregation that met up the road in Barony St, Edinburgh. He forgot to tell me that all the women would be wearing hats. They were graciousness itself in overlooking my bare-headedness. Even as a young child I had loved to be present in worship services, for they intrigued me—what was happening and why? But, even for such a nerd as myself, this one proved a hard test, in length, in lack of action and in the less than comfortable pews. But I remained touched by their welcome and refusal to make me uncomfortable about the hat thing (I had been made uncomfortable in various places at various times over this issue), and as I grew to understand them a little more, by their deep loyalty to their congregation coupled with a refusal to panic about falling numbers and a clearly seen imminent end. That God's kingdom was bigger than their movement was a conviction they held to, and the loss of their community, while sad for themselves was not felt as a failure of the work of God. This conviction, though none of the congregation probably realised they had conveyed it to me, has remained deeply important.

The story of the Glasites was a constant backdrop to my childhood and adolescence: 'Shh, Dad's working on his thesis'; 'why don't we go out to Loch Leven (a local nature reserve) and leave him in peace to work'; 'no, he's not coming on holiday for the first week, he's going to work on the thesis' And then the great day when he graduated, and we had a day out to St Andrews.

The publication of the thesis as a book was long talked of, but there were other things to do—other books to write, life to live, communities to minister to, a family to encourage, care for, be proud of. But eventually, thanks in no small part to David Bebbington, faithfully urging it over many years, and Robin Parry, providing a 'way in' in recent years, the thesis was rewritten, and updated, and supplemented by new research, personal reflection, other people's discoveries generously shared.

During the pandemic lockdown, Zoom conversations provided the family with time to talk together—and my apologies now to various members of the family for the way that comparing notes on our books (for I was trying to finish one too) rather dominated and filled our short times together. But the work on the text gave my father pleasure and satisfaction. The editing ready for printing less so, and was delayed and avoided, and loomed large.

And in 2022, he became ill and died. My last coherent conversation with him allowed me to give him a copy of the book I had been finishing during lockdown—and to promise that now that was done, and with that experience to hand, I would see to getting his script ready for handing over. I am sad that he didn't live long enough to see me do it. But it is done. And here it is. Those who read carefully will notice that some of the citations, especially of manuscripts, are incomplete. No research is ever finished; this is the sign of incompletion in this one. I did not have the resources to complete what he had left unfinished. If you need to follow up on the material, the archive in Dundee University has all this material, but you may need to search it out.

In the acknowledgements, he thanks all those—so many—who have helped to make this possible. Here, I want to add my thanks—to David Bebbington for encouraging it, and for writing the foreword; for the friends at Wipf and Stock for being so patient and encouraging as I have tried to do these last tasks; to Lorna, Ann and Paul, Alice and Amy, and Ian, who put up with our filling of the conversation with 'here's what I've been writing—what have you been doing?'

And to my father, for giving me courage to write, taking me places I wouldn't have gone, teaching me more than I will ever remember, and being himself. Thanks, Daddy.

Rev Dr Ruth Murray Gouldbourne

Acknowledgments

THIS BOOK HAS BEEN contemplated for a very long time and I have been indebted to many people. My first thanks must go to the later elders of the Edinburgh Glasite Church, Mr William Ferguson and Mr Gerard Sandeman, who welcomed me to their homes and shared knowledge and books with me. The Glasites were private folk and I was privileged to be treated so kindly. All who would understand the church are grateful to Dr Geoffrey Cantor for his works on Faraday and the wider Sandemanian Church. I was able long ago to welcome him to my home, and other visitors who have become friends include Dr Lynn McMillon of Oklahoma, Professor Dyron Doughrity of Pepperdine University, Professor David Mullan, lately of the University of Cape Breton. Dr Brian Bowers, formerly of the Science Museum in London, Dr Charles Waterston of Edinburgh, and Rev. Dr Douglas Somerset of Aberdeen have shared resources with me. Henry Stuart Fothringham, Esq., helped with genealogical detail. Dr Ford Stanley kindly sent me a copy of his thesis. Josh Jeffrey of the website Glasite.org supplied me with many sources, some of which I had once owned but lost when my home was flooded in 2016. The University of Dundee Archive has the largest collection of Glasite material and I am grateful for the help that I have been given. My thanks also to the National Library of Scotland and the Bell Library in Perth. The Dundee Central Library, the Edinburgh Central Library and the Library of New College in Edinburgh yielded much information and I am grateful to the Massachusetts Historical Society in Boston for allowing me on a brief visit to see original letters of Sandeman.

My supervisor at the University of St Andrews, the late Professor J. K. Cameron, dealt patiently with me many years ago and guided my research.

Professor David Bebbington of Stirling University has gently persuaded me over the years to write this story, and Andrew Muirhead has read the manuscript and given invaluable help, encouragement and mild correction, and Ken Drysdale has helped with formatting, and deserves much thanks.

Abbreviations

BQ	*Baptist Quarterly*
CBRF	Christian Brethren Research Fellowship
DSCHT	Dictionary of Scottish Church History and Theology
JEH	*Journal of Ecclesiastical History*
ODNB	Oxford Dictionary of National Biography
RSCHS	Records of the Scottish Church History Society

Introduction

EVEN IN SCOTLAND, THE country of their origin, mention of the Glasite or Sandemanian movement elicits blank looks and, often, scant interest. Let it be made clear at the beginning of the story, that Glasites and Sandemanians are two names for the same body of Christians. In Scotland they are known as Glasites,[1] after their founder, John Glas, once minister of Tealing, near Dundee. Everywhere else they are called Sandemanians after Glas's son-in-law, Robert Sandeman, whose writings and travels spread the church. Yet this always small and usually reticent movement has attracted devoted followers in Scotland, England, Wales, New England, and Nova Scotia. Although all its meetings have now ceased, and its writings been consigned to library shelves, it deserves to be remembered and its history and theology ought not to be ignored. At the outset it is helpful to realise that there were two facets of Sandemanianism which must be distinguished. There was firstly an intellectualist definition of faith, and secondly there was a carefully set out church order, seeking to emulate the 'primitive' church of the first Christians. This church order both separated the followers of Glas and Sandeman from all other churches and was maintained almost rigidly for the whole life of the churches. From time to time we come across those who are influenced by their views of faith, but who do not follow the order of the Church, such as Samuel Newton of Norwich, the Independent minister who tutored William Godwin. It took a great deal of commitment to live 'by the rule' and become true Sandemanians. We can follow the process in the epistolary correspondence[2] between Robert Sandeman and Samuel Pike, a

---

1. Spelt this way on the notice board of the Edinburgh Meeting House, but often found as 'Glassites'. I will use the church's own spelling, except when quoting contemporary documents. In his foreword to the third volume of his history of the Scottish Church, Dr James Bulloch establishes the spelling 'Glas' and not 'Glass' for the founder of the movement. See Glasite.org for more, a site that contains much of great value to any student of the movement.

2. Pike, *Epistolary Correspondence between S. P. and R. S.*

London Independent minister who was almost reluctantly drawn into full acceptance of the Church, becoming an elder in it, having lived through a split in his original congregation.

Comments, For and Against

Michael Faraday, its most famous member, in a letter to Ada, Countess of Lovelace, who had enquired about his faith, wrote 'I am of a very small and despised sect of Christians, known, if at all, as *Sandemanians*.'[3] Friendly comments appear in several histories. A standard work such as Ferguson's '*Scotland, 1689 to the present*' characterizes them thus: 'the Glasites were never numerous, but they had a wide influence, with their emphasis on Christian life rather than Christian dogmatics. They practiced a spiritual communion, held the Lord's Supper weekly, and owing to their love-feasts became known as "kailites".'[4] We shall see how accurate this description was as the story progresses. E. P. Thompson, in *The Making of the English Working Class* implies that Sandemanians were a working-class sect, which was only partly true.[5] T. C. Smout, in his *A History of the Scottish People 1560–830* writes of the 'Glasites, with their stress on Christian love and their belief in the voluntary nature of religion'.[6] H. Grey Graham, in his *Social Life of Scotland in the Eighteenth Century*, remarks that

> without the little body of Glasites, founded by the simple-heart-
> ed minister of Tealing in 1730—with its abstinence from things
> strangled, the kiss of greeting, the love-feasts of homely broth
> which gained for it the vulgar title of the 'kail-Kirk'—Scotland
> would have lost some of the quaintest aspects of social life.[7]

Dr John Macleod of the Free Church College, in his *Scottish Theology in Relation to Church History* includes a section on John Glas and another on Sandemanian faith which are accurate and quite sympathetic.[8]

Drummond and Bulloch refer to Glas and his Church in an apprecia-tive manner in all three of their volumes, showing a real acquaintance with twentieth-century Glasites. 'Glas', they write,

---

3. Cantor, *Faraday*, 5.

4. Ferguson, *Scotland, 1689 to the Present*, 131–32.

5. Thompson, *Making of the English Working Class*, 39.

6. Smout, *History of the Scottish People 1560–1830*, 217.

7. Graham, *Social Life of Scotland in the Eighteenth Century*, 382.

8. Macleod, *Scottish Theology*, 185–88.

had no interest in making converts and the number of his followers was always small, but they survived and still receive an
occasional addition to their numbers, usually from the ranks
of the educated.[9]

I have not found any evidence of converts in the late twentieth century
and the few new members have come from Glasite families, like the Baxters,
who are referred to in the third volume. Dr Henry Sefton, in his chapter in
Studies in the History of Worship in Scotland, notices the adaptability of the
Glasites in their composing, compiling and singing spiritual songs as well
as psalms.[10] In the volume on religion in the series *Scottish Life and Society*
there is a precise and accurate account of the Glasite Church in Scotland.[11]
Dr Callum Brown refers to the remarkable number of Glasites in Dundee
in the 1790, and quotes the writer of the *Old Statistical Account* 'on the indispensable law of the society enjoining early marriages'.[12] Andrew Muirhead in his recent *Reformation, Dissent and Diversity* gives a very succinct
and accurate account of the movement,[13] and Professor David Bebbington,
comments on the Sandemanian view of faith, 'once more the sway of reason
showed itself, affecting, for example, the way in which their leading light
Michael Faraday conducted his scientific experiments.'[14]

Other writers can sound quite bewildered. Fernandez-Armesto and
Wilson, in their *Reformation* commenting on the churches and family life,
write:

> Sandemanians in the eighteenth and nineteenth centuries spent
> so long together on Sundays, what with prayers, exhortations,
> common meal and Lord's Supper that the day of the week nor-
> mally reserved for family activities was almost monopolized by
> the Church. As if to emphasize the pre-eminence of the Church
> family over the nuclear family, since only adults were admitted
> to full communion, children were left to eat sandwiches in the
> pews while the fully-fledged members of the community with-
> drew for their love-feast.

9. Drummond and Bulloch, *Scottish Church, 1688–1843*, 45–47; *Church in Victorian Scotland, 1843–1874*, 52; *Church in Late Victorian Scotland, 1874–1900*, 132.

10. Sefton, "Revolution to Disruption," 72.

11. J. A. Whyte, in MacLean and Veitch, *Scottish Life and Society*, 12:238–39.

12. Brown, *Religion and Society in Scotland*, 29.

13. Muirhead, *Reformation, Dissent and Diversity*, 106–7.

14. David Bebbington in Larsen and Ledger-Lomas, *Oxford History of Protestant
Dissenting Traditions*, 3:349.

This is not false. It just seems the emphasis falls in the wrong place, and their later comment on a split over the eating of blood quite misses the point, seemingly confusing the Lord's Supper with the ban on the eating of blood.[15] John Henry Newman, in ironic vein, accuses Matthew Arnold of illiberality for excluding from his ideal church Jews, Papists and Quakers . . . 'why not space for Socinians and 'Sandemonians [*sic*] too?'[16] Werner Stark, suggesting antinomianism amongst sectarians, comments that 'the English and Scots Baptists or Sandemanians also played with fire [sc. sexual], and so did the Moravians and the Methodists.'[17]

That intrepid Victorian explorer of all sorts of London religions, Rev C. Maurice Davies, in his book *Unorthodox London*, recounts his visit to the Sandemanian meeting house in Barnsbury Grove in alarmingly gloomy terms. His description of the long service, of the preaching elder weeping for no apparent reason, and his conclusion, 'all hope abandon ye who enter here', contrasts with his further remark that many of its members had a substantial and intellectual appearance and that there were many pretty girls in the congregation.[18] John Betjeman's poem on the Sandemanian Meeting-House in Highbury Quadrant written in the early 1930s perhaps catches the ethos more tellingly:

> Psalm-singing over and love-lunch done,
> Listening to the Bible in their room for meetings
> Old Sandemanians sit hidden from the sun.[19]

More specialized writings, such as Escott's *A History of Scottish Congregationalism*[20] and its predecessor, Ross's *A History of Congregational Independency in Scotland*[21] give longer and more accurate accounts of the church. These writers acknowledge Glas as, probably, 'the founder of Scottish Congregationalism'. A concise and accurate account of the church is found in Alan Sell's article on John Chater, London Sandemanian elder and novelist, in the *Baptist Quarterly*.[22] The best and most comprehensive account of the church is the 1936 Edinburgh University PhD thesis of J. T. Hornsby, 'John Glas (1695–1773)'. I was told by Gerard Sandeman, the last

---

15. Fernandez-Armesto and Wilson, *Reformation*, 211.

16. Quoted in Gilley, *Newman and His Age*, 99.

17. Stark, *Sociology of Religion*, 2:193.

18. Davies, *Unorthodox London*, 284–92.

19. Betjeman, *Collected Poems*, 15.

20. Escott, *History of Scottish Congregationalism*, 17–23.

21. Ross, *History of Congregational Independency*, 24–31.

22. Sell, "John Chater," 100–117.

elder, that Hornsby had done his research just in time to catch the church in a certain amount of strength. After the Second World War few of the younger generation joined the church, although some of them were in attendance to the end.

Professor Geoffrey Cantor, in his study, *Michael Faraday, Scientist and Sandemanian,*[23] and in his essay 'Reading the Book of Nature: The Relation Between Faraday's Religion and his Science in Faraday Rediscovered,[24] has put all students of Sandemanianism deeply in his debt. He has carefully described and understood Faraday's faith and related it to his work, and at the same time provided a splendid overview of the life of the Church, especially in London. John Howard Smith has published *The Perfect Rule of the Christian Religion*[25] which deals well with the founding and early years of the Church in Britain and its expansion into New England and Nova Scotia. Ford Stanley's Oxford DPhil thesis 'The Glasite-Sandemanian Movement in the Eighteenth Century British Atlantic World'[26] along with Smith's work cover the American dimension in a careful and detailed way. Contemporary comments on Glasites could be wry and amusing. Here is John Ramsay of Ochtertyre, writing to an anonymous friend on 7 January, 1800:

> I thank you for your news particularly for the excommunication story which makes me rejoice I am no Glassite. I have seen William Sandeman who was a great-grandfather early in life. Young ladies who are no Glassites ought to ponder well ere they reject a good offer which in Glassite style means a bonny young lad.[27]

Rev James Hall, an Anglican clergyman and traveler, who had studied at St Andrews, published his *Travels* in 1807. He came across Glasites in Newburgh and comments that they marry young, saying that the Lord will provide, and are very virtuous in truth and reality. He also remarks that the community of worldly goods is frittered away to nothing. Mr Hall's travels are full of gossip, as when he confuses the Bereans with the Glasites, but his comments are at least amusing.[28]

On the other hand, in 1765 James Scott of Dundee records his surprise and delight in discovering the Glasite Church.

---

23. Cantor, *Faraday.*
24. Cantor, "Reading the Book of Nature," 69–82.
25. Smith, *Perfect Rule of the Christian Religion.*
26. Stanley, *Glasite-Sandemanian Movement.*
27. Horn, *Letters of John Ramsay, 1799–1812,* 7.
28. Hall, *Travels in Scotland,* 217.

Everything about the Glasites appeared new and surprising to
me—I was struck like one in a Dream being accustomed to the
National worship and to the Seceders which are complete imita-
tors of the National. I was at first confounded to find nothing
like them—the very singing, Prayers, Preaching etc. all quite
in a different manner attending to the whole that I had been
a perfect stranger to. At the same time a simplicity and godly
sincerity without a mask that made me conclude that God was
with them for a truth. At the Lord's Supper the Elders' desk only
covered and all the rest of the brethren in their usual seats, the
Elder who presided had the bread set before him by one of the
deacons, rose up, and taking the bread in his hands spoke to the
people to this purpose. . .'

The communion prayers were then given verbatim and at great
length.[29]

Despite their small numbers and avoidance of undue publicity, the
Glasites did draw adverse criticism, especially from those who most nearly
resembled them. In the *London Christian Instructor* for 1819 a critic, presumably from a Congregationalist background, thus characterizes the
Church. After a brief history and an acknowledgement that in the writings
of Glas and Sandeman 'there are many things deserving of attention, and
that they boldly contended, especially at their outset, for some of the grand
principles of the kingdom of Christ', yet it is pointed out that 'the genius of
this system has been distinguished from a very early period by its spirit of
contradiction and opposition.'[30] Exclusive, hypocritical, 'the antinomianism
of the north' are some of the epithets used, and we will see as the story develops how accurate or otherwise they were. E. K. Simpson, in an *Evangelical
Quarterly* article on Independency comments that in Scotland 'the Glassite
movement gave birth in Scotland to a bastard form of the sect, frigidly fini-
cal and exclusive.'[31]

A writer in the *Eclectic Review* for 1838 sought to provide the epitaph
for the Church:

Although many of our readers who may never have heard of
the sect of the Sandemanians and others who have heard but

29. Scott, *Notebook*, 192.

30. Anon., "Historical Sketch," 144–45. Regarding Glasite documents, the manuscripts in the University of Dundee Archive 9/4/1, 318, 364, and Acc M. include letters,
diaries, and pamphlets. There are also items in the Dundee Central Library, including a
first edition, 1749, of *Christian Songs*, and several recent acquisitions from 1728–2000.
These continue to be added as members of Glasite families discover them.

31. Simpson, "Independency and Its Eclipse," 373.

little of them may both be inclined to ask whether it were not as well to leave them to enjoy undisturbed repose in the tomb of all the Capulets as to bring them before the public; yet we are disposed to think that considerable interest attaches to their history, and we feel confident that their reliquiae are well worth preservation, both as theological curiosities, and a beacon to the churches and pastors of the present age. Church history, as well as natural history, may have its museums for the preservation of moral petrifactions and specimens of extinct races.'[32]

Yet the Church persisted to the very end of the twentieth century.

More extensive critical studies were not long in appearing. The Baptist minister John Brine,[33] writing in 1758 from a High Calvinist position, and John Wesley, writing from an Arminian standpoint, were both acerbic critics of the influence and teaching of the movement, especially of Sandeman's Letters. Wesley is particularly harsh. In his *A Sufficient Answer, to Letters to the author of Theron and Aspasio, in a Letter to the Author* Wesley wrote:

> So your youth may in some measure plead your excuse for such a peculiar pertness, insolence and self-sufficiency, with such an utter contempt for all mankind, as no other writer of the present age has shewn . . . I object first that you are a gross, willful slanderer, . . . and fourthly, that you have no charity, and you know not what charity is.

Wesley is particularly scornful of Sandeman's dismissal of Guthrie, Marshall and Doddridge and ends his diatribe:

> God be merciful to thee a sinner! And shew thee compassion, though thou hast none for thy fellow-servants. Otherwise, it will be more tolerable, I will not say for Seneca or Epictetus, but for Nero and Domitian in the Day of Judgement than for thee.[34]

As we consider the movement, we may think that Wesley has been less than just to it!

The eminent Baptist theologian Andrew Fuller met what he considered to be excessive influence of Sandemanianism in the writing of his friend Archibald McLean, and both in his appendix to his magnum opus *The Gospel Worthy of All Acceptation* published in 1785 and in his 'Strictures on Sandemanianism' of 1812 acutely criticized Sandeman and McLean, while

---

32. Anon., "Sandemanians," 519.

33. Brine, *Animadversions upon the Letters on Theron and Aspasio.*

34. Wesley, *Sufficient Answer,* 12.

admitting some virtues in their teaching.[35] These influential writings will be examined in more detail later.

The notice board of the Barony Street Meeting House in Edinburgh of the 'Church of Christ, commonly known as Glasite or Sandemanian' gave the times of the morning and afternoon service and added 'All Welcome'. Yet in its last years only those interested in the church and its history found their way into the Meeting Room, described in the Edinburgh volume of the *Buildings of Scotland* as being 'very severe, the interior unchanged, like a faded Victorian photograph'.[36] Even fewer found their way into the Love Feast room on the upper floor, and in the last years perhaps none into the bedroom, kept fully furnished until the church closed, for any visiting elder. The liturgy, unchanged for at least two centuries, although truncated for lack of men to take part, was slow, deliberate, and totally lacking in any surprises. The people stood to pray, with their hands uplifted. The psalms were sung slowly to tunes introduced by an elder with a pitch pipe. All the words of several chapters of the Authorised Version of the Bible were read, sometimes, when there were unfamiliar names, with some difficulty, and the prayers and the exhortation were largely in words of scripture. All was logical, dry and without obvious emotion, despite what Davies claimed to have witnessed in London, and the only animated episode was after the service when the members greeted each other with a perfunctory kiss. The really surprising thing about the church was that it survived so long.

One reason for its longevity was its family basis. Sandemans, Waterstons, Baxters and Barnards from the early eighteenth century onwards intermarried and cherished their family connections and their family faith, and members of these families were in the church almost until the end. When Patrick Sandeman, the last deacon, died, his daughter Mary, a well-known folk-singer, remarked in her obituary of her father published in the *Scotsman* that, although he lived latterly in Perthshire, he had been sustained through life by a small family church, and others, who had been brought up in the church, have told me that wherever their ecclesiastical journeys had later led, they still looked back to their Glasite roots and to the knowledge of the Bible they had absorbed. There were no Sabbath Schools, although Faraday attended a singing school attached to the London Meeting House. Children grew up sharing in the services of the Church, and in the Edinburgh Meeting House the pews still carried the carved initials of many of them.[37]

35. Fuller, *Strictures on Sandemanianism*, 256.

36. Gifford et al., *Buildings of Scotland, Edinburgh*, 337.

37. Sadly, no longer, as the pews have been stripped out in 2018.

The works of Glas and Sandeman were widely read amongst serious Christians in the eighteenth century and later. The influence of their views on faith and less often their Biblicism and customs must not be ignored. In the mid-eighteenth century the Scotch Baptists and the Old Scots Independents were both deeply indebted to these writings, and later they were influential with the Haldanes and with Alexander Campbell and the Churches of Christ, although this remains a contentious matter for some. The followers of John Barclay, the Bereans, were also influenced.

The Scotch Baptists

Robert Carmichael was minister of an Anti-Burgher Secession Church in Coupar Angus who, having become unsettled on the matter of church government, was drawn to the writings of Glas and Sandeman, being regarded as rather a catch for the movement and becoming an elder in Glasgow. Carmichael, always referred to in Glasite sources as 'Dr' although there is no evidence of a doctorate elsewhere, was ordained over the Anti-Burgher Church in Coupar Angus on 21 August 1751. Although the church flourished for a few years this did not continue, and on 1 November 1761 Carmichael was brought before the Anti-Burgher Presbytery of Auchterarder by complaint of his Session and congregation. He was alleged to have taught,

1. Faith is not the instrument but the fruit of justification;

2. that there is no authority in Scripture to make the Gospel call universal; and

3. in exhorting unbelievers about what they are to do to escape the wrath and curse of God we only encourage them to work out a righteousness of their own.

He was also accused of holding that there was no warrant in the New Testament for national churches or national covenanting, and that the Presbyterian system of church government did not exist until Calvin. The case went to Synod, Carmichael was suspended and went to Dundee. He was finally deposed in April 1763, by which time he was an ally of Glas.[38]

On 16 November 1761 Glas wrote to Carmichael,

> Very Dear Brother, Though I was clear you should take the first opportunity to show your non-subjection to the authority of what Seceders call their reverend presbytery—yet as by this time I suppose you have done this, and find yourself standing out of

---

38. Small, *History of the Congregations*, 2:565.

connection with any thing that you can call a Church of Christ;
I begin to hesitate upon this,—whether you be exercising the
ministry of the Word, for which I doubt not the Lord has fitted
you, in the order that he hath prescribed. Far be it from me to
forbid you to preach Christ, because you follow not with us.[39]

Glas is glad to welcome a new recruit, so long as he follows the order of
the Glasite churches. And Carmichael did, at least for a time.

'18 January 1762, Dr Carmichael preached the whole Sabbath on Acts
9 verse 20, about 50 minutes and Mr Glas in the afternoon on Jonah 2 verse
4. We gave Mr Glas half a guinea, he would take no more, and Dr C the
same', wrote Robert Cant to Robert Sandeman.[40] In the Glasite Church in
Glasgow Carmichael met Archibald McLean, a printer and already a student of the Scriptures. McLean had been converted under the ministry of
the Church of Scotland evangelical, Rev John Mclaurin of the Ramshorn
Church in Glasgow, having been previously impressed at the Cambuslang
Revival and by the preaching of George Whitefield. He read the *Testimony
of King of Martyrs*, John Glas's most influential work, 'which led him to call
in question the propriety of national establishments of Christianity' and in
1762 he attached himself to the Glasgow Glasite meeting.

Carmichael and McLean did not remain long in that connection.
They found themselves in disagreement with Glas, who had been sent for
to decide on a case of discipline in the Church, and they left the fellowship,
amidst tears. Carmichael became the co-pastor of an independent church in
Edinburgh, probably an offshoot of the Glasites, and McLean continued his
printing career. In 1765 they discussed baptism and concluded that the New
Testament taught baptism of believers only. Carmichael, knowing of no
other Baptists in Scotland, went to London and was baptised in the Barbican
Baptistry by the famous Dr John Gill. Thereafter he returned to Edinburgh,
baptised seven others in the Water of Leith at Canonmills and formed the
church known today as Bristo Baptist Church. In 1767 McLean found a
position at the well-known Edinburgh printers and publishers, Donaldson,
and coming to that city was baptised and joined with Carmichael as co-
pastor of the Baptist Church.[41]

Despite such a short sojourn with the Glasites, or the 'First class of
Independents' as they were sometimes called, these first Baptists carried
over many traits of their former friends. Two other elders joined McLean
in the early days of the Edinburgh church. Henry David Inglis (1757–1806)

---

39. Macintosh, *Letters in Correspondence*, 93.
40. Morison, *Supplementary Volume*, 14.
41. McLean, *Works*, 1:xxiv.

whose great grandfather on his mother's side was Colonel Gardiner, friend of Philip Doddridge, and who was born into a lawyer's family, became Clerk of the Bills in the Edinburgh Courts. He was drawn towards a Christian life by the preaching of Dr John Erskine of Greyfriars, and 'the writings of Glas and Sandeman were also useful to him'. He was deeply interested in the spiritual welfare of prisoners condemned to death and his Letters to the Public Respecting W. Mills, one such prisoner, were often reprinted. In an appendix to his account Inglis printed the hymn sung by the doomed man on the scaffold, which was "Tis finished" (song number 53 in the Glasite *Christian Songs*).[42] The third elder, William Braidwood, (1751–1830) came to the Baptist church by way of the Independent fellowship where Robert Carmichael was pastor before he adopted Baptist views.

Leadership in all the Scotch Baptist Churches was by lay elders, and college training was not deemed necessary; the Lord's Supper was celebrated every Sunday afternoon, and there had to be at least two elders to constitute the church, to attend to the Supper and to discipline. Services followed the Glasite pattern, with many scriptures and prayers and the singing of psalms, and also hymns, including several from the Glasite hymnal, in their early hymn books; foot-washing when appropriate; abstinence from blood; the kiss of charity; a view of faith as simple belief; and, of course, complete separation from the state. As the question of the eating of blood was so important in the Glasite story it is worth noting that in the household of the William Holms Coats, the Paisley Scotch Baptist, in the middle of the nineteenth century, the 'biblical prohibition on things strangled and from blood was observed'.[43]

Scotch Baptists did not follow the Glasites in their exclusiveness of Christian fellowship, and McLean was very active in promoting the early work of the Baptist Missionary Society. They objected to what they considered the levity of the Glasites in social matters, such as attendance at theatres and balls, and to what they considered Pharisaism.

The oldest Baptist Church in Scotland was founded before McLean and Carmichael even discovered the Glasites. In 1750 Sir William Sinclair, second baronet of Dunbeath, who had succeeded to the title in 1742, returned from service in the army to his ancestral estate in Keiss, Caithness, the most northerly county in mainland Scotland. The Sinclair family of landowners in Caithness were mostly Episcopalians, but Sir William, somewhere in his travels, had become a Baptist, and on his return to his home country immediately began to preach. The bishop of Ross and Caithness, Robert Forbes,

---

42. Murray, "Henry David Inglis," 316.
43. Binfield, "Coats Family and Paisley Baptists," 2.

visited Lady Sinclair, a member of the Episcopal Church, and was horrified to discover that her husband was

> the preaching knight, a wrongheaded man confessedly by all who know him best, for he has taken up that odd way of strolling about and preaching without commission or appointment of any man or any set of men whatsoever, and vents the wildest and most extravagant notions that ever were hatched in the most disordered brain.

Sinclair did not stand when the bishop said grace. This was a rather unflattering portrayal of the man who succeeded in founding a Baptist church on his estate which has endured. The little church first met in Keiss castle, and like the Glasites, had weekly communion, and a Love Feast. Sir William is said to have washed his followers' feet, and he composed a book of hymns for his people in 1750, which was used in the Keiss Church for many years and is the first hymnbook after Glas's *Christian Songs* of 1749 to have been produced in Scotland. In 1763 Sir William moved to Edinburgh, probably to escape his creditors. The Sinclair lairds were notoriously litigious, and sometimes extravagant, and Sir William had to abandon his castle and his church and take refuge in the Sanctuary of Holyrood in Edinburgh. He was able to attend Glasite worship for some time, to hear Sandeman preach and to read his writings. However, he disagreed with some of the teaching, specifically on 'the obedience of Christ, the law of the spirit of life, and the nature of that perfect love that casteth out fear.' In January 1764 he wrote to Sandeman to this effect and Sandeman replied a few days later:

> As to your choosing to attend our public doctrine for some weeks and then choosing to withdraw, we have no charge to bring against you and no title to enquire after your reasons. You was [*sic*] welcome to attend while you inclined, and welcome to withdraw when inclination ceased, as we pretend no right whatever to call you to account for you conduct.

Sinclair replied, claiming that illuminations and exercises of the mind were necessary to believing, and there the contact seems to have ceased. Sinclair died in Edinburgh in 1768, but his church continued.[44]

---

44. Johnstone, "Memoir of Sir William Sinclair," *Evangelist* 1 (May 1847) 245–46. Quoted in Lumsden, *Rich Inheritance*, 31.

The Old Scots Independents

Another new church influenced by Glas and Sandeman was known as the second class of Independents or more commonly as the Old Scots Independents. Their rise was in two parallel movements, one in the rural parts of East Fife and the other in Glasgow. The pioneers in Fife were James Smith, minister of Newburn Parish, and his immediate neighbor to the east, Robert Ferrier, minister of the parish of Largo. Smith was an elderly man when in 1768 he renounced his benefice. He was born in 1708 and educated at Aberdeen, becoming the minister in Newburn in 1735. He is described as a 'well-favoured person, of good manners and unquestionable piety, of a tender holy walk, zealous and prudent, and of a good stock of learning'. Sandeman's *Letters* fell into his hands and greatly influenced his thinking, some time after their publication in 1757. He then adopted the practice of weekly communion without the assistance of other ministers and in 1765 published what was in effect a statement of the Independent scheme of church government, entitled *A Compendious Account, taken from Holy Scripture, of the Form and Order of the Church of God . . . also of the Nature Design and Right Manner of Observing the Eating of the Lord's Supper.*

His neighbor was a much younger man. Robert Ferrier was born in 1741, the ninth son of the minister of Largo, John Ferrier, who was there from 1724–1764. Robert joined his father as colleague and successor in August 1764 and told his own story in the Preface he contributed to his republication of Glas's *Testimony* in 1777.

> When as a clergyman of the Established Church, I was going on, like others, without enquiry, in the beaten track, preaching what I had learned from systems, and writings of men; baptizing every child in the parish, whatever the parents were, because it was born in a Christian country; prostituting the holy ordinance of the Supper to everyone who was not just obnoxious to the civil law as an atrocious criminal; jugging myself in a good living and thinking that all was well . . . I was stopped short in my career by a most affecting occurrence . . .

A dying clergyman of the neighborhood pierced his conscience with an account of his opinions that he had stifled.

> [C]ontrary to the dictates of his conscience he had stood connected to the National Church, in which he was fully convinced the truth concerning the Son of God which gives hope to sinners, was not understood, nor in any way the bond of their

union, because the evidence of knowing that truth, viz BROTH-
ERLY LOVE, was utterly a stranger among them . . . .

This minister in his last days spoke to others in the same way, recom-
mending them to read Glas's *Testimony* and to compare it with the Scriptures. Who this clergyman was can only be surmised. Beaton asserts that
he was a neighbor of Ferrier. The only person who fits the description was
Andrew Waddell of Anstruther Wester, born in 1735, ordained in 1761,
who died, unmarried, in 1767. We have a glimpse here of earnest men discovering the work of Glas, thirty-five years after it had been written.[45]

Ferrier obeyed the dying wish of his colleague and read the *Testimony*.
Previously he had had no very high regard for Glas and his works, but now
the writing stirred his conscience, and he began to understand the nature of
Christ's kingdom for the first time. He found that Smith had come indepen-
dently to similar conclusions, and they both felt there was only one course
open to them, to resign their charges and follow their new understanding
of the Word of God. Accordingly, they submitted their resignations to the
Presbytery of St Andrews on 17 August 1768, and although the Presbytery
were reluctant to act, the two ministers left their charges on the following
Sunday, and began to hold meetings at Balchrystie, a farm on the boundary
of Newburn and Largo, said to be a very early Christian site. They published
their reasons for their course of action in a pamphlet, *The Case of James
Smith and Robert Ferrier truly represented and defended*. In it they explained
their change of views concerning Christ's kingdom. They acknowledged the
truth of most of the Westminster Confession, but they had to dissent at
certain points.

1. The eternal Sonship of Christ. They admit that the Savior is spoken
    of in Scripture as the only-begotten of the Father but claim that he
    is never described as eternally begotten. McLean also held this view,
    one which recurs amongst those who have held a very high view of
    Scripture.

2. They reject the *filioque* clause in the Creed. In this they may have been
    unique. Glas did not hold either of these views.

3. They agree with Glas and Sandeman on the nature of saving faith.

4. They reject the authority of the magistrate in ecclesiastical affairs.

5. They reject the civil magistrate's power to call synods and church
    courts.

---

45. Glas, *Testimony*, 15–16 (Ferrier's preface).

6. They hold that the power of church censure and discipline should be in the hands of the whole congregation and not of officers only. They then argued for the adoption of an Independent Church Order, and the adoption of primitive customs as the Glasites did.[46]

Glas approached them with a view to discussion but Smith had a rooted dislike to him, and this for a while influenced Ferrier. Shortly afterwards Ferrier encountered Glas, severed his connections with the church at Balchrystie, and for a time officiated as an elder of the Glasite church in Dundee, and then in Glasgow in 1769. In 1786, having been widowed he married a remarkable woman, Catherine Waterston née Sandeman, whom we shall meet again. He joined the family business, that of a wax chandler, and had, because of a second marriage, to resign as an elder.[47] He became a teacher of classics in Edinburgh until his death in 1795.[48]

The second movement, which began at the same time as the 'Balchrystians' was associated particularly with David Dale of Glasgow. Born in 1739 in Stewarton in Ayrshire, he prospered in Glasgow in the linen trade, and built up a series of businesses in the west of Scotland and beyond. He is best known as the founder of the mills at New Lanark, afterwards operated by his son-in-law, Robert Owen. All his adult life Dale was involved in the church. He joined the College Church of Scotland in Glasgow, where the evangelical Dr John Gillies was minister, and then in a series of moves came to an Independent position, and in 1769 a church was formed with him as an elder. For a short time Ferrier assisted him, and the church grew, being provided with a building sitting five hundred people. Despite losses to the Glasites and the Scotch Baptists it continued to flourish in Dale's lifetime. The order of the church was very similar to that of the Glasites, but Dale's outlook was much less restricted, and he was active in all good Christian causes. Amongst other offices he was treasurer of the Glasgow and West of Scotland Bible Society until his death in 1806. Another church was formed in Dundee, and several others in the northeast and in Lanarkshire, but lacking the discipline of the Glasites the movement declined and in 1814 the remaining churches formed a union with the remnant of the Inghamites[49] in northwest England.[50]

---

46. Escott, *History of Scottish Congregationalism*, 25.

47. It was a Glasite principle that an elder must resign if after being widowed he married again.

48. Glas, *Testimony*, 17–19 (Ferrier's preface).

49. Followers of Benjamin Ingham who had split from the Methodists.

50. Escott, *History of Scottish Congregationalism*, 34.

The Bereans

There is one other native Scottish dissenting church that must be noticed. They had some things in common with the Glasites, including having suffered at the hands of historians because of their quaintness. They have died out and left little trace, despite an interesting article on their beliefs in the *Encyclopaedia of Religion and Ethics*,[51] and some of the writings of the eccentric Presbyterian Rev William Thom of Liverpool, who held doctorates from Heidelberg and Jena. The group owes its origin to John Barclay, who studied in St Andrews under Professor Campbell from whom he seems to have learnt one of the main tenets of his theology, that knowledge of the existence of God is drawn from revelation and not from nature or reason. In 1763 Barclay moved from an assistantship in Errol to a similar position in Fettercairn, where his preaching drew great crowds. 'He had a luxuriant fancy and a great taste for poetry. His taste however was not very correct, and he lacked sound judgment', wrote the historian of Fettercairn.[52] In 1766 he published a paraphrase of the psalms, insisting that the laments spoke of the suffering of the Messiah and not of David or of Christians. In the following year he published *Rejoice Evermore*, which brought him under suspicion of heresy, and in 1769 came *Without Faith, Without God*, in which he attacked the whole system of Scottish education, because it is founded on the premise that there is such a thing as natural revelation. 'Pretended reason murders faith' was the refrain. He held strongly that real faith brings assurance, a rather different belief from that of the Glasites, who were very wary of any talk of assurance.[53]

When the parish of Fettercairn became vacant in 1773 the people wanted him as minister, but the Presbytery refused him even a certificate of character and he forthwith separated himself from the Church of Scotland. A church, which was to be well attended, was built for him in the village of Sauchieburn, although he soon went to Edinburgh, and thence to London, where he had followers. The Assembly at Sauchieburn became a Congregational Church in 1809, and most of the other churches had dwindled by the 1840s. The Glasgow church in 1860, according to James Brown, was

> of a mixed communion. The majority are Paedobaptists, yet a small minority of Baptists worship with them. On baptism—its mode and subjects—they mutually agree to forbear . . . their

51. Hastings, *Encyclopaedia of Religion and Ethics*, 2:520.

52. Cameron, *History of Fettercairn*, 201.

53. For an attractive description of the Bereans see Philip, *Evangel in Gowrie*, 231–58.

union as one body was recently much disturbed by the introduction of a widely-entertained topic—the future reign of the Lord Jesus—whether it would be a personal one on earth or a continued spiritual one in heaven; and the friends who could forbear on baptism separated on a question of doubtful interest.[54]

Thom republished Barclay's works in Glasgow in 1852, using a bequest from a late deacon, James Carswell, to allow them to circulate without charge. Escott concludes his account of these Bible loving Bereans thus: 'It must be admitted that the Bereans did dress religion in the homespun of the people and related it to their daily lives and habits'.[55]

James and Robert Haldane were instrumental in many evangelistic efforts from the end of the eighteenth century, when they abandoned their aristocratic lifestyle, and travelled the country preaching the Gospel and scandalizing the more sedate leaders of the Scottish churches. As laymen and first as Independents and then as Baptists their itinerancy, teaching, controversial writings, and disdain for parish boundaries helped to establish the Congregational and Baptist denominations in Scotland. But they were not immune to Sandemanian influences. Alexander Haldane, their biographer, writes:

> To many of the principles of Glas and Sandeman, and especially to their bitter intolerant spirit, both the brothers were at all times strongly opposed. There were indeed some parts of their writings which were regarded as exhibiting noble views of the freeness of the Gospel and the simplicity of faith, but, as a whole, the Glasite or Sandemanian system was abhorrent to their principles and feelings.[56]

Their ally in many of their enterprises and the leader of the nascent Congregationalism in Scotland, Greville Ewing, introduced the works of Glas and Sandeman to his seminary in Glasgow, seeking to approximate his followers to the ideal model of primitive Christianity, and was duly rebuked by James Haldane in a letter of 1801. Yet in his *View of Social Worship* published in 1805, James Haldane advocated some Glasite practices in the worship of the church, such as the mutual exhortation by the brethren in the morning service, and a plurality of pastors in each church. These were men who were in the main employed in secular business. Not only exhortation but also discipline, he contended, should take place publicly in

---

54. Brown, *Religious Denominations of Glasgow*, 38–39.
55. Escott, *History of Scottish Congregationalism*, 42.
56. Haldane, *Lives of Robert and James Haldane*, 381.

the Sunday services. In this point he went beyond Glasite precedent, for in that church discipline took place at the Love Feast, which was confined to members. But 'no dispensing power has He given us respecting any of his ordinances', wrote Haldane. This insistence led to a parting of the ways. Ewing, once interested in Glas and Sandeman, and rebuked for that interest by Haldane, now repudiated their influence. Both the brothers Haldane, who were baptised as believers in 1808, remained estranged from Ewing and the Congregationalists. The divisions in the churches do not concern us here, except that the continuing influence of Glas and Sandeman is evident, and in this controversy a vigorous evangelical movement in Scotland was seriously weakened.

The Haldane churches formed a new strand in the growth of the Baptist movement in Scotland, and the flirtation with Glasite customs was soon forgotten, although the practice of holding communion every Sunday, still quite common in Scottish Baptist Churches, probably is a legacy of the experience of the Glasite churches. The search for the true, primitive church developed in a new way in the United States, particularly in the early nineteenth century in the churches associated with Alexander Campbell. Among the historians of the Disciples of Christ and the Churches of Christ, who in various branches have several million members in the United States and indeed throughout the world, there have been serious disagreements about the possible influence of Sandemanianism on these churches. We shall consider these in a later chapter of this study.

Opponents in Britain

Andrew Fuller (1754–1815) was one of the most influential Baptists of his period. His seminal work, *The Gospel Worthy of All Acceptation* was published in 1785 and he played a large part in the founding of the Baptist Missionary Society, and the spread of a moderate, evangelistic Calvinism. In his travels to raise awareness and finance for the Society he came to Scotland and found a fellow worker in Archibald McLean, the Edinburgh Scotch Baptist elder. McLean was deeply influenced by Sandemanian thought and practice, although he differed from them in his missionary enthusiasm. But he took issue with Fuller on some points and Fuller devoted his *Twelve Letters to a Friend* to *Strictures on Sandemanianism*, published in 1812 in both England and New York, which began with a sharp rebuke to McLean for the spirit of some of his remarks on Fuller's theology, and developed into a survey of the Sandemanian positions on faith and church practices which has been often quoted in quite recent times and held to be the final coup de grace on the movement. It is doubtful if McLean read the book as he died in the December of the year it was published.

Fuller writes:

> The principles taught by Messrs Glass and Sandeman about half a century ago did certainly give a new turn and character to almost everything pertaining to the religion of Christ, as must appear to anyone who reads and understands their publications. . . . It is a distinct species of religion. If Mr Sandeman and his followers had only taught that faith has revealed truth for its object, or that which is true antecedent to its being believed, and whether it is believed or not—that the finished work of Christ, exclusive of every act, exercise, or thought of the human mind is that for the sake of which a sinner is justified before God—that no qualifications of any kind are necessary to our believing in him—and that the first scriptural consolation received by the believer arises from the gospel and not from reflections on the feelings of his own mind towards it, they would have deserved well of the church of Christ.[57]

Fuller quotes Ecking as another who criticizes the popular preachers and especially Thomas Boston in his *Fourfold State* for using dangerous language about grace, and Fuller seems to agree. In other letters he examines Sandeman's teaching on justifying faith, repentance, and other doctrines, and condemns the exclusive and loveless spirit of the movement and its spokesmen.

When, in *Letter 9* he writes of the customs of the Sandemanians he again damns with faint praise.

> It has appeared to me that there is a greater diligence in endeavouring to understand the scriptures, and a stricter regard to what they are supposed to contain, than among many other professors of Christianity. They do not seem to trifle with either principle of practice in the manner many do. There is something even in their rigidness which I prefer before that trifling with truth which often passes under the name of liberality among other professing Christians . . . but Religion as exhibited by them (those fully in the system,) resembles a rickety child whose growth is confined to certain parts: it wants that lovely uniformity or proportion which constitutes the beauty of believers.[58]

---

57. Fuller, *Strictures*, 8, 9.

58. Fuller, *Strictures*, 159.

In *Letter 12* he condemns the harsh and sarcastic spirit of Sandeman's writings. 'Is there no medium between flattery and malignity?' And then he refers to Braidwood's[59] criticism of 'Simplex,' (John Young) whose sermon James Boswell heard and disapproved.[60]

Fuller's 'Strictures' are important in themselves, for showing, among other things, how almost a hundred years after the beginnings of the movement its teachings attracted criticism. They are also important because other more recent writers have taken their cue from Fuller when they are attacking what they see as Sandemanian tendencies in the modern, particularly evangelical churches. Foremost among those was Dr Martyn Lloyd-Jones, a very influential figure in evangelical circles, particularly associated with strong Calvinist theology. In his book on *The Puritans, their Origins and Successors*, he follows Fuller and Dr John McLeod of the Free Church of Scotland in outlining what he sees as the errors of Sandeman's view of faith and he quotes the Welsh preacher, Christmas Evans, who was for some time influenced by Sandemanianism and who described its 'quenching of the spirit of prayer for the conversion of sinners'. Lloyd-Jones, having set out the orthodox doctrine of faith as involving trust that is far more than intellectual acceptance, warns against the tendency in some contemporary evangelical circles to overemphasize bare belief.[61]

A number of writers have taken their cue from Lloyd-Jones in the last fifty years, and the most recent is David Gay, whose 2016 book, *The Secret Stifler. Incipient Sandemanianism and Preaching the Gospel to Sinners*, has the merit of giving long quotations from Sandeman's Letters, while dismantling their argument point by point at great length. The Glasite people I met would have been quite surprised to discover what a menace to true gospel preaching they are in the twenty-first century![62]

59. William Braidwood was the third elder of the Edinburgh Scotch Baptist Church.

60. Fuller, *Strictures*, 212.

61. Lloyd-Jones, *Sandemanianism*.

62. Perform an Internet search for 'Sandemanianism' for many examples of present-day use, or abuse, of the term!

1

The Church in Scotland at the
Beginning of the Eighteenth Century

JOHN GLAS BEGAN HIS public ministry in the Angus parish of Tealing, a few miles north of Dundee, in 1719. Presbyterianism had been established as Scotland's national form of Christianity in the complex legislation following the flight of James VII and II in 1689 and the accession of William of Orange and his wife, Mary Stuart, Protestant sister of the departed Catholic King. Since 1560 the Church of Scotland had alternated between Episcopalianism of different forms and Presbyterianism, and now it seemed the latter had finally triumphed. The idea of a national covenant between God and the Scottish people can be traced back to that great reformer John Knox, who, 'when considering a whole kingdom, thought of a covenanted people based upon the Old Testament kingdoms of Israel and Judah'.[1]

Central to the debates of the early eighteenth century which we shall try to follow were two remarkable documents, the *National Covenant* of 1638, and the *Solemn League and Covenant* of 1643. Without an outline of these landmarks, which are so often cited in the controversies which surrounded Glas and his contemporaries, we shall easily lose our way. The National Covenant, signed by nobles, lairds, ministers, and lay men and women, first in Greyfriars Churchyard in Edinburgh, and then on copies sent out throughout Scotland, was an expression of revolt against the ecclesiastical policies of Charles 1 who attempted to bring Scotland into ecclesiastical conformity with England. The reading of the Liturgy in St Giles Kirk in Edinburgh on 23 July 1637 was the final insult to Scottish Presbyterianism,

---

1. Dawson, *John Knox*, 204.

and the Covenant, a long and largely historical document mainly drawn up by the Presbyterian lawyer Archibald Johnston of Warriston, was the outcome. It did not condemn episcopal government explicitly, but, having reviewed many of the changes over the years it roundly condemned what it called 'Novations' in the government and practice of the Church. It bound the individuals who signed it to each other as well as to God. It was not anti-monarchical but anti-Charles's Monarchy.[2] Soon there ensued the Civil War, which does not directly affect our story.

The Solemn League and Covenant of September 1643 was really a treaty between the Scots and the English Parliamentary party. It was not a mere civil bond which the English would have preferred, but a statement representing the Presbyterian desire for the imposition of uniformity in doctrine, worship, discipline, and government on the three churches of Scotland, England, and Ireland.[3] These are the two documents over which Glas and Willison, one of the ministers of Dundee, amongst others, were to disagree and which were to overshadow much of the controversy leading to the deposition of the minister of Tealing.

The scene, then, in 1689/90, at the Revolution Settlement, was not so simple. Although the bishops of the former regime kept a low profile, having failed to convince the king of their loyalty and their right to remain in their places, there were still many parishes where the minister remained committed to Episcopalian views. At least until 1715, and the first Jacobite Rising, in counties such as Angus many incumbents remained relatively undisturbed outside or on the fringes of the Presbyterian system.[4]

The re-establishment of Presbyterianism was by no means a straightforward or inevitable process. It was closely associated with political changes. On 14 March 1689 the Estates of Scotland met as the Convention, shortly to be transformed into Parliament. On 4 April they declared the throne of Scotland vacant and on 11 April offered it to William and Mary and ordered them to be proclaimed at the Mercat Cross of Edinburgh. All ministers were instructed to pray publicly and by name for their new sovereigns, those in Edinburgh on Sunday 14 April, others south of the Tay on 21 April and those north of it on 28 April. The Westminster Confession of Faith was reinstated but not the National Covenant nor the Solemn League and Covenant. Episcopacy was abolished, because it was 'contrary to the inclinations of the generality of the people'. This may or may not have been true and there are various estimates of the relative strength of committed Presbyterians and

2. Dickinson and Donaldson, *Source Book of Scottish History*, 95–104.

3. Dickinson and Donaldson, *Source Book of Scottish History*, 122–25.

4. Drummond and Bulloch, *Scottish Church, 1688–1843*, 8.

Episcopalians. Certainly, there were Presbyterians mainly in the south west of Scotland who excluded themselves from the settlement, and who later coalesced as the Reformed Presbyterian Church, and there were Episcopalians who were loyal supporters of the Stewart cause. King William could not afford to be intolerant and is reported to have hesitated at the clause in the coronation oath which obliged him 'to root out all heretics and enemies to the true worship of God'. He only accepted it on the understanding that it did not require him to persecute.[5]

The nature of the Revolution Settlement was dictated by the desire for political stability, rather than by the clear consent of the majority of the Scottish people, although it must be allowed that Presbyterianism had the best organized and most vociferous supporters and the Episcopalians were committed by their bishops to Jacobitism, for loyalty to James became to them what amounted to a first article of faith. William's main adviser in his ecclesiastical policy in Scotland was William Carstares, a man of moderating influence, who added to a covenanting background a breadth of culture and wisdom denied to some of his colleagues. In June 1690 after much negotiation the Presbyterian Government of the Church was established, ratified, and confirmed, an act was passed abolishing patronage and the right to call a minister was transferred to the Protestant heritors and elders of the parishes.

In 1693 the Scottish Parliament passed an Act for Settling the Peace of the Church which demanded that all ministers should acknowledge by oath that William was king de jure as well as de facto. No one who did not swear that oath could be a member of the Assembly. This Erastian[6] Act infuriated strict Presbyterians and must have raised Episcopalian hopes. Queen Anne's accession in 1702 and English Acts, such as the Occasional Conformity Bill of 1711, which limited the freedom of dissenting churches in England, caused more anxieties. The complex discussions and stratagems leading to the Act of Union in 1707 did not allay Presbyterian fears which persisted even although the Act for Securing the Protestant Religion and Presbyterian Church Government was passed alongside the Treaty. There was widespread, if ineffective, opposition to the Union amongst many sectors of the Scottish people, but under Carstares' guidance the Church as a body did not oppose it. Many individual ministers and some presbyteries did. Thomas Boston of Ettrick, who was in 1707 engaged in removing there from Simprin, spoke for many when he wrote in his *Memoirs*:

5. Drummond and Bulloch, *Scottish Church, 1688–1843*, 5.
6. Erastianism elided the distinction between church and state.

On the first day of May I was admitted minister of Ettrick; a day
remarkable to after ages as the day in which the Union of England and Scotland commenced. . . . I had frequent occasion to
remember it, the spirits of the people being embittered on that
event against the ministers of the Church which is an occasion
of much heaviness to me, though I was never for the Union but
always against it from the beginning to this day.

Thereafter in his farewell sermon at Simprin, on 7 June 1707, Boston
said:

I give my testimony to the covenanted work of Reformation
and believe that the National and Solemn League and Covenant
were of God; and I exhort you to cleave thereto, against popery,
prelacy, superstition and ceremonies. And mourn for this that
by this Union a nail is sent from Scotland, to fix the Dagon of
the English hierarchy in its place in our country.[7]

Boston was not alone in fearing undue English and Episcopalian influence, and soon ominous legislation ensued. The new British Parliament
was denounced as a monstrous affront to Presbyterian principles, with prel-
ates—an abomination in themselves—in the House of Lords confounding
the strict separation of civil and spiritual spheres.

Other affronts to strict Presbyterians soon followed. In 1709 James
Greenshields, an indulged Episcopalian minister, opened a meeting house
opposite St Giles Kirk in Edinburgh, and used the *Book of Common Prayer*
in his services. He was harassed and arrested but won his appeal to the
House of Lords.[8] The Tory government at Westminster proceeded to pass
several rather alarming measures. On 3 March 1712 the royal assent was
given to the Act of Toleration for Episcopalian clergymen who took an oath
of allegiance. The offence that this caused was compounded by the demand
that Presbyterian ministers should also take the oath which was frankly
Erastian. Then the church's power of excommunication was deprived of
civil sanctions, thus diminishing the authority of the church. The Assembly protested, but in vain. Worse was to follow. The right of presentation to
parishes was restored to patrons, and this led to numerous disputed settle-
ments throughout the eighteenth century and indeed until the Disruption
in 1843.[9] Despite the Toleration Act hard times came to the Episcopalians,
who were riven with internal disputes and lost support, especially after the

---

7. Boston, *Whole Works*, 4:456.

8. Drummond and Bulloch, *Scottish Church, 1688–1843*, 17–18.

9. Whitley, *Great Grievance*, 124–27.

'15' Jacobite rebellion was defeated. Many laity now came to adhere to the national church and helped to liberalise its life. The 1745/6 Jacobite rebellion, when many Episcopalians were on the losing side and after which meeting houses were destroyed, reduced the church of the bishops to 'the shadow of a shade'.[10]

Scotland was changing rapidly in the early eighteenth century. Famine in the years 1695–1699 carried off one fifth to one third of the population in some areas, and the Darien scheme which attempted to seize for Scotland a slice of the profitable overseas trade became a melancholy failure by 1702.[11] Gradually thereafter the country began to recover, thanks partly to the Union, and by 1740 the country was moving towards the Industrial revolution. The manufacture of linen cloth, Scotland's premier industry, and one in which several early Glasite families were to become involved, rose threefold in output and fourfold in value between 1736–1740 and 1772. The tobacco trade flourished. There was a growth in the banking system. The Bank of Scotland was founded in 1695, the Royal Bank of Scotland in 1727, and the British Linen Bank, entirely at this stage financing the linen trade, in 1746. Coal and lead mining increased in volume. Farmers used improved implements and stock, and the population began to increase rapidly, especially in the towns. In 1755 when Dr Webster produced an estimate of the national population, partly to satisfy government requirements and partly to assist in the computation of a pension scheme for ministers, he settled on the basis of parish returns on approximately 1,265,000 people.[12] In 1801 the census return was 1,608,000. Large scale emigration offset the natural increase, and it was in the towns that the most dramatic rises occurred. Between 1707 and 1801 the population of Paisley rose from 4,500 to 31,000, Glasgow from 13,000 to 77,000, Arbroath from 2,000 to 5,000, and Dundee, in the years from 1755 to 1801, from 12,500 to 27,000. These were towns where dissent was strong and where Glasite and allied churches were modestly to flourish. As people moved in from surrounding villages and farms the traditional religious discipline slackened, the towns provided a freer atmosphere for discussion, and the circulation of religious and political literature, although the rural population of Scotland had had a long tradition of treasuring spiritual books.

---

10. Scott, *Guy Mannering*, chapter 37.

11. Watt, *Price of Scotland*, tells the story in detail.

12. Whyte, *Scotland before the Industrial Revolution*, 113.

The Religious Climate in Early Eighteenth-Century Scotland

John Glas's move from the orthodoxy of his training and upbringing did not come without precedent and was to some extent a consequence of subtle changes in the religious climate of his time. Scotland was not immune to general currents in Europe. Wodrow's letters and clerical diaries like that of George Ridpath of Stitchell, near Kelso,[13] show the wide extent of reading and the eagerness with which books were exchanged and ideas were transmitted from France and the Low Countries to rural manses in Scotland. New ideas produced new emphases in doctrine and life style within the church. There was a certain weariness after the times of persecution which induced a more relaxed theological atmosphere both in Scotland and among English nonconformists, with some of whom the Presbyterians had felt kinship during the years of persecuting prelacy. As we shall see, although Independents had not been altogether welcome in Scotland during the Commonwealth, the writings of their judicious theologians, especially John Owen, were studied and admired.

Not long after the Revolution heterodox sentiments began to appear in the Church of England, and also among some nonconformists, particularly the Presbyterians and General or Arminian Baptists. Those who held such views, variously referred to as Socinian or Arian, claimed that they were returning to the bare word of Scripture from man-made creeds and confessions. It was held that as the word Trinity was not in Scripture, it should not be used as a test of orthodoxy. On 31 March 1717 the bishop of Bangor, Benjamin Hoadley, preached, in the presence of King George 1, a sermon entitled *The Nature of the Kingdom, or Church, of Christ*. Its text was John 18:36: 'Jesus answered, "My Kingdom is not of this world"', and thus sparked the Bangorian controversy whose echoes were heard in Scotland.[14] That text was also the foundation of Glas's most important work, *The Testimony of the King of Martyrs*. In February 1719 the nonconformist ministers of London met at Salter's Hall to discuss questions from the Exeter Assembly of Nonconformists, and resolved, by fifty-seven votes to fifty-three, that 'no human compositions, or interpretations of the doctrine of the Trinity should be made part of those articles of advice' to be sent to Exeter.[15] From Arminianism to Arianism to Socinianism, the road seemed to lead to Deism, which saw Christianity as the 'Republication of the Religion of Nature'. That such a

---

13. Paul, *Diary of George Ridpath.*
14. Starkie, *Church of England and the Bangorian Controversy*, 77.
15. Watts, *Dissenters*, 375–76.

narrative was neither a chimera nor a purely English phenomenon is shown by the Act of the General Assembly of 1696 against 'Atheistical Opinions of the Deists and for Establishing the Confession of Faith.' Thomas Halyburton, professor of divinity at the University of St Andrews, who had been troubled in his student days by Deism, wrote to controvert Lord Herbert of Cherbury, a noted Deist writer. In a posthumous work published in 1714 Halyburton wrote, 'The infection [sc. of Deism] spreads and many are daily carried off by it both in England and in Scotland. Though it must be owned that Scotland is as yet less tainted with that poison'.[16] That atheism was considered a danger is evidenced by a popular work of George Sinclair, professor of philosophy in Glasgow. In 1685 he published *Satan's Invisible World Discovered*, which was reprinted into the nineteenth century and was for a long time a constituent part of every cottage library in Scotland. He considered it necessary to assert belief in demons and witches, 'especially now, while atheism and Quakerism, that sink of folly and madness, out of which is not a great leap into the other doth now so much obtain'.[17]

The haunting fear that the clergy had of atheism disguised as deism must be the reason for the harsh treatment given to Thomas Aitkenhead, the son of an Edinburgh surgeon, and a student at Edinburgh, who was tried and executed for blasphemy in 1697. He was charged with saying that theology was a 'rhapsody of feigned and ill-invented nonsense', and it was alleged that he had called the Old Testament 'Ezra's Fables', and the New Testament 'the History of the Impostor Christ'. At his trial he did not deny these words but said he repented of them and was willing to make amends by his subsequent conduct. Nevertheless, the court, with the agreement of at least some of the Edinburgh clergy, sentenced him to be hanged.[18] Until the end of the seventeenth century the persecuting spirit survived. Witchcraft trials from the same period show an equally rigid interpretation of both Scripture and the law.

In 1726 Wodrow wrote:

> We have the Marrou on the one hand who print and scatter papers and sermons very cheap through the country and are popular and spreading and gaining ground in some places. In the North we have Popery not born down, and very much increasing. In the West we have Mr Simson's unhappy affair. To say

---

16. Thomas Halyburton, *Natural Religion Insufficient*, 32, quoted in Torrance, *Scottish Theology*, 231.

17. Dunlop et al., *Miscellany of the Scottish History Society* 6, 282.

18. Chambers, *Domestic Annals of Scotland*, 160–66.

nothing of Mr Glass and Archibald in Angus; and the nue-lights
and Preachers legal shall I call them or Arminians.[19]

Wodrow's survey introduces some of the theological attitudes and
ecclesiastical themes that can be distinguished in the first half of the eighteenth century, which can shade into each other and leave some leaders not
easily classified.[20] Firstly, there were the scholastic Calvinists like Principal
James Hadow of St Andrews, who were equally opposed to all deviations
from orthodoxy, whether in the direction of a warmer evangelicalism, such
as was manifested by the 'Marrow' men, or to speculative theology such as
that of Professor Simson of Glasgow. Hadow and those who thought like
him stood for total loyalty to the Westminster Confession, particularly to
the sections dealing with predestination. In the controversy over the place
of Law in the Christian life, which was part of the Marrow matter, they were
so afraid of antinomianism that they leaned towards the Neonomianism associated with the writings of the English Puritan Richard Baxter, a doctrine
which stated that our 'evangelical righteousness . . . consisteth in our own
actions of faith and gospel obedience' and talked of performing the conditions of the gospel. This doctrinal formulation had been much debated in
English nonconformity and in Scotland in the late seventeenth century, and
while the orthodox party did not hold it explicitly, they came near it in their
defense of the Confession.

The second attitude bears most closely on the theology of the Independents. It was that of those who may be called evangelical Calvinists, of men
who were zealous for free grace, loyal to the Confession, yet making a wide
and warm-hearted gospel appeal to their hearers. James Hog of Carnock,
Boston of Ettrick, Willison of Dundee, soon to be an opponent of Glas,
Davidson of Galashiels and the Erskine brothers were men of this stamp.
They were to be condemned by Robert Sandeman as 'popular preachers',
who preached to the hearts of men and reached beyond the strict bounds
of predestinarian theology in their offer of the gospel and their anxiety that
their hearers should 'close with Christ'. Whilst it would be anachronistic to
speak at this stage of an evangelical party in the Kirk, the events of these
years drew together men of like mind and temper. Drummond and Bulloch
see connections between the preaching of those ministers and theologians
and the Anabaptists and Mennonites and those other groups whose emphases on conversion and the gathered church were in many ways alien

19. Wodrow, *Analecta*, in *Correspondence*, 3:360.

20. I follow here the chapter by Mechie in Shaw, *Reformation and Revolution*,
258–72. For another classification of attitudes see Ahnert, *Moral Culture of the Scottish
Enlightenment, 1690–1805*, 17–33.

to the traditional way of the Reformed church.[21] At the great communion seasons people flocked together from neighboring churches and there is a line of revivals from Kirk o' Shotts in 1630 through the Great Awakening in America in 1734 to the Cambuslang 'Wark' of 1740 and the following years, although it must be noted that the Evangelicals such as Ebenezer Erskine were very wary of 'revivals'.

Some of the formative influences for this tradition can be isolated. Praying Societies were in existence and looked upon coldly by the General Assembly as early as 1640 but this did not stop their development and popularity in certain parts of the country. Often those who joined such groups were dissatisfied with the ordinary ministrations of the parish, but occasionally the minister and session were the moving spirits in promoting the spiritual welfare of the people in these gatherings. At Tealing in the late 1720s John Glas gathered some seventy-two people into a disciplined society within the parish. Other societies were to become the nuclei of the Secession congregations. These praying societies did not set out to oppose the National Church. They were the Scottish part of a European movement for closer fellowship in small groups within the parish structure. Phillip Jakob Spener in Frankfurt in 1675 had set in motion by the publication of his 'Pia Desideria' the movement which by 1694 was established in the new University of Halle, and which became known as Pietism. There is a link through Zinzendorf and the Moravian Church with John Wesley and the class meetings of the early Methodists. Wodrow records in 1724 that a friend 'joyned in a privat fellowship meeting which convened every Monday about six of the clock, and spent some hours in prayer and conference, where he was much refreshed'. He adds that 'there were multitudes of these meetings, both of young men and of elder persons in London'.[22] Some of these groups were organized for charity as well as for prayer.

In the second decade of the eighteenth century, rules were drawn up for entry into and continuance in the societies, and guidance given about suitable subjects for discussion. The weak in gifts were welcomed, but the unsound in principle could be kept out. In Ebenezer Erskine's society in Portmoak rule eleven states, 'The members of the society shall pray by turns according to the alphabetical order of their names; and at every meeting three or at most five or six shall pray, except when providence calls for more than ordinary wrestling'.[23] There was nothing new in small fellowship groups meeting for mutual comfort, instruction, and exhortation. The

21. Drummond and Bulloch, *Scottish Church, 1688–1843*, 49.

22. Wodrow, *Analecta*, in *Correspondence*, 3:371.

23. Fawcett, *Cambuslang Revival*, 69.

Independents did not invent the *ecclesiola in ecclesia*. Where Glas went far beyond the common practice of his contemporaries was in celebrating the sacrament of the Lord's Supper in a small elect group.

The third attitude is that of those who may be called 'early moderates', or New Lights. They were men influenced by the liberal but still orthodox temper of William Hamilton, who was professor of divinity in Edinburgh from 1709–1732. He had been baptized at a conventicle, and had an impeccable covenanting background, yet his teaching, while guarded and orthodox, was not of the old school. Wodrow was suspicious of him, and he may well be seen as the teacher of the Moderates, along with Frances Hutcheson, who became professor of moral philosophy at Glasgow in 1730. These men were able to keep silent on certain controverted points and they were for toleration in the church. Hamilton was unwilling to press for the condemnation of either Simson or Glas. He presumably had little sympathy with Glas's stance, but he was anxious not to offend the Independent churches in England and he did not wish to drive an earnest and learned man out of the church. Dr Wallace, who succeeded him in leadership in the church, 'seems to have been not unsympathetic' with much that Glas had done, but he considered that Glas had been imprudent and should have 'let the Covenants sleep for some years longer'. He would have had Glas restored to the exercise of his ministry in Tealing, holding that his differences with the Church were merely speculative.'[24] Men like these took up strongly the defense of Christianity against infidelity, arguing not from the proclamation of a full Christian faith, but from its intrinsic excellence and the great benefits conferred on society by its divine origin and authority.

The fourth group consists of Professor John Simson and the Glasgow men who were believed to have accepted at least part of his teaching. Wodrow wrote to Cotton Mather in New England in 1716, 'This poor church, since the Reformation has been entirely free of any dispute on point of doctrine, and I pray that this may end so as truth may prevail'. The 'this' he mentions was the process against Simson, an old correspondent of Wodrow's who had been pursued since 1714 by James Webster of the Tron Church, Edinburgh, a stalwart, and sometimes reckless, champion of orthodoxy. Simson was the son of one of the antediluvians, that is the ministers restored to office in 1690. He had been educated at Leyden and was appointed to the chair of divinity at Glasgow in 1708. He was charged with heresy at the Assembly of 1717. From all accounts he was an unlikely heresiarch, timid and colorless, and by the end of his second ordeal ill and confused. Yet his teaching

24. Sefton, "Rev Robert Wallace," 3.

frightened less rigid men than Webster. Basically the charge against him was of teaching Arminianism, and he was alleged to have taught

> that by the light of Nature and the works of providence and cre-
> ation, including tradition, God has given an objective revelation
> unto all men of his being reconcilable to sinners; that the hea-
> then may know this; that it is probable that none are excluded
> from the benefits of the remedy for sin provided by God, and
> published twice to the world, except those who by their actual
> sin exclude themselves; that nothing is to be admitted in religion
> but what is agreeable to reason; that the souls of infants since
> the Fall are pure and holy; that were it not for the prospect of
> happiness we could not and therefore would not serve God.[25]

He apologized for unguarded language, but he was certainly sailing close not only to Arminianism, but to Deism, and to a form of natural religion.

He was exonerated in 1717, but in 1726 he was again in the limelight. All this time he was teaching a large number of divinity students, many of them from Ulster, to which they returned and where they have been held to be responsible for spreading Arianism. At the Assembly of 1726 a strong committee was set up with powers to suspend Simson from teaching if they deemed it necessary. The case was at last settled in 1729 when Simson was suspended but not deposed. He was relieved of his duties but left with his salary. His teaching was cloudy and imprecise and possibly often misunderstood but influenced as he was by the writings of Samuel Clarke and John Locke, he was held to have been a bad influence on young men.[26] The contrast between the relatively light sentence on Simson and the harsh treatment of Glas a year later was noted by Glas's friends.

Two Contrasting Controversies

There was still in Scotland in the early eighteenth century a popular interest in theological controversy and experimental religion. The 'Marrow Contro-versy' approached very near the hearts of believers. In 1717 the Presbytery of Auchterarder, afraid of Baxterian Neonomianism, required a candidate for license to affirm 'that it is not sound and orthodox to teach that we must forsake sin in order to come to Christ'. The student saw in these words more than a hint of Antinomianism and appealed to the Assembly which upheld him and condemned the Presbytery. Thomas Boston observed to

---

25. Dundas, *State of the Processes Depending against Mr John Simson*, 220.
26. Boston, *Memoirs*, 416.

John Drummond of Crieff who was sitting next to him at the Assembly that he had recently read a book which he had discovered in a cottage in Simprin. This book was *The Marrow of Modern Divinity*, by Edward Fisher, published in 1646 and brought to Simprin by a soldier returning from the Civil War. Boston's friends read it and were so impressed that they brought out a new edition in 1718, with a preface by James Hog of Carnock. Hadow of St Andrews smelt the taint of Antinomianism and attacked the book in a pamphlet, and by 1720 several propositions in the book were condemned in the Assembly. The author uses a paradoxical style, and its format, of a discussion between those of differing views, allowed him to state firmly what he did not necessarily believe. Where Simson's case showed the rise of a broader-based theology, the Marrow Controversy brought the second group in the church into prominence as the 'Evangelical Party' opposed both by the strict Calvinists and the Moderates. There were twelve original Marrowmen, who sought unsuccessfully to have the condemnation removed at the Assembly in 1721. No action was then taken against them, but the seeds of the Secession were sown, and it is interesting that James Adams (1682–1734) minister of Kinnaird from 1707–1734, claims that there was a direct relationship between the Marrow men and the Glasite Church. In his tract *The Independent Ghost Conjur'd* published in 1728 he wrote 'some years ago we were stuff'd and cram'd, even to nauseating, with the "Marrow of Modern Divinity", smoothing the Antinomian doctrine to us; and now by a rump of the same men we have got some of the worst part of the Independent Scheme brought upon the Stage'.[27]

James Adams's career is worth noting as it comprehends many of the competing currents of religion in that part of Scotland. Kinnaird is a small parish in Perthshire whose laird, Sir David Thriepland of Fingask, was in 1700 a Jacobite, in touch with the court of the Chevalier. In 1715 he came out with the rebels, and there are stories of the devotion of the people of the district to the Old Pretender. Adams denounced the rebels from the pulpit. He was an admirer of the Covenanters and so opposed to his chief heritor, Sir David. Adams, as we have seen, had little time for the *Marrow*, although he conceded that its author, Fisher, was 'no contemptible man,' but his book was 'stuff'd with Errors and erroneous Insinuations'. The book pretended to light where the Westminster Divines saw none and tended to Antinomianism. He accuses Fisher of teaching downright Arminianism on the subject of Christ's sin-bearing.[28] In Glas's *Narrative* there is a tangled account of letters containing twenty-six queries which had been put by Adams, largely

---

27. Adams, *Independent Ghost Conjur'd*, iv–v.
28. Adams, *Independent Ghost Conjur'd*, 44.

upon the status of the Covenants, to which Glas replied in many counter-queries. Adams was only one of the local ministers who took issue with Glas but there were several who took his part.

The Marrow doctrine was that of a warm evangelicalism. The search for peace with God was the abiding principle, and an important strand was re-introduced into Scottish Calvinism. It stated that when a man once comes to believe that all his sins, past, present and to come, are freely and fully pardoned, and God in Christ graciously reconciled to him; the Lord would hereupon so reveal his fatherly face unto him in Christ and so make known that incredible union betwixt him and the believing soul; that his heart becomes quietly contented in God, who is the proper element of its being. The Westminster Confession was already becoming too narrow a vehicle for Christian experience.

In the northeast of Scotland around Aberdeen Presbyterianism had only a slender hold. There was no Synod until 1697 and only three presbyteries were organized by that date. There was an interest in mystical doctrine among some ministers and leading lay folk. Here Henry Scougal wrote *The Life of God in the Soul of Man* and here also the teachings of Madame Bourignon, a Catholic writer who shared some ideas with Quakers and Pietists found followers. Dr George Garden and other 'Aberdeen Doctors' were influenced by her and by the Quietist Madame Guyon.[29] They were duly condemned in 1701 for a variety of heresies, notably that of denying the doctrines of election and reprobation, the assertion of the sinful corruption of Christ's nature, of a state of perfection attainable in this life, and of the view that generation would take place in heaven. Halyburton preached against it in 1707, and in 1714 Wodrow condemned it as 'enthusiastical foppery'. Scotland was not theologically homogeneous, nor was it cut off from continental trends of thought.

By 1730 the ecclesiastical scene in Scotland seemed ripe for new developments. On the one extreme were the 'old dissenters' organized in societies and able in 1743 to form a Presbytery of the Reformed Presbyterian Church. They were strongest in the southwest, but both Boston in Ettrick in the Borders and Glas in Tealing were troubled by them. On the other extreme there were rumors of revived Romanism, particularly in the north, and in many places, as we have noted, Episcopalianism remained strong. Both Presbyterian and non-Presbyterian dissent were responses to the challenges of the time. The former resolved to keep the faith pure by seceding from the Church of Scotland, and the latter seeking scriptural warrant for the

---

29. Henderson, *Religious Life in Seventeenth Century Scotland*, 220–31. The mystical teaching of the Quietists did not accord with Scottish Calvinism.

constitution of the church, was led into forms of Independency. The First Secession, known as the Associate Presbytery, was formed at Gairney Bridge near Kinross in December 1733, by men deposed from their parishes in the previous months for attacking the declension of the church and Patronage in particular. Soon praying societies and other groups formed congregations, to preserve the true faith. The Seceders, in their *Judicial Testimony* of 1736, condemned general slackness in the Church. The 1736 repeal in Parliament of the Acts of Assembly condemning witchcraft was denounced, and attention was drawn to the arbitrary and unfairly harsh treatment of the Marrow-men, and the Presbytery of Auchterarder, and the contrasting lenient treatment of Simson and others. The leading Seceders, Ebenezer and Ralph Erskine, had been Marrow-men, but not all their fellow-sufferers left the Establishment. For eight years after 1732 the Assembly attempted to win back the Seceders, leaving them in possessions of their manses, churches, and stipends. The Church of Scotland had a deep-rooted horror of schism, but the Secession continued and drew in an increasing number of earnest folk, mostly in the Lowlands.

Independency in Scotland—The Beginning

Glas's position in 1730, while appearing revolutionary, was not quite new in Scotland. We shall examine the process by which he became disillusioned with the Kirk, and was driven, almost unwillingly, into an Independent position as the leader of a new kind of church. But there were precedents. The first recorded Independent in Scotland was a refugee from England, Robert Browne, who gave his name to early Congregationalists in England. Fleeing from persecution he and a few companions landed at Dundee late in 1583 and were favorably received by Andrew Melville in St Andrews. They proceeded to Edinburgh where they had a much less cordial reception. Browne was examined by the Presbytery, whose jurisdiction he refused, and he appealed to the magistrates. He was briefly imprisoned and although he claimed to have travelled widely to study the church, he achieved nothing and left, probably in 1584. His comments on the Scottish Church, that the regime of pastors, doctors and presbyters produced 'instead of one pope a thousand, and instead of some lord bishops in name a thousand lordly tyrants in deed', would scarcely have endeared him to the Kirk. The Welshman John Penry also fled to Scotland in 1589 and had no more success.[30]

In the early seventeenth century 'Brownists' were mentioned in the Register of the Privy Council in Scotland as forming conventicles, particularly

30. Escott, *History of Scottish Congregationalism*, 3–5.

in Edinburgh, where John Mein, a merchant, was noted as a leader. Similar reports came in the next twenty years from Stirling and Aberdeen. Books by Puritans and Independents spread into Scotland but the experience of Scottish delegates at the Westminster Assembly strengthened their opposition to Independency and Anabaptism. In his book *Cromwell and Scotland* R. Scott Spurlock gives details of several dissident groups who in the 1650s questioned the Presbyterian form of church government and the Covenants. In a time of uncertainty and conflict Alexander Jaffray, a substantial citizen of Aberdeen, who later became a Quaker, sent a letter to the Protestors, the most radical faction of the Presbyterian church, stating that the Church of Christ, rather than including the masses and then weeding out the clearly degenerate, should start by gathering together true believers:

> To us it seems, for aught we can search in the Word, that none should be admitted as constituent members of a visible church, but such as with a profession of the Truth join such a blameless and gospel-like behaviour, as they may be esteemed in a rational judgment of charity, believers, and their children. Such were the churches founded by the apostles.[31]

The national church saw the 'saints' as the invisible elect among the visible church. Jaffray and his friends believed that the church should be composed of those who showed signs of grace. The only solution they could see was separation from the Kirk, although that was far from their original intention, sharing as they did the deep dislike of schism in the Kirk.

This decision took place in 1652, while the Commonwealth armies occupied Scotland and army chaplains like James Brown and others were free to proclaim, in pulpit and debate, Independent and even Baptist teachings. Despite the opposition of the Kirk, small independent gatherings were noted throughout Scotland, particularly in Aberdeen and the northeast. The recall of English troops in 1658 renewed pressure to rejoin the Kirk and the further radicalization of some towards Quakerism spelt the end of Scottish Independency for sixty years. There is, however, a tantalizing glimpse in the *Fasti* of an eccentric minister, James Farquhar. He was born in 1666, educated at Marischal College, Aberdeen, and in 1701 ordained to the Parish of Tyrie, in Aberdeenshire. 'He demitted office on 31st August 1709, as he entertained scruples regarding Congregational Church government, which he renounced before 30th April 1715'. He was called in 1717 to Nigg, near Aberdeen, and remained there until his death in December 1754. 'He was a man of great muscular strength, and as a young man was frequently employed in preaching churches vacant which had been in the hands of

---

31. Spurlock, *Cromwell and Scotland*, 123.

the Episcopalians'.[32] Perhaps his scruples were of the nature of a youthful indiscretion. Apart from the meetings held by Gabriel Wilson and Henry Davidson, which are mentioned in passing, Independency seems to have been otherwise unknown until the beginning of the Glasite movement. It is worth stressing how repugnant such teachings were to the great majority of the leaders of the Kirk. Glas was treading in very dangerous territory.

In 1730 Thomas Ayton, minister of Alyth in Perthshire, published a long book entitled *The Original Constitution of the Christian Church: wherein the Extremes on either hand are stated and examined; to which is added an appendix, containing The Rise of Jure Divino Prelatists, and an answer to their arguments by Episcopal Divines*. Professor Thomas Torrance, who became a leading twentieth-century theologian and whose first charge was Alyth, has written a very full appreciation of this work, especially its contribution to the debate between Presbyterians and Episcopalians which was still acute in certain parts of Scotland. Ayton attempts to vindicate Presbyterian order and government by a series of courts, from Session, to Presbytery, to Synod, and ultimately to General Assembly, in Torrance's view with success. He pays less attention to the other area of dispute, the Independent scheme, for which Glas forfeited his parish in that same year, although he does mention that Ayton did not really consider the 'claim of the Congregationalists that the local congregation is an outcrop and manifestation of the one Catholic Universal Church'.[33]

Glas, who had already set forth Independency in his tract *A Congregation or Church of Jesus Christ, with its presbytery, is, in its discipline, subject to no jurisdiction under heaven*, published in 1728. In 1730 he published *Some Observations upon the Original Constitution of the Christian Church in a letter to the author of a book bearing that title*. In this he seeks to refute Ayton point by point and with great patristic and reformation learning. He controverts his assertions of a primitive Presbyterian order by a close exegesis of passages in the Acts of the Apostles and in the Epistle to the Ephesians and seeks to establish Independency of some sort as the primitive form of the church. In 1731 he replied to Ayton's *Remarks on the Review of the Observations* in which he further asserts the rights of the individual congregation, and this seems to be part of an ongoing controversy. We shall return to this theme in a discussion of Glas's principles in chapter 2.

32. Wodrow, *Correspondence*, 2:224n2.

33. Torrance, in Shaw, *Reformation and Revolution*, 297.

2

John Glas

ON 6 MAY 1719 John Glas was ordained and inducted to the parish of Tealing near Dundee, and in March 1730 at the meeting of the Commission of
Assembly, after a long and complicated process, he was deposed from the
ministry of the Church of Scotland. By this time he was so far removed
from the life of the national church that when in 1739 his deposition was
reversed, not at his request, and he was informed that he was considered a
Christian minister, but not of the Church of Scotland until he made peace
with it, he paid no attention to the Church's change of heart.[1] Between 1719
and 1730 Glas's thought and practice developed in new and relatively un-
charted directions.

John Glas was born on 21 September 1695, the fifth generation of a
clerical lineage, son of Alexander, minister of the parish of Auchtermuchty
in Cupar Presbytery, in the county of Fife. When he was quite young his
father moved, in April 1700, to the parish of Kinclaven, in Perthshire, where
John Glas began his education, later moving to Perth Grammar School, and
thence to St Leonard's College in the University of St Andrews. He graduated M.A. on 6 May 1713 and proceeded with his father's recommendation
to theological study in Edinburgh.[2] Later he reflected that he had never
given serious consideration to anything other than the ministry but had a
lack of confidence in his fitness for the work.

---

1. See Raffe, "John Glas and the Development," 527–45. Raffe sees this recognition
of Glas as a 'minister of the Gospel of Christ and exercise of that Holy Function but not
as a minister of the Church of Scotland' as an important step towards the recognition of
religious pluralism in the hitherto united national church.

2. Mullan, "Early Career of John Glas," 234.

In his paper on the 'Early Career of John Glas'[3] David Mullan has traced his journey through the long and arduous process towards ordination, which he describes as a 'procedural thicket.' It was at the urging of the Presbytery of Dunkeld, that Glas (despite his own misgivings, and his comparative youth) began the journey in August 1717. The Synod of Perth and Stirling gave permission for the usual licensing trials, in October 1717. He then went back to his theological studies in Edinburgh, afterwards returning to the presbytery to give public demonstrations of his fitness for the ministry. On 20 May 1718 he signed the confession and formula and after promising subjection to 'this and any other presbytery where providence should cast his lot' he was licensed to preach the gospel as a probationer. At this time he was happy to accept the Westminster Confession of Faith in its entirety and the conviction of the scriptural basis and authenticity of the church's doctrine, worship and polity and to make the promises 'never to endeavour, directly or indirectly the prejudice or subversion of the same'; and never to follow any 'divisive course from the present establishment of this church.'[4]

On 25 March 1719 Glas, having become the unanimous choice of the parish of Tealing, preached before the Presbytery of Dundee, and on 15 April he underwent extemporary trials, offered analyses of Hebrew and Greek texts, being thoroughly approved by the whole body. He was appointed to be ordained as the minister of the Parish of Tealing on 6 May and was preached in by Rev James Marr of Muirhouse (now Murroes) who was to continue to be his friend. In all this Glas behaved as, and was accepted as, a perfectly orthodox minister of the Church of Scotland, and soon he was taking part in the activities of the Presbytery.

It was not long before he entered the stormy path which led to his deposition. J. T. Hornsby noted that the 'Kirk Session records reveal that there was great need for the exercise of church discipline in Tealing. As in many parish records of this time, there are cases of swearing, violence, antenuptial fornication and irreligious expression.'[5] After his deposition some members of his congregation wrote warmly of his labors in his parish, saying that

> he had found the Parish almost void of any Thing of the Form of Religion, and overspread with ignorance, but since they have Ground to bless the Lord, that they have found a very desirable change, by the Lord's Blessing on his Labours.

3. Mullan, "Early Career of John Glas," 233–62.
4. Mullan, "Early Career of John Glas," 235–36.
5. Hornsby, "Case of Mr John Glas," 116.

His predecessor, Hugh Maxwell, (1703–1717) wrote in 1709 to Wodrow, complaining that

> the English service continues with us, and that Liturgy is in great vogue and esteem with many amongst us, especially our gentry, who seem to be disposed to receive any thing that's against the Established Church, her doctrine, worship and government; and that's against the truth that is according to godliness' and that 'iniquity abounds among us, the love of many waxeth cold, great deadness seizes this generation.[6]

Perhaps Glas's 'youth and inexperience and idealism meant that he was unprepared for the sometimes sordid grind that parochial discipline could entail', writes Mullan.[7] But this was an unruly and uncertain time in Scotland, and surely Glas, growing up in a country manse, would have known something of the difficulties of parish life.

Opposition to Glas partly came from some parishioners who were influenced by the Cameronian party. They were particularly angered by the fact that the Kirk had submitted to the Oath of Abjuration of 1711, an anti-Jacobite measure which supported the Revolution settlement and entailed recognition of a monarch who was member of the Church of England. This measure left no room for the reinstatement of the covenants, and the Cameronians 'magnified the former covenanting days, and prophesied of great days to come, by the reviving of the covenants'.[8] Glas was led by this pastoral problem with some of his parish to examine the whole question of the nature of the kingdom of Christ, and to attempt to settle the matter based on Scripture. He had earlier looked at the Episcopal system and rejected it. At that time he had not investigated congregationalism's arguments, assuming the usual prejudices that it is 'mere confusion and the Mother of all Sectaries'. Experience led him in time to look at congregational Independency. He sought to set up a select church within his parish and thereby showed that he wanted to build a community of saints and erect a fence around the committed few with restricted access to the Lord's Table, where only the visible saints, defined ultimately in the style of congregational Independency, might approach.

In the event he did gather together a group of real believers, an *ecclesiola in ecclesia*, an *imperium in imperio* according to William Jones,[9] where

---

6. Wodrow, *Correspondence*, 1:79.

7. Mullan, "Early Career of John Glas," 239.

8. Mullan, "Early Career of John Glas," 237.

9. Jones, *New Evangelical Magazine* 9, 282. Jones was a Scotch Baptist based in London who edited a series of magazines and often reprinted Glasite material.

his teaching was appreciated and where a real fellowship could develop. This group, of around seventy-two persons, whose addresses are the farmtouns of the parish, eventually met monthly for communion in a way that was not customary in the Kirk and were also recommended to meet in societies for prayer, exhortation and discipline.[10] The only parallel to this proceeding was in the Scottish Borders where Henry Davidson, minister of Galashiels from 1714 until his death in 1756,[11] and Gabriel Wilson, minister of Maxton from 1709 until 1750,[12] who were both involved in the Marrow controversy, renounced sacramental communion with the established church. They continued to preach, baptize, and catechize in their parishes, but declined to dispense communion to their people. Around 1736 they started to hold communion services in Maxton on Sunday evenings with a select group in what Escott describes as a congregational church,[13] and this they did undisturbed by the Kirk for around twenty years. Small quotes the Caledonian Mercury:

> A new church has sprung up in the parish of Maxton. They have frequent meetings for prayer and conversation. At their last meeting it was debated whether in the sacrament there ought to be distinct blessings of the bread and wine, and if it was agreeable to Scripture to celebrate the ordinance once every week. Men and women are allowed to give their opinions.[14]

The *Fasti* calls this meeting 'Glasite'[15] but this is unlikely as there is no mention of it in Glasite records. Henry Davidson who was a 'Marrow' evangelical, was interested in Glas and his preachers. He wrote to an unnamed correspondent, 'I was told you was a hearer of one of Mr Glas's licensed preachers; pray how did he and what is Mr Glas himself doing?'[16] After they died the church continued to meet for a few years and formed a connection with the Old Scots Independents. From the same district George Byres, the minister of St Boswells (son-in-law of Gabriel Wilson) joined the followers

---

10. Murray, "Social and Religious Origins," appendix, gives a list of the members of this society.

11. *Fasti Ecclesiae Scoticanae*, 2:178.

12. *Fasti Ecclesiae Scoticanae*, 2:185.

13. Escott, *History of Scottish Congregationalism*, 24.

14. Small, *History of the Congregations*, 2:565–66.

15. *Fasti Ecclesiae Scoticanae*, 2:185.

16. Mackelvie comments, 'Mr Wilson, though maintaining his incumbency in the Established Church, built a chapel in his parish upon Independent principles and in it alone dispensed the Lord's Supper, on which occasions he was assisted by Mr Davidson of Galashiels.' Mackelvie et al., *Annals and Statistics of the United Presbyterian Church*, 521.

of Glas, setting up a church at Kippielaw, in Bowden parish, in 1738, which later moved into Galashiels and survived into the twentieth century.

Glas was also critical of the ministry of some of his colleagues, particularly John Willison of Dundee, a notable Evangelical minister whose devotional writings retained their popularity for many generations of pious Scots. Glas considered that Willison was self-satisfied and that he designed to impose an authoritative religious scheme on ordinary folk, seeking to prevent the common people from reading and interpreting the Bible for themselves. In his 1734 letter to Willison Glas defends his 'illiterate preachers' (that is unlettered in the ancient languages, not without the ability to read and write English) and accuses Willison of weakness in defending the gospel.

> You have Infidels to deal with in Dundee; but what did you, beyond raising an use of lamentation in the pulpit. And telling them in private, that they should be hanged? An illiterate man would have taken another course; he would have plainly told them the evidence he himself saw in the Gospel, and how the atheism and infidelity of his own heart was quelled by the Word of God; and if he prevailed not, he would pray for them, and shew them the truth of Christianity in his life, and even in deeds of good will to them.[17]

In his *Narrative* (1728) Glas states:

> It is a business of much more grave consideration with me, to find Protestants, adhering to the Covenants, abjuring all the errors of Popery, and charging them who differ from them about our Covenants, as being favourers of Popery and Perjury; yet beginning to speak of the Old and New Testament in the Popish Dialect, as if the People were not in safety to search for themselves, and could not come to know the mind of the Author of them in the use of means because they are dark, and different senses put upon them, and the people have not Clergy enough for them.[18]

Glas was set on the road to abandon the ideas of National Covenanting, and of a chosen nation especially favored by God. He did speak favorably of the covenanting martyrs of the reigns of Charles II and James VII. They had testified to the kingdom of Christ to the effect that the church had no earthly head, and that its officers must be authenticated by Christ. But they were wrong when they made Christ's kingdom a worldly entity. Glas said he

---

17. Glas, "Letter to Mr Willison," *Works*, 2:272.

18. Glas, *Narrative*, 205.

would honour the martyrs as far as they followed Christ, asking, 'Is there no Mids between Madness and unerring Wisdom? Or are worthy Ancestors to be followed any further, than as they follow Christ?'[19] He was reported as saying that 'our Martyrs died as Fools and they were self-murderers'. An illustration of the almost superstitious reverence paid to the covenanting heroes occurred in 1726 when the bones of some of the martyrs of 1681 were reinterred in Edinburgh. Willison spoke of them

> for a testimony against the opposition now made to the Covenants and against the present apostasy. Such a story as this was firmly believed by some well-meaning people in Dundee, that the spot of ground where the heads of these Martyrs lay bore the finest flowers, and when Mr G—s began to speak against the Covenants, the Flowers withered. The heads of the Martyrs, when taken up, were perfectly fresh so that their faces could be known.[20]

In this atmosphere Glas's limited veneration of the martyrs was dangerous talk and was one of the factors which led ultimately to the Synod of April 1728 suspending him from the exercise of his ministry. Glas was willing to affirm the Presbyterian polity of the Formula he had signed at the beginning of his ministry, but he could not adjudge it to be *iure divino*. He 'trembled at the thought of adding anything to the Words written in the Book of God'.

At the General Assembly, 11 May, the case was referred to the Commission of Assembly which continued the suspension but declared it might be lifted by the Synod upon receipt of satisfaction. But by now Glas did not care what the courts of the Church did or said, and he continued his ministry. The minister sent to supply Tealing was kept out of the church and thought there was no use going back to give any further disturbance to so resolute people as they are. Glas's obduracy strengthened and became a liability. Opposition to him solidified, and Glas moved further and further from the mainstream of the Church.

Only one other minister shared Glas's views and left his parish. This was Francis Archibald, who had been minister of Guthrie, near Brechin, since 1716. He had favored the Cameronians, and he was questioned in 1726 by his Presbytery (Arbroath) whether he had been with Rev John MacMillan, the great Covenanter apostle, in Fife a fortnight earlier. It was alleged that Archibald had travelled a long distance to be married by him, and Wodrow, also in 1726, noted his connection with MacMillan and that he had read the

19. Glas, *Narrative*, 99.
20. Glas, *Narrative*, 80.

Covenants on the fast-day before the sacrament.[21] This seemed to be the climax of his connection with the Cameronians. By 1728 he had joined Glas as an elder, forming a church first in Guthrie and then in the larger centre of Arbroath. Later he became chaplain of the Orphan Hospital in Edinburgh.

James Gray, minister of Kettins in Perthshire was a noted opponent of Glas. In 1729 he published *The Naked Truth*, a hostile account of the controversy sparked by Glas. Wodrow had claimed that 'Mr Glas's father was not very fond of his son's tryalls and said to some that he was not pleased with him'.[22] This allegation was repeated by Gray, who objected to Glas's description of Tealing, and claimed that neighboring ministers had told him that they had never heard of any concern among the people about the Covenants until Mr G. himself began it. He went on to tell the story, as he had heard it of 'Mr Glas's behaviour since he was deposed'.

> I understand that he preaches ordinarily in the house of Tealine [*sic*], sometimes in Dundee, sometimes in the parish of Guthrie. He preached once in Montrose on a week day and his hearers were for the most part Meeting House people and some others who were very indifferent about anything in religion. Mr Archibald preached there with him and they gathered a collection which was about 50 pounds Scots. They preached at Brechen [*sic*] by means of one Marjory Low, a young woman of that town, they got into the Meal Market out of which the magistrates turned them and their hearers when they went into the close of a publick tavern kept by Low's father.[23] Mr Archibald made another sermon, and both went out of town that night, their hearers were not many and those mostly Meeting House People, and the very scum of those who go to Church, but no one that ever had a profession except that Marjory Low. . . Mr Glas preached once in Perth since his deposition (as he had done sundry times while under suspension) in a private house: his hearers were very few, most of them light people and school boys, some of whom climbed on a ladder up to the windows without, so that it was a kind of religious mob.[24]

Meeting House people were almost certainly the Episcopalians of the district, expelled from the Parish Church but still numerous.

---

21. Wodrow, *Analecta*, in *Correspondence*, 3:358.

22. Wodrow, *Analecta*, in *Correspondence*, 3:323.

23. Glas firmly denied this. 'And it is the Naked Truth that I know nothing of preaching in the Clois of a Publick Tavern.' *Narrative (Further Continuation)*, 67.

24. Gray, *Naked Truth*, 37 (Second Letter).

Despite the opposition of prominent ministers, the work of building what became a new church continued. Glas's thought and teaching developed remarkably quickly. *The Testimony of the King of Martyrs* was published in 1729, at the height of the struggle with the Courts of the Church. His strong conviction was that he must be guided by the Scriptures, and he seeks in this seminal work to define the nature, extent and purpose of the kingdom of Christ. Thomas M'Crie, the editor of Wodrow's *Correspondence*, claimed that 'the Testimony was, in fact a treatise by Dr Owen, given a new form, without due acknowledgement'.[25] M'Crie seems in turn to have borrowed this comment from Bogue and Bennett's *History of the Dissenters*, a work that is not sympathetic generally to the Glasites. Owen taught that the spiritual kingdom of Christ is paramount and civil government must be subordinated to those high ends. Glas taught an absolute division between the kingdom of Christ and the rulers of this world and he based this on his typological interpretation of the Bible. He was certainly aware of the English Independent thinkers, and he occasionally quotes Owen, but his thought took him in a new and different direction. Owen had taught that the magistrate had a real obligation to support the Christian religion. 'If it once comes to that, that you shall say, you have nothing to doe [sic] with religion as Rulers of the Nation, God will quickly manifest that he has nothing to doe [sic] with you as rulers of the Nation'.[26] Owen showed that persecution of people who held erroneous opinions had never achieved any good, and that God's Word does not require the punishment of heretics unless they caused civil disorder.

Glas's text for his book was John 18:36–37, 'Jesus answered, "My Kingdom is not of this world: If my Kingdom were of this world, then would my servants fight"'. This is the text at the head of chapter 1. At the head of the short Preface are two other verses; 'Come and see . . . ' John 1:46, and a much more ominous text, Rev 16:10; 'and the fifth angel poured out his vial on the seat of the beast; and his Kingdom was full of darkness, and they gnawed their tongues for pain'.[27] Fortunately he does not expand on this and the whole treatise is an explication of the words of Jesus before Pilate. On 31 January 1717 Benjamin Hoadly, Bishop of Bangor, had preached before the king on the same text, arguing that 'the Kingdom of Christ was synonymous and coterminous with the church of Christ "over which Christ was King to the exclusion of earthly authorities," and that there are "no judges over the Consciences or Religion of his People'. James Adams, minister of Kinnaird

---

25. Wodrow, *Correspondence*, 458n1.

26. John Owen, cited in Mullan, "Early Career of John Glas," 255.

27. Glas, *Testimony of the King of Martyrs*, 1:v.

in Perthshire, in one of his memorably named pamphlets, *The Independent Ghost Conjur'd*, and John Willison in his *Defence of National Churches* both stated that Glas drew his opinions from Hoadly, and there are certainly similarities, but Glas would not have been at ease with Hoadly's pronounced latitudinarianism, which in the event gave rise to a prolonged controversy in England.[28] Nevertheless, Walter Wilson in volume 3 of his *History and Antiquities of Dissenting Churches and Meeting Houses* states that his work was highly esteemed by the London Sandemanians.[29]

While Glas was certainly acquainted with the work of John Owen and other Puritans, David Mullan suggests a more potent influence. He quotes another pamphlet which suggests that a Glasite production was alleged to contain 'the plain language of the Sectaries'. He goes on to show that many of Glas's typological interpretations of Scripture have much in common with those of Roger Williams, and that Glas may have read *The Bloody Tenent of Persecution* which Williams published in 1644. Williams made

> a thoroughgoing typological distinction between the earthly types of the Old Testament and the heavenly and spiritual anti-types of the New; the impossibility of another earthly Israel with national covenants; an absolute rejection of any molestation based upon belief or worship; and an interpretation of the parable of the tares which excluded all grounds for persecution.[30]

For Glas quite categorically, the 'New Testament speaks nothing of a National Church'. Therefore, Scotland could not be a new Israel, covenanted to God, despite all that the *National Covenant* and *The Solemn League and Covenant* claimed. There was no scriptural warrant for the Presbyterian system of church government 'of this national church'. This was dangerous doctrine, and it was stated quite unambiguously by Glas in his speech before the Commission of Assembly on 11 March, 1730.[31] Whatever were the sources of his beliefs about church and state, Glas was declaring himself to be an Independent, although there were important differences between his views and those of the English Independents.

Hornsby suggests that it may seem strange that Glas's attempt to re-introduce Independency into Scotland received no support from Congregationalists in England. Shortly after the formation of the first Glasite churches, one of Glas's principal supporters, without his approval, wrote to

---

28. See Starkie, *Church of England*; and Gibson, *Enlightenment Prelate*.
29. Wilson, *History and Antiquities of the Dissenting Churches*, 3:268.
30. Mullan, "Early Career of John Glas," 257.
31. Glas, *Works*, 1:275.

Dr Isaac Watts soliciting the interest and help of Independent ministers, but the approach was coldly received. Glas wrote:

> Then they seemed more afraid of their own honour as they stand in connexion with the Presbyterians, and of the loss of their good name with the Church of Scotland to which they professed the highest regard, and indeed shewed themselves to be more acted by this fear than by the Fear lest the meanest appearance of the Cause of Christ, and Christian Liberty should suffer.[32]

In 1737 Glas was asked by a Congregational minister in Newcastle if either he or Mr Archibald could be prevailed on to go to a people in Sunderland wanting a minister. Such influence as could be attributed to the English Nonconformists came through their writings, especially from John Owen, whom Glas quotes from time to time.

What sort of a man was John Glas? Friends and opponents provide quite different estimates. Some have accused him of a domineering spirit, and represented him as an autocrat, resentful of criticism and impatient of advice. We have seen how McLean and Carmichael left the Glasite church in Glasgow over a case of discipline in which they saw Glas interfering. Carmichael, once such a welcome addition to the church, is quoted by Glas himself as having 'a masterful and lordly spirit'. James Duncan of Glasgow, who later withdrew from the Glasite Church to become a leader of the Scotch Baptists in the city takes Glas to task in a long letter of March 1771. He accuses him of intermeddling in the affairs of the churches in Glasgow and Paisley. 'Sure I am, that should any man presume to act the same part towards the church of which you are a member, you would spurn at him with the most contemptuous disdain'. Glas was certainly dogged and assertive in his struggle with the church courts. But Robert Ferrier, once believing that Glas was arbitrary and tyrannical, changed his views on meeting him. 'Justice and truth oblige me to say that I never beheld a character more the opposite of this, or one more like the little child than Mr Glas appeared to me, when acquainted with him'. So long as any proposition could be shown as Scriptural, 'it immediately received his hearty support, whatever might be the self-denial it would lead to, or whoever might be its proposer'.[33]

Although he did not place any emphasis on academic learning as a qualification for the ministry, he himself was a man of thorough education and wide erudition. He had studied classics, philosophy and divinity and often in his many works gives evidence of wide reading and a fluency in the biblical languages. Among his works is *A Literal Translation of the true*

32. Glas, *Works*, 1:275.
33. Glas, *Testimony of the King of Martyrs*, v (Ferrier's preface).

Discourse of Celsus, as far as it can be gathered out of Origen's eight Books against him, published ca. 1753, followed by eighty-five pages of notes.[34] In these notes he gives a careful definition of faith.

> Faith is a way we have of knowing things, different from the way of knowing the principles from which we reason, which is called intuitive knowledge by instinct or inward sense, different from the knowledge we come to by reasoning, which may be called science, and different from the knowledge we take in by our senses, which may be called experience. This knowledge of things by testimony, which, in distinction from the other ways of knowing, is called faith or belief, takes place only where other ways of knowing fail.

Later he says:

> The prophets and apostles declared this testimony of God to the consciences of men. And it is set forth in their Scriptures, in an agreeableness to the tradition that prevailed universally among mankind concerning God's being reconcileable to men by sacrifice. This testimony of God, declared by the prophets and apostles, is, that God is well pleased in the sacrifice of Jesus Christ his beloved Son, delivered to death for the offences of all sorts of sinners, and raised again for their justification. . . . [D]o not examine but believe, and thy faith will save you.[35]

In 1745 he published *A View of the Heresy of Aerius*,[36] an obscure heretic mentioned by Epiphanius as a companion of Eustathius of Sebaste who subsequently left him and founded his own ascetic movement around AD 375. Glas found that he had taught the following articles:

1. That a presbyter differs not in order and degree from a bishop;

2. That there is no Pasch remaining to be observed or celebrated among Christians;

3. That fasts ought not to be prefixed to certain and stated annual days;

4. That prayers are not to be poured out and made for the dead.

Glas sees Aerius as a man who continued the primitive teaching of the church into the late fourth century. That Presbyters and bishops hold the same office Glas has argued elsewhere and the other heresies Glas sees as

---

34. Glas, *Works*, 4:305–452.

35. Glas, *Works*, 4:378, 380.

36. Glas, *Works*, 4:453–538. Not to be confused with Arius.

truths which were obscured by the fourth century. He seems to hold that the Pasch, that is Easter, is not binding upon Christians, and no Scottish Protestant would think of praying for the dead. The orthodox clergy of Glas's time called for National Fasts on certain occasions and Glas in *a Letter on National Fasts appointed by the Clergy*, written in 1735, and in two *Fast Sermons* in 1740 and 1741 sees them as reassertions of the Covenants. 'They fast, because they have it not in their power to knock everyone on the head, who finds himself, in conscience, openly and obstinately to dissent from them. They fast because every man has the same freedom with them to worship God, and to practise accordingly'.[37] Thus Aerius become a champion of Independency. That Aerius was not unknown in Scotland at that time is evident in a letter of Wodrow to L. Campbell in 1702. An Episcopalian clergyman had preached in Glasgow on Lam 4:20:

> . . . making King Charles a martyr for episcopacy, and to be murdered by the sectarians. He pretended to refute a sermon of Mr D. B. [David Brown, minister of Blackfriars, Glasgow] . . . quherin Mr B proved prelacy had noe foundation in the scripture. He said that this was ane upstart opinion and defended by none in primitive times but the heretic Aerius who was burnt. This last particular anent Aerius you know is a terrible blunder in matter of fact.[38]

Glas also, in a letter of March 1759, gives his opinion of John Hutchinson's *Philosophy and Divinity*. He admits that he was at first impressed with 'a new world-maker, and a quite new scheme of the workmanship of God, offering to succeed the Newtonian, that had set aside and succeeded former schemes'. But then he began to wonder how no one had seen the meanings in Hebrew words and the teachings of Moses before and he warned his correspondent of the dangers of the system. As Samuel Pike had written a Hutchinsonian tract before he became a Sandemanian, this was not a matter remote from Glas's work, and the fact that Hutchinsonianism was strong among certain Scottish Episcopalians did not escape him. He refers to Lord President Forbes as the only man that could make Hutchinson intelligible by our common capacities.[39] Glas was a man of wide culture and learning, alert to the cross-currents of thought in Enlightenment Scotland and beyond.

Glas's sermons were long, logical and doctrinal. While the good Scots word 'dour' might describe some aspects of his character, his general disposition was genial. He was a good conversationalist and companion, and

---

37. Glas, *Works*, 2:329.

38. Sharp, *Early Letters of Robert Wodrow, 1698–1709*, 254–55.

39. Glas, *Works*, 2:426–36 (*Of Mr Hutchinson's Philosophy and Divinity*).

he was different from the solemn clerical type of his day. His manners, we are told, were free and easy, utterly devoid of professionalism. Once when he was teased about his seeming levity he is reported to have quipped, 'I too can be grave at times, when I want money or want righteousness'. His attitude to balls, routs and theatrical performances was quite different from that of most church folk. He objected to making laws where Christ had not made them. It was this seeming laxity that horrified the staider and more traditional McLean.

His life had many sadnesses. He outlived his wife who died in 1749, and all his fifteen children, including his seafaring son George, predeceased him. George had been active in the London church and was on a trading voyage to the Canaries when he was murdered.[40] In a memoir of Mr John Glas, published in the *New Evangelical Magazine* of 1818 the author, almost certainly the Scotch Baptist Elder William Jones, who edited the magazine, wrote:

> His primary concern about the gospel originated in his anxiety to find a remedy for his own troubled conscience under that distress in which the real misery of guilty mortals always consists and the want of righteousness adequate to the requirements of the divine law. He saw the command of God to be exceeding broad, and the enquiry 'how shall man be just with God' was to him of all others the most important.

Both his sermons and his public prayers excited extraordinary attention. 'There is in the possession of the writer of this memoir a folio volume of his sermons, in MS. All of which were preached by him in Tealing in 1722 and 1723. No text was left unexhausted'. There were in this collection, twelve discourses on 2 Cor 5:14–15, followed by twelve on 2 Cor 5:17. 'His esteemed father-in-law frequently told him that the purity of communion which he was in quest of was altogether unattainable, but he uniformly answered, "that if he could only get a dozen shepherds to unite with in the love of the truth, at the foot of the Cydla [Sidlaw] hills he should be happy"'.[41]

John Glas and Robert Sandeman—Theology

The Glasite churches never became large or influential. On the first of January 1782, when the church was probably at its largest extent, there were in Scotland 633 members, with about two hundred in England and

---

40. For the story of this tragedy, see Macintosh, *Letters in Correspondence*, 94–97.
41. Jones in *New Evangelical Magazine*, September 1818, 282.

one hundred in America.[42] There were also many hearers, or occasional at-tenders, and some churches such as Dundee were full every Sunday, with up to six hundred people. Comparatively few took the step of 'confessing the faith'. But the theological writings, particularly of Glas and Sandeman, had a wide circulation, and they should be taken seriously. Theirs was a system, to use a word often applied by their critics, which professed to give a real and true understanding of the Bible. They were of course writing and studying before the rise of modern biblical criticism, and so shared with the other churches of Scotland a belief in the clarity of Scripture, and the necessity of obedience to its teaching. Theology was a staple of the mental diet of eighteenth-century Scots with a serious turn of mind, and although belief was no longer a matter of life or death in this world, as it had been in the seventeenth century, there was still a ready audience for a well-argued theological case.

Glas's thought has been described as rational Calvinism, and certainly the core of his thought is Genevan. In an age where such eminent Christian leaders as John Wesley believed in miraculous healings, providence, visions, witchcraft, ghosts, and the spiritual significance of dreams, and in the in-vestigation of such phenomena along the lines of the experimental method, Glas and his followers are silent on these matters, and proceed by logic and intellect, even if their exegesis sometimes seems a little fantastic to us. They were also opposed to the reductionist Deism which alarmed so many or-thodox Christians in the Enlightenment Era. Sandeman was vehement that he had found the true way, and that the 'popular preachers' had misled the people. What to us may seem minor verbal differences were to them matters of eternal salvation. Glas's original point of departure was his questioning of the idea of Scotland as a chosen nation, bound by its Covenants to God, and this is what perturbed his colleagues in the ministry. Independency could well co-exist with Calvinism, as it did in the life and writings of John Owen, and the Glasites believed in the sovereignty of God, in particular re-demption, in limited atonement, and the other tenets common to reformed theologies of their era. So, let us look at the particular teachings.

---

42. Macintosh, *Letters in Correspondence*, 125–26. In the Census of Religious Wor-ship, 1851, Sandemanians are recorded as having, in England, 6 places of worship, 439 present in the morning, 256 in the afternoon and 61 in the evening. In Scotland there were also 6 places of worship, 429 present in the morning, 554 in the afternoon and 100 in the evening. This must have included hearers as well as members. Currie et al., *Churches and Churchgoers*, 216, 219.

1. The Primacy of Scripture

Glas's commitment to Calvinism did not mean the acceptance of all the Westminster standards. He claimed that he went beyond the teachings of even such giants as Calvin and Owen to the Scriptures themselves. Scripture is final and plain and open to the person who will search in its pages for the Will and Word of God. The order of the church was there, especially in the Acts of the Apostles. It would have been strange if Christ had not left instructions for the minutest matters of behavior of his followers. As far as I know, no other church has ever given so much space in its worship to the reading of the whole Bible, and the form of exhortation as it developed in the churches emphasised the subordination of the words of men to the Word of God.

Robert Sandeman in his forceful way commends the primacy of Scripture over all human works of devotion.

> Now seeing it is the fashion to commend religious books I am willing to comply with it for once. If anyone chooses to go to Hell by a devout route, rather than by any other, let him study to form his heart on any one of these four treatises, Mr Guthrie's 'Trial of a Saving Interest in Christ,' Mr Marshall's 'Gospel Mystery of Sanctification,' Mr Boston's 'Human Nature in its Fourfold State,' and Mr Doddridge's 'Rise and Progress of Religion in the Human Soul.' If any profane man, who desires to be converted, shall take pains to enter the spirit of these books, it will be easy to show from the New Testament that he thereby becomes twofold more the child of Hell than before. On the other hand, if anyone has got an ear for the truth of God, and desires to have his mind established therein, let him read the history of Jesus Christ, and the Acts of the Apostles recorded by the four evangelists. Would he be skillful in distinguishing the ancient Gospel from all counterfeits, and so expert in fighting the good fight of faith? Let him read Paul's epistles. Would he know what is pure and undefiled religion before God, in distinction from talking about it? Let him read James. Would he learn sobriety and patience in suffering for the truth, and have his veneration for the greatest name in the Antichristian world abated? Let him read Peter and Jude. Would he be satisfied that his spiritual joys are not the joys of the hypocrite, but that they arise from fellowship with the true God, so are the sure pledges and real beginning of life eternal, let him read the epistles of John. Would he know the true state and appearance of God's Kingdom in this world and the world to come, and so have his mind fortified against all modern men's visions and

prophecies? Let him read the Revelation of the last-mentioned apostle. Would he have a safe and authentic commentary on the Old Testament to prevent him being imposed upon by the deceitful glosses of ancient and modern Jews? Let him consult all those apostolic writings together.[43]

This is a fairly comprehensive rejection of what Sandeman, and Glas before him, called the popular preachers and a commendation of the whole New Testament. Yet Glas did not discard earlier writers and he quoted from time to time church fathers such as Tertullian and Cyprian, and of course both writers often referred to the Old Testament, although Sandeman was suspicious of Jewish commentators. 'To the Books and to the Testimony' became a motto, and what the Scriptures commended, such as the sacredness of the lot, the Glasites sought to obey and what was not forbidden, such as theatrical performances, they tolerated. 'Simplex,' the pseudonym of John Young, Edinburgh lawyer and elder in the late eighteenth century, sums up their attitude to scripture thus:

> The scriptures of the Old and New testaments were indited by the Spirit of God. Being the Word of God, they must of course be perfect and wisely adapted to the circumstances and necessities of His people. Christians accordingly hold that these scriptures contain not only a complete system of all the doctrines necessary for salvation but also a perfect code of laws, and an infallible code of behavior for them in all ages, and under all possible circumstances.[44]

All their views and customs, beliefs and hopes came directly from Scripture, and they insisted on its simplicity and coherence, and on a common sense and unmysterious approach to doctrine. This approach cannot be unrelated to the ideas current in the mid-eighteenth century, deriving partly at least from Locke and the Deists. Such words as plain, clear, obvious, had an attraction for men tired of scholastic Calvinism and its opponents, and weary of the emotional excesses of the 'popular preaching'.

2. The Doctrine of Revelation

The Westminster Confession taught that natural revelation, and the 'works of creation and providence' give men enough light to be inexcusable, but that this was not enough, and therefore the Scriptures, the special revelation

---

43. Sandeman, *Letters*, 5:373–74.
44. Simplex, *Church of God*, 162.

of the love and activity of God were necessary, and they were the source of knowledge of divine things, and the touchstone whereby truth was to be judged. Glas and Sandeman agreed with this but Sandeman put his view of revelation thus:

> All divine revelation rests on supernatural facts. . . . God hath awakened attention by some supernatural appearance, so as to produce in the mind of the observer the question of surprise, what meaneth this? Hereupon he hath always provided, by means equally above the power of nature, a clear and satisfying account of that which occasioned surprise, so as the result should be the joint appearance of divine wonder and divine power to the mind of the observer. . . . [T]his is contrary to the general expectation and reasoning of mankind. . . . [T]here is one capital or central fact, which collects the evidence of all that went before, and is supported by all that follows, even the resurrection of Jesus. Here all the lines of divine revelation are united.[45]

Then Sandeman gives scriptural proofs, firstly from 2 Peter, before he turns to the transfiguration and resurrection accounts. For Sandeman the subject of revelation and the object of faith is the resurrection of Jesus, which is what attests his divine claims. At the beginning of editions of *Christian Songs*, the Glasite hymnbook, is *The Evidence of Christ's Resurrection versified for the help of the memory*.

> This fact demands with awful pow'r
> My faith, yea faith divine;
> As it declares to me O God
> The Glory that is Thine.
> No fact or word did ever show
> So much of God before.[46]

3. The Doctrine of Saving Faith

In the *Testimony* Glas defines faith as 'divine Faith receiving divine testimony'. This intellectual view of faith is one of the most distinctive tenets of Glasite theology, and like their views of church order arises from what they saw as fidelity to Scripture. It is also influenced by the conviction that Christianity is not to be wrapped in mystery, and it arose in reaction to a

45. Sandeman, *Letters*.
46. *Christian Songs*, 9.

strong emphasis put on the place of the emotions in the preaching of the 'popular preachers'. Like any Calvinist, Glas believed that man is a sinner, unable to save or justify himself. Only God can justify the ungodly. How is man to come to faith and how is that faith to be defined?

Faith comes by hearing and hearing by the Word of God. Faith is receiving the truth of the gospel. Man's part in his salvation is confined to receiving the truth. Glas in tracing the history of justification by faith in the early church found it hard to discover any of the fathers who preserved the doctrine in its pure form, although he made an exception of Clement of Rome and the *Letter to Diognetus*. When the church was established by the Roman Empire, the truth was still more obscured, though 'wherever the testimony of God, and the import of Christ's death and resurrection in the apostolic scriptures was heard of, there might be some taught of God, and saved, so coming to the knowledge of the truth'.[47] At the Reformation the truth was rediscovered and proclaimed but soon overlaid by an insistence on

> free electing grace, but especially on the efficacious power of that grace, working unfeigned faith on them, and turning them to God in a sincere repentance. . . . [T]he effect of this strain of doctrine upon them that hearkened to it, was their seeking peace with God and rest to their consciences by what they might feel in themselves, the motions of their hearts and the exercise of their souls, in compliance with the call of faith and repentance, under the efficacious operation of grace, which they hoped to find in using those means whereby they supposed it to be conveyed.[48]

That is, faith had become confused with its effects and had become a 'work'. James Allen, in his *Treatise on Redemption*, wrote, 'The justification of a sinner is an act of grace and mercy. The actual justification of God's elect took place in their substitute in the resurrection of Christ from the dead; and the justification obtained in the conscience by the knowledge of the truth is a participation with Christ in the fruit of his obedience unto death'.[49]

In his *Notes on the Discourse of Celsus* Glas wrote:

> As faith is the credit we give to a testimony, the knowledge we have of things by it must be accorded to the testimony. We are used from our infancy to the knowledge of many things by the testimony of men; and we know some things this way with great certainty. But as the testimony of God must be greater than

47. Glas, *Works* 5:358.
48. Glas, *Works*, 5:358.
49. Allen, *Treatise of Redemption*, 43.

man's; so must our faith of his testimony, when we hear him, be greater than our belief in the testimony of men.

He expanded on this:

> The prophets and apostles declared this testimony of God to the consciences of men. And it is set forth in their scriptures, in an agreeableness to the tradition that prevailed universally among mankind concerning God's being reconcilable to men by sacrifice. This testimony of God, declared by the prophets and apostles, is, that God is well pleased in the sacrifice of Jesus Christ his beloved Son, delivered to death for the offences of all sorts of sinners, and raised again for their justification. And every one that believes this, hears in his conscience, the voice of the same God, whose wrath was known there, declaring himself well pleased; and so is saved from his misery, and becomes happy in peace with God.[50]

This view of faith as a simple intellectual act is not very different from that held by other Scottish Calvinist divines. John Erskine of Carnock, minister of Greyfriars in Edinburgh, laid stress on an intellectual view of faith, 'following the pattern set by John Locke in his *Reasonableness of Christianity*: faith was logical, and need not be a form of enthusiasm if the mind was presented with overwhelming evidence to convince it of the reliability of the proposition that Jesus Christ is the Son of God'. But Erskine was emphatic that his view of the matter was not that of the Glasites. He held that faith was a 'supernatural revelation of knowledge that should be more pragmatic than theoretical'.[51]

It was what he saw as their perversion of the doctrine of faith that made Robert Sandeman attack the teaching of the 'popular preachers so vehemently'. Faith is a simple thing and the evangelical preachers had complicated its meaning and obscured its truth. Sandeman elaborates on Glas's teaching, at some length and with some asperity, but in fact adds little to it. The whole tenor of the Sandemanian presentation of the Gospel was anti-emotional, to the point of coldness. The great enemy was Pharisaism, self-righteousness, or any form of trusting in oneself for salvation. Sandeman sought support for his teaching from John Locke. He wrote

> Mr Locke shows at large from the scriptures, with great perspicuity, that man obtained eternal life, believing that Jesus the Christ is the Son of God. But not knowing the truth which the

---

50. Glas, *Works*, 4:380.
51. Yeager, *Enlightened Evangelicalism*, 99, 102.

apostles understood by these words, so not finding any ground of acceptance with God in them he very plainly rests our justification before God in the homage we pay him in giving credit to any promise of truth he is pleased to reveal, as that Abraham should have a son or rather in putting together these two words and affirming, in any sense we please that Jesus is the Christ, together with our best endeavours to obey the precepts delivered by him.[52]

But neither Locke, nor Erasmus, nor Mandeville, all of whom Sandeman quotes, had the truth.

Sandeman seems to equate belief with the thing believed, faith in the atonement with atonement itself. His doctrine of faith represents an extreme position in the attempt to apportion salvation between the actions of God and those of man. Under the influence of early eighteenth-century rationalism Glas and Sandeman assumed a sharp division between man's action and God's action. Knowledge of the atonement was planted in man by the Holy Spirit according to the divine decree of absolute predestination. It is no wonder that William Godwin, looking back to his days at the Dissenting Academy, remarked that Sandeman was a thoroughgoing Calvinist. 'Where Calvin damned 99 out of 100 of the human race, Sandeman damned 99 out of 100 Calvinists'.[53] This is scarcely a considered judgement, but it does point up the logic of Sandeman's position, Salvation is by belief in the testimony but is only possible to the elect. Sandeman was attacked for incipient Antinomianism, but he insisted that genuine faith would issue in works of love, and the mutual love of believers is often stressed.

One consequence of this was that the way into a Sandemanian assembly was by declaration of belief, and acceptance by the whole membership based on the correctness of the applicant's faith. In other forms of Independency the postulant related her experience of grace, and so was accepted. Sandemanians saw this as 'going about to establish one's own righteousness' and therefore it was the intellectual acceptance of propositions concerning Jesus the Christ and the consequences in church life and discipline that became the touchstones of acceptability.

4. The Nature of the Church

John Glas derived his Independent views of the nature and government of the church from his insistence on the bare word of Scripture, uncorrupted

52. Sandeman, *Letters*, 1:250.
53. Cited in Fleisher, *William Godwin*, 139.

by the traditions of men. If all things necessary to faith are present and evident in the Bible, then so must be all things necessary to the life of the church, and that life must conform to the pattern laid down by the teaching and example of the apostles. Of course, Episcopalians and Presbyterians also wished to restore primitive simplicity and correct church order. The form of Presbyterial church government the lawfulness of Church Courts is set out in the Westminster Confession.[54] For Presbyterians, full power and authority lay in the church courts, local and national. For the Independents the local congregation possessed the rights and powers of the visible church.

In his seminal writing, *The Testimony of the King of Martyrs* Glas deals with the setting up and advancing of Christ's kingdom in this world. It cannot be introduced by the sword or the civil power. This is totally opposed to its genius. It is set up by the truth, and witness to the truth. The truth is the facts concerning Christ and especially his resurrection. Salvation is by 'divine faith receiving the divine testimony'. The crucifixion of Christ and his resurrection are presented as evidence, and 'everyone that is persuaded upon this evidence sees with his own eyes'. Thus early does the peculiar Glasite notion of faith appear. In the last chapter of the *Testimony* Glas deals with the subjects of Christ's kingdom. His text here is 'everyone that is of the truth hears my voice'. He sets out again his characteristic view, 'the scripture notion of faith agrees with the common notion of faith and belief among men, a persuasion of a thing upon a testimony'.[55] This faith must produce good works. Christ's subjects hear his commands, obey his voice, and follow his guidance. Glas sees the church as a spiritual society, distinct from the nation, and that only those who are persuaded of the truth about Christ are qualified to become its members.

In the answers that he supplied to the queries set to him during his trial before the Synod of Angus and Mearns in April 1728, Glas was more specific on several points. He clearly denied the magistrate's power concerning church matters. The Westminster Confession in chapter 23 states, 'The magistrate hath power to call Synods, to be present at them, and to provide that whatsoever is transacted in them be according to the mind of God'. Glas rejected this function of the magistrate.

> If the Church be of this world, or if it be national, and established by the law of the kingdoms of this world with civil sanctions . . . but in the kingdom of heaven, or in the church of Christ which is not of this world, the magistrate's power, whether he be Christian or not, has no place.

54. Westminster Confession of Faith, 1958 edition, 406.
55. Glas, *Works*, 1:137.

In a later query, 'Is it your opinion that those who suffered in the late times for adhering to such national covenant engagements were so far un-enlightened or not?' he answered, 'It is my opinion; while at the same time I highly honour and value them, and the light they had and their sufferings for Christ.'[56] 'A congregation, or Church of Jesus Christ, with its Presbytery, is in its discipline, subject to no jurisdiction under heaven,'[57] he replied to a later question and this became a watchword for Independency. Glas claimed that his view, that there is no other church besides the universal church ex-cept a congregation is acknowledged in the *Scots Confession of Faith*, article 18, which he quotes thus 'wherefore then these former notes are seen, and any time continue, be the number ever so few, about two or three, there, no doubt is the true Church of Christ, who according to his promise is in the midst of them'.

John Barnard, the former Independent minister in London who be-came a leading Sandemanian, spelt out his views on church order, which accord with those of Glas, in his short book *The Nature and Government of the Christian Church*, published in London in 1761 and reprinted in Perth by James Morison in 1855. His subtitle is indicative of the contents: *gathered only from the Word of God without regard to the tradition of men, in which are considered its formation, union, discipline, officers, and ordinances, to which is added a summary declaration of the faith*. The text is Ezek 43:10, which reads, 'Thou son of man, shew the house to the house of Israel, that they may be ashamed of their iniquities; and let them measure the pattern'.

'We are forbidden', he wrote, 'to think of an earthly establishment of his Kingdom, or of temporal honour for his followers'.[58] Lordship and pre-cedency have no place in Christ's kingdom, and its subjects are 'collected by the influence of His Word in a way of sovereignty'. The word "church" is used for an assembly of disciples meeting in one place to eat the Lord's Supper and to observe all things whatsoever he hath commanded them'.

> An accidental assembly met together for worship is not called a church for those of whom we read that they were that day added to the church at Jerusalem were made a part of the assembly before they believed and were added to the Lord.

In the church there must be union of heart and sentiment. If there is a difference of opinion in the 'main thing', that is the reason of their hope, both parties cannot be right. He asks, 'Does a society founded on the truth cease

56. Glas, *Works*, 1:187.
57. Glas, *Works*, 1:192–93.
58. Barnard, *Nature and Government*, 5.

to be a church of Christ if there is division in it? I answer, "no" any more than a body ceases to live immediately on its having a dangerous disease in it'.[59] General rules for conduct are laid down in 1 Cor 14 and 16, and Phil 2, and mutual conference is commended in Heb 10:24 and in 1 Cor 14:26–35. All brethren and no women ought to speak. Prophesying is an extraordinary gift, Rom 12:6, and so inimitable by us who have no extraordinary gifts (which are held to have ceased.) Discipline, dealing with both private and public offences, is a mark of the church, as is abstinence from blood. 'Some indeed seek to evade it by calling it a little thing and conclude there can be no immorality in it, as it doth no injury to the rights of society. But so one reasons about self-murder'.[60] Brotherly love means amongst much else not going to law between members.

So the church is to be united in belief and action and to seek perfect obedience to the clear commands of the gospel as recorded in the New Testament. Jots and tittles are important, and although division should be avoided as much as possible there are occasions, as we shall see in the chapter on schisms, when deep and hurtful divisions become necessary.

5. The Officers of the Church

In the church at Tealing John Glas, according to the tenets of the Church of Scotland, was the teaching elder, and there was a group of men who were ruling elders. When the church moved to Dundee the regime began to change, piece by piece.

> Mr Glas took great delight in telling his friends that he frequently got hints in the church assemblies from the poorest of the brethren which served to open and explain many scriptures that he had not before understood. In 1730 he went to the Highlands in the summer season for the benefit of his health. During his absence the church assembled as usual on the Lord's day; and in the evening the deacons laid the cover as usual for the Lord's Supper. But some of the brethren moved a difficulty how they could eat the Lord's Supper in the absence of their pastor.

There were elders, who were rulers, not teachers and preachers. So they summoned Glas and he and the church searched the New Testament and concluded that elders must be apt to teach. 'The ruling Elders were all laid aside' and only Glas and Archibald were left. After fasting and prayer,

---

59. Barnard, *Nature and Government*, 18.
60. Barnard, *Nature and Government*, 39.

early in the morning for many days they sought light on this matter and only held the Supper when both the elders were present.

> At length they unanimously called James Cargill, a glover, and William Scott, who was almost blind, to the office of Elder, and they were set apart by fasting and prayer, and the laying on of hands of the presbytery.[61] They were both well instructed in the scriptures. James Cargill was colleague to Mr Glas in Dundee, and W. Scott to Mr Archibald in Arbroath.

Thus runs the memoranda in *Letters in Correspondence*.[62]

The next innovation was to hold the Lord's Supper weekly instead of monthly, or once or twice a year as in the National Church. Again the Scriptures were searched and Acts 20 verse 17 settled the matter. They agreed to observe the Lord's Supper every first day of the week. This led to denunciation by the ministers of the district, who accused the Glasites of stripping the ordinance of due solemnity, as the new custom dispensed with fast-days, preparation, and thanksgiving days.

Glas defended his position in his tract, *Of the Unity and Distinction of the Elder's Office*, published in 1731. The work of the apostles was done when the New Testament revelation was complete, and we now have the records in the New Testament. With the evangelists, the assistants to the apostles, they are the extraordinary officers of the church. The ordinary officers are two only, elders or bishops, and deacons, with whom is reckoned the deaconess or the widow ministering to the sick. Barnard writes that teachers communicate instruction whether elders or not. All elders must be teachers, but not vice-versa.

Glas equates elder with bishop and says that 'the Lord Jesus hath appointed a plurality of bishops in every church, all of them apt to teach, and able, by sound doctrine, both to exhort and convince the gainsayers, all of them stewards of God'.[63] Each has particular, complementary gifts, so that the church is built up. This insistence on a plurality of elders was sometimes questioned, and sometimes meant elders and their families being sent quite

---

61. That is, Glas and Archibald at this time.

62. Macintosh, *Letters in Correspondence*, 117. Wodrow in a letter of February 1730 to Hugh Maxwell Glas's predecessor in Tealing, now in Forfar, laments Glas's actions, 'spreading schisms and innovations in a peaceable and united society contrary to his solemn vow and subscription. I am of opinion (under correction) that Dr Owen, the Mathers and other pious Independents would never have approved his practices.' In a letter of January 1731 to a minister in Ireland, he laments that Glas is advancing tradesmen to the ministry, and turning out the soberest members of his congregation with much imperiousness' (Wodrow, *Correspondence*, 459, 481).

63. Glas, *Works*, 2:213ff.

long distances to make up a presbytery, but it remained the practice of the churches until the end.

6. The Order of the Church

Much attention was always paid to the details of church worship and life, sometimes described as 'going about the ordinances of the Church'. These matters arose from the doctrine of Scripture, and the assumption of its clarity and its enduring relevance. Nothing laid down in the New Testament could be ignored or modified. John Walker, the 'Separatist', also laid down these principles, and a few of his own, but in the last days of his churches there were modifications and an opening to the practices and people of other similar churches such as the Brethren.[64] The Glasite liturgy shrank, as the members, particularly the male members, became fewer, and therefore there were less prayers by the male members, and towards the end only the elders prayed and exhorted, but there was no real change in essential elements of worship and obedience to the commands of Scripture. The kiss of peace was mandatory, although the practice led to somewhat ribald comments and to the occasional scriptural essay. The Washing of Feet, while often mentioned by opponents as a peculiar custom, seems to have been observed as necessary, if, for example, a brother had walked a long way to the meeting. It was necessary for every member to attend the Love Feast which in early days, before the acquisition of Meeting Houses, was held in the homes of members. This was not unique to the Sandemanians, although its almost sacramental nature was, and into the twentieth century other small denominations such as the Scotch Baptists provided a meal between the morning and afternoon services, for fellowship and for the convenience of members who had a long journey to gather on a Sunday.[65] For them also it could be the occasion of discipline although that came to be administered at the Communion Service in later years, and that indeed is still the custom in many Baptist churches.

The Order of Service was full of Scripture. In the morning and afternoon services only psalms[66] were sung, several verses of a particular psalm at a time, interspersed with prayers and Scripture readings, five chapters in the morning and three in the afternoon. The portions of the psalm were often sung to different tunes. At the Communion Service John Glas's paraphrase of Rev 5:9–10, Song 16, was sung, and was indeed an appropriate

64. Martin, *Recollections of the Walkerite*, 2–10.

65. Personal recollection of an old member of Baptist Church, Kirkcaldy, in 1966.

66. In the version by Robert Boswell.

hymn.[67] The other hymns, or songs, were sung in rotation at the Love Feast. Exhortations were largely in the words of Scripture, to guard against the intrusive wisdom of men. There was an unemotional atmosphere, a very rational performance of a fixed liturgy, and the changelessness of Glasite worship for two hundred and seventy or so years was a remarkable feature of the church's life.

Elegies were sung to mark the death of members and eleven of these are included in the sixth edition of *Christian Songs*. Other elegies are found among the *Manuscripts*, some attached to the names of prominent members. Certainly in the eighteenth and early nineteenth centuries the deaths of Nonconformist ministers and prominent laypeople were marked by elegies, some of them quite lengthy, but only the Glasites continued the custom into the twentieth century.

7. Eschatology

While it would scarcely be correct to claim that Glasites were an Adventist body, nevertheless the study of prophecy was a continuing theme, and the expectation of the Lord's coming never quite died away. Glas himself wrote extensively on the subject. In volume four of his works there is *A General view of Revelation*, *The Vision of the Sealed Book*, and *The Two Witnesses prophesying in sackcloth, One Thousand two hundred and sixty days, overcome and killed by the beast, and then reviving at the end of three days*. These writings take up two hundred and twenty-three pages altogether and are devoted to studies of Daniel and Revelation.

The Westminster Confession outlined a map of the future in its last two chapters, concentrating on the resurrection of the dead, eternal bliss or punishment, and the second coming of Christ. *The Larger Catechism*, Question 191, on the petition 'Thy Kingdom come' is more precise, stating that in this petition we pray 'that the kingdom of sin and Satan may be destroyed; the gospel propagated throughout the world, the Jews called, the fulness of the Gentiles brought in . . . that Christ would rule in our hearts here and hasten the time of his second coming'.[68]

Glas did not abandon the Westminster documents but he expanded on them, seeing history fulfilling prophecy, and interpreting with great

---

67. The first stanza is worth quoting: 'Thy worthiness is all our song, / O Lamb of God! For thou wast slain; / and by thy blood brought'st us to God, / Out of each nation, tribe and tongue. / To our God mads't us kings and priests, / And we shall reign upon the earth.'

68. Westminster Confession of Faith, 1958 edition, 274–75.

ingenuity the whole history of the church in the light of the prophetic scriptures. He often quotes Joseph Mede, the seventeenth-century exegete whose schemes and their variations had great influence well into the next century. Glas was convinced that he lived in the end-times, and while he is not dogmatic about the millennium, he inclined to believe that Christ would return first, to reign with his saints for a thousand years upon the earth. This may not seem consistent with the care he took over church order and worship, until it is seen that the Glasites saw themselves as a sort of microcosm on earth of the church in heaven. Purity of communion is necessary in view of the approaching return of Christ.

The important points in history according to Glas's scheme were

1. the occluding of pure doctrine almost immediately after the death of the apostles,

2. the conversion of Constantine, with the consequent corruption of the church by its connection with the State, the growth of the power of the Roman Church,

3. the fall of the Western Empire,

4. the bravery and insight of the Waldensians and the Bohemian Brethren, about whom he knows a great deal, and whom he prefers to Luther, and the Reformation.

He sees also a place for the rise of Islam and indeed for most of the main events of history. He gives an elaborate interpretation of the ten kingdoms of Dan 6 and Rev 13, with criticism of the views of Sir Isaac Newton. His interpretation of the mysterious number 666 deserves to be noticed. As the one hundred and forty-four of the one hundred and forty-four thousand to be sealed is the square of twelve, the number symbolizing apostolic truth, so 666 is the square, as near as may be of twenty-five, a number of evil import in Ezekiel, and the number of parishes into which Rome was divided and from which twenty-five cardinals, the opposite of the twelve apostles, took their titles.[69] Such speculative calculations were part of eighteenth-century piety but the conclusions Glas drew gives them more importance. The very smallness of the number of those convinced by the truth became a matter of pleasure, as the Glasites identified themselves with the persecuted little flock. Present insignificance would give way to future power and glory. 'We shall reign upon the earth' is a line from Glas's hymn which was sung at every Communion Service. Many of the *Christian Songs* allude to the

69. Glas, *Works*, 4:127–28.

'good time coming'. Suffering of the faithful and corruption of the so-called church are signs of the End.

> How long shall it be, ere thy saints Lord with thee
> As kings and priests exalted shall reign
> O when shall the time come that thou'lt bring them all home
> With thee in thy glory for aye to remain.[70]

This historicist treatment of prophecy must have had its effects on the minds of those who felt disadvantaged in this life. In the *19th Century Exhortations* published in Dundee in 1910 are several expositions of prophetic texts, applied to the signs of the times, and in a pamphlet, *The Second Coming of the Son of Man—Is It Nigh?* printed in 1894 an anonymous editor published a work of George Sandeman composed in 1871, and gave as his reason the 'unusual degree of interest in the fulfilment of prophecy'.[71] The author draws attention to many scriptures and to the need to be vigilant. There is a summary of the predictions in Matt 24:

1. His disciples shall be hated of all men for the name's sake;

2. false prophets shall arise and deceive many;

3. iniquity shall abound and cause the love of many to wax cold;

4. the gospel shall be preached in all the world;

5. the sun shall be darkened;

6. the moon shall not give its light;

7. the stars shall fall from heaven;

8. the powers of the heavens shall be shaken.

The first three signs were fulfilled in the 1,260 years when the true church sojourned in the wilderness. The fourth sign is complex. The church was soon corrupted, and Jerome translated the Scriptures into Latin when that language was becoming obsolete for the general body of the people. Nearly eight hundred years elapsed before the Bible was translated into the vulgar tongue, and the invention of printing allowed the Scriptures to be promulgated among the nations generally. Before this the monasteries both preserved and hid the Word. The two testaments are the two witnesses coming to life and the still small voice of the everlasting gospel is heard by those who are granted a hearing ear.

---

70. *Christian Songs*, 77.
71. G. Sandeman, *Second Coming of the Son of Man*, 1–17. Acc 364/4/9.

There is not a more widely spread fallacy than the popular expectation that the result of missionary work now going on will sooner or later be the Christianization of the whole or nearly the whole nations on earth. This is opposed to the doctrine of the Grace of God who hath mercy on whom he will have mercy.

The last four events are applied to revolutions, the unification of Germany and Italy and the fall of kings and dukes. The last part of the pamphlet speculates, by using Daniel's days, that the second coming will be either in 1890 or 1935. But the author repeats warnings about date setting.[72]

Here the hope of victory and a glorious second coming is balanced with the typical Glasite opposition to missions and a High Calvinist favorite text, Rom 9:18, and an attempt to match world events with prophetic scripture, something not confined to the Glasites of that time. The Edinburgh Elder George Waterston's *Notes on the Book of Revelation* which was published in 1893 is much less complex and elaborate. He sees the series of prophecies in Revelation not as giving a continuous account to be aligned with historical events but as overlapping and supplementing each other. He concludes:

> If therefore we give up the idea of continuity in these prophecies, we can study each in the light of the others, and take the same broad view of this period that Christ does in Matthew 24 and Luke 21; while the continuous method would lead us to examination of obscure periods of history in search of what are after all private interpretations.[73]

The teaching of Glas and other writers on such subjects as eschatology can be challenged and a much simpler approach suggested. Waterston says several times that the aim of prophecy is to keep us alert to the wickedness of the world and to establish our hope for the victory of Christ.

8. Baptism

The Glasites were paedobaptists. In his '*Dissertation on Infant-Baptism*', published in 1746, Glas writes:

> The whole plea against the baptizing the infants of Christians comes to this, that there is neither particular express precept not indisputable example for it in the New Testament, where baptism is inseparably connected with a profession of faith, which infants are not capable to make. All this may be owned at the

72. G. Sandeman, *Second Coming of the Son of Man*, 19.

73. Waterston, *Notes on the Book of Revelation*.

same time that the inference from it is denied.'[74] He maintains that the sacrament so perfectly expresses the truth of salvation that there is 'no remarkable error about baptism but what has foundation in some great error as to the truth which is signified in Baptism.'[75]

He dismisses those who would deny water-baptism, presumably the Quakers, and those who consider that baptism was only necessary at the beginning of Christianity, presumably the Socinians, and he roots the doctrine of baptism in the doctrine of the Trinity. He denies baptismal regeneration and condemns those who reject infant baptism on the same grounds, that the thing signified in baptism is wrongly understood. Glas sets out his arguments in favor of infant baptism in terms which are not unusual in more recent debates. For example he points out that the baptized households mentioned in Acts must have included children, and that Peter's words at Pentecost, 'the promise is to you and your children' imply the inclusion of children. He examines very carefully 1 Cor 7:14 and asserts that the word 'holy' has a different meaning when applied to children and the wife. One believing parent makes the child holy, sharing the same status as the parent. By referring to Col 2:11–13 he argues that what circumcision was to the Old Covenant, baptism is to the New, and he shows from history that infant baptism was the universal custom of the church until the time of Tertullian, who was mistaken in his idea of faith and therefore gave unwise advice about the postponement of baptism.

The Presbyterian standards clearly state that the baptized are within the visible church. With this Glas disagrees. As the visible church consists only of conscious and accepted believers, infants could not be part of it. They are baptized onto the invisible church, into Christ who is the Head of the Body. There is no necessary connection between baptism and church membership. Writing to Gabriel Wilson, a Dundee elder, he said:

> This baptism makes the baptized debtors to do all the commands of Jesus Christ the Lord, and so to become members of a visible church where these commandments are observed, as soon as it shall be in their power.[76]

Baptism was for the Glasites an essentially private and individual act whereby the promise of the gospel is conveyed to believing parents. 'One may indeed baptize—this is doing nothing to the Church' wrote Glas to an

---

74. Glas, *Works*, 2:359.

75. Glas, *Works*, 2:356.

76. Hornsby, "John Glas, (1695–1773)," citing an unpublished letter.

English correspondent, 'baptism not belonging to a particular church but to the visible members of that one body into which all are baptized, though not members of any visible church.'[77] Glas presses to the limit the distinction between the visible and the invisible church. The visible church is confined to companies of people under discipline and walking in the ordinances of the Lord's house. So baptism is often administered in the home and there is no record of public baptism of infants although some applicants for membership who had not been baptized as infants may have been baptized in the presence of the church.

9. The Lord's Supper

The Glasites knew that the central act of worship to be carried out each Lord's Day, was the communion, or as they preferred to name it, the Lord's Supper. In his *Letter on Frequent Communicating*, published in 1749, Glas writes, 'I know of no law in the Church of Scotland, to hinder any minister from having the Lord's Supper in his parish every first day of the week if he will', and he maintains this is a dominical command. 'Christ has made it once-a-week at least'.[78] This was a surprising position, given that communion was celebrated only once or twice a year in most parishes, and that the communion season lasted several days, with many sermons. This was the era of revivals at Cambuslang and elsewhere which were based on the communions to which people came from the parishes around. Glas is very clear that those who take part in communion must be believers and must be in harmony with each other. If the church is divided, or there are unsolved problems of discipline, or if there are not two or more elders present, communion cannot take place. Glas looks back to the primitive church. 'While the Christian churches continued stedfastly in the Lord's Supper once-a-week at least, the Christian discipline continued with it as its fence'. Occasional communion and the admission of the unsaved were marks of the declension and corruption of the church. Purity of faith and unity of believers are necessary for the true Lord's Supper. In answers to a series of queries put to Glas by the Synod of Angus and Mearns in 1728 he states,

> None can be admitted to communion in the Lord's Supper with a congregation of Christ, without the consent of that congregation, and there must be a profession of mutual brotherly love in them that partake together in that ordinance. . . . And this

77. Macintosh, *Letters in Correspondence*, 47. And see Murray, "Eighteenth Century Baptismal Controversy," 419–29.

78. Glas, *Works*, 2:300.

is a remarkable difference betwixt baptism and the Lord's Supper; for though we be all baptized into the same body of Christ, the true church, which is represented in the Lord's Supper, . . . but the nature of the Lord's Supper will not admit of a believer receiving it alone . . . and therefore there is no instance of it in the New Testament.[79]

In his large *Treatise on the Lord's Supper* of 1743 Glas expounds the centrality of the sacrament. The covenant in Christ's blood is declared in his supper and is the new covenant in contrast to the old covenant with Israel which was only temporary. The new covenant of grace can give eternal life not because humanity can have perfect obedience but because of God's gracious gift. The blood of the new covenant is shed for the remission of sins, in which the promise of God is confirmed to us. Glas quotes Jer 31 as three divine promises: that God will make a new covenant, that all would know the Lord from the greatest to the least, and that God will remember the sins of his people no more. These are the promises of the shed blood of communion. In what is a very rich exposition of the communion Glas reminds Christians that they are to remember Jesus' poverty, pain and suffering of both body and mind. 'The remembrance of him in the holiness of his life, when he dwelt among us, serves to possess us with a true notion of a holy life and to keep us from being misled by false examples'. His disciples today must behave as he did, in obedience to the Father. Jesus' love to his disciples is the pattern of love required of his disciples one to another. As Jesus washed the feet of his disciples as an expression of humble love, so are we to do the same even as the ministering widows or deaconesses did in 1 Tim 5:10. Likewise the 'kiss of charity' was an expression of brotherly love one to another and should be practiced by believers.[80] Glas, and after him Sandeman maintained that in their practice and doctrine of the sacraments they were returning to the ways of the primitive church.

There is an interesting essay on 'The Centrality of the Lord's Supper' in a recent book produced by the American Churches of Christ. In it the Restorationist scholar[81] Lynn A. McMillon quotes extensively from Glas's *Treatise*, describes the practice of the communion as he observed it in Edinburgh in 1985 and makes clear the freshness of Glas's teaching and its relevance in the development of the Churches of Christ. Not the least interesting part of this chapter in the book is the warm response of the Methodist New Testament scholar, I. Howard Marshall, who writes:

79. Glas, *Works*, 1:188.
80. Glas, *Works*, 5:33.
81. That is, a member of the Churches of Christ.

Most of the points mentioned in the paper would be generally accepted by all Christians holding to an independent form of church polity. Certainly John Glas himself was something of a scriptural literalist, demonstrated by his insistence that the Lord's Supper, as he rightly called it, should be celebrated in the evening, thereby canonizing what may have been an adventitious circumstance in Corinth into an ecclesiastical rule.

He also affirms most strongly that the presence of an ordained minister is not required, and that the emphasis on Jesus 'poverty is unusual but appropriate'.[82] McMillon remarked that on his visit he could not share the communion and Marshall deplores this. 'As soon as an assembly or denomination refuses the Lord's Supper to other Christians who love the Lord, then something drastically has gone wrong with their self-understanding as part of the body of Christ'.[83] This exclusiveness was a feature of the Glasite churches almost from the beginning, and a closed communion table is also a feature of Strict and Particular Baptist churches and the more exclusive branches of the Brethren movement.

10. Pure and Undefiled Religion

In some comments on the movement it is suggested that the Glasites practiced a form of communism. This is easily shown to be an anachronism, but it is true that they were exhorted not to lay up treasures on earth but to hold their possessions available to those of the fellowship in need. Glas's treatise *A Plea for Pure and Undefiled Religion* is probably his most attractive writing and expresses well the theme of brotherly kindness which is at the root of his teaching on Christian life in this world. The *Plea*, first published in 1741, is dedicated to the 'Honourable Colonel James Gardiner'. It is unusual for Glas to make such a dedication, but significantly Gardiner, who was famously defeated by the Jacobite army at the Battle of Prestonpans in 1745, was the subject of a biography by Philip Doddridge which tells the story of a young army officer halted in his thoughtless life by reading *The Christian in Full Armour*, and thus becoming an evangelical hero.

Glas's text is 2 Cor 8:9: 'Ye know the grace of our Lord Jesus Christ, that though he was rich, yet for your sakes he became poor, that ye through his poverty might be rich'. Glas begins, 'The gospel of Jesus Christ slams the pride of man's glorying, and excludes boasting on his part, when it proclaims the glory of the divine perfections in his salvation'. He condemns the

82. Baker, *Evangelicalism and the Stone-Campbell Movement*, 151–63; 206–11.

83. Baker, *Evangelicalism and the Stone-Campbell Movement*, 207.

corruption of the church and the pursuit of wealth and shows that the laws of the gospel are not designed for the prosperity of 'a nation of this world' but of a people whom God is pleased to take out of every nation, for his name. Commenting on the story of the rich man and the beggar Lazarus, Glas says, 'We see the rich man damned for spending that on his pride and vanity and his luxury, that should have relieved poor Lazarus'.

> This Lazarus would have been a very fit person for the public care, or for being laid on some of those hospitals and mortifications, which are sacrifices to the pride and vanity of the mortifiers; and so he might have been removed, as a grievance, from the sight of the rich man, whose daily work it should have been to pity and relieve him.[84]

Another parable that he alludes to, that of the rich fool, makes the point that the rich man has honestly earned his wealth but lays it up on earth and so is not rich towards God. He goes on to show from Scripture that wealth may be used wisely, as by Joseph in Egypt, and in various proverbs, but he contends that right motives in using wealth are necessary.

> There is indeed a great noise made about charity and alms in the Roman church; but as in that worldly kingdom they are far enough from keeping themselves unspotted from the world, so by the merit that is there placed on alms deeds, these are stated in opposition to the mercy and grace of the Father, and the righteousness of his son Jesus Christ, and the fatherless and the widows in their affliction are not the chief objects of their alms, but the enriching of the worldly church, and cherishing the swarms of sturdy holy beggars is the great work of their charity.[85]

The true Christian if he would indeed lay up for a time of infirmity and for old age or for widows and fatherless children ought to keep himself unspotted from the world. Laying up treasures on earth for sickness, old age and for their wives and children after them suggests a lack of trust in God's word, that 'he that giveth to the poor, shall not lack' (Prov 28:27).

Amongst the ministers who opposed Glas in the early years of his movement was Wodrow of Eastwood, that indefatigable gatherer of news from all the churches. He wrote that those who were found not ministering according to the ability God had given them, came to be judged of by the Lord's doctrine concerning covetousness, Matt 6; in consequence some of the most wealthy, under specious pretenses, withdrew. A young man, who

---

84. Glas, *Works*, 2:6.
85. Glas, *Works*, 2:4.

had shown much attachment and some personal kindness to Mr Glas, was the occasion of the piece entitled *A Plea for a Pure and Undefiled Religion*. 'He, as also did another young man, went away sorrowful, for he had great possessions'.

Later, in Danbury and the other New England Churches this became a divisive matter. Around 1788 it was held that

> whenever any of the brethren proposed to lay by their earnings to buy land and increase their property it was looked upon as an evidence of covetousness which is idolatry. It was universally understood and practiced that if by our industry in business we had more than was necessary for the support of ourselves and families that Surpluss must be given to the poor.

This was Glas's teaching and it is worth noting that the American churches were involved in the buying of land to an extent that the British churches, almost entirely urban, were not. Trouble soon came to the American churches soon after Oliver Burr moved from Newtown to Danbury and proved a prosperous merchant. By 1788 he proposed to build a new home on land he had bought. The church at first thought it wrong but gradually a majority were won over to Burr's way of thinking. Benjamin Hoyt, an elder, and Joshua Benedict, a deacon, called Burr's conduct forbidden by scripture, and they were excommunicated. There was a deep divide for a few years. Daniel Humphreys, a prominent member sold his house and costly furniture and gave the proceeds to the poor and was excommunicated, apparently for standing by the teaching of Glas, but eventually most of the churches returned to the original view of the sinfulness of laying up treasures on earth.[86]

In *The Plain and Full Account of the Christian Practices observed by the Church in St Martin's le Grand, London*, this teaching of Glas is set out in practical terms.

> We reckon it unlawful to lay up treasures on earth by setting them apart for any distant, future, uncertain use, but think it incumbent on us to lay up treasure in heaven, by giving alms and readily doing good to all men and especially to those of the household of faith. Everyone therefore is to look upon all that he has in his possession and power as open to the call of the poor and the church, and to contribute according to his ability as everyone has need. And as all of the several churches in connection with us have one cause at heart aiming to maintain a cordial friendship and open fellowship with each other as much as possible, so

---

86. Smith, *Perfect Rule of the Christian Religion*, 134.

they all think themselves bound to contribute liberally for their
mutual assistance and support as occasion may require.[87]

At Communion the members of the Church gave their Fellowship,
the offering for the work of the church. In Edinburgh there was a box at
the door for offerings for the church fabric, to which all could contribute,
but the Fellowship, like the Supper, was confined to members. In the most
recent edition of Pike's work published in 1908 it was suggested that members should not take out Insurance as that showed a lack of trust in God's
providence. There are several letters thanking churches for their contribu-
tions to a church in need, and the Bishops in their tour carried gifts from
America for poor churches, hoping to obtain an elder for their communities
in return. The churches maintained their own poor, as indeed in the eighteenth and early nineteenth centuries did the Scotch Baptists. I was told by
a friend of Glasite descent that a member whose tobacconist shop had been
destroyed by fire and who had no insurance was rescued by an elder who
temporarily became financially embarrassed. This could have unintended
consequences. Another friend told me that his grandfather had been an
elder in the Edinburgh Church, and had fallen on hard times. My friend's
father resented being helped by the richer families and had left the church
in consequence of what he saw as condescension by the more fortunate.[88]

11. The Lot

The lot was considered sacred and therefore games of chance were strictly
forbidden. We shall see how the Bishops on their transatlantic crossing kept
clear of such games and how Sandy Waterston watched his school friends
play Monopoly. 'Senex', writing in *Old and New Glasgow*, tells of Mr John
Glas Sandeman, who would not allow his son, enrolled at the city's grammar
school to have his place in class drawn by lot, and asked for him to be placed
at the foot of the class, from which he always rose to the top by merit.[89]
The allegation that places at the Love Feast were drawn by lot seems to be
apocryphal. If the lot was considered sacred and its use in worldly enterprises was forbidden, the Glasites did not consider entertainments such as
the theatre and balls as sinful. Writing in 1764 to Edward Gorrell of Newby
Glas made this very clear.

87. Pike, *Plain and Full Account*, 10–11.
88. Personal notes.
89. Reid [Senex] , *Old Glasgow*, 3:409.

We cannot approve of any games wherein the lot takes place; because the whole disposal thereof is of the Lord, whose providence is not to be played with. We allow not the game of cards and dice; we condemn your bets and wagers, or cock-fighting or Horse-racing, as offensive and unlawful ways of gaining or losing money. But at the same time we cannot find ground to condemn the amusements or diversions of music and dancing; or even the reading or hearing of plays, though the Methodists and suchlike plead much religion in abstinence from all these more than in strictly following every command of God and the testimony of Jesus.[90]

Indeed this apparent 'worldliness' was one of the differences that Archibald McLean emphasised when he distinguished the Scotch Baptists from the Glasites. 'They will not pray with you, but they will accompany you to the theatre', wrote McLean, and indeed he was speaking for the majority of Scottish Christians. Faraday enjoyed the theatre and read to his family from Shakespeare and the novels of Scott. This was surprising in the early 1800s when even Samuel Taylor Coleridge held that 'Walter Scott's novels are chargeable with . . . ministering to the depraved appetite for excitement'.[91] There was what might be called sumptuary advice regarding appearance and dress. Robert Boswell wrote in 1783, commenting on 1 Cor 11:7–10, that a man should not 'wear his hair very long or dressed in any mode in the shewy way like a woman'. He does admit that there is 'no difference between man and woman as to the matter of their acceptance with God. Galatians 3:28'.[92]

Unlike the Quakers and the General Baptists, the Glasites did not insist on marriage within the church. In a letter of 1762 to James Allen Glas writes:

As the New Testament forbids not the marriage of a professor with an unbeliever we dare not forbid it, however great the disadvantages may be. I cannot understand 'in the Lord' 1st Corinthians 7:39, to mean a believer in the Lord, for then I might say that one who can receive that saying, marrying a believer who cannot receive it yet marries in the Lord; or that one marries in the Lord who marries a believer within the forbidden degrees; yea that one committing fornication with a believer in the Lord did so in the Lord. Therefore I must take it to mean in subjection to the Lord and dependence upon him, with due regard to his

90. Macintosh, *Letters in Correspondence*, 88.
91. Davie, *Gathered Church*, 69.
92. *Few Sandemanian Fragments*, 29.

authority in all that he hath ordered in relation to marriage; as without this marrying a believer is not marrying in the Lord.[93]

In 1730 Glas published a pamphlet which contained an argument with the Presbytery of Dundee 'concerning the lawfulness of JB's marriage with JM his former wife's grandniece in 1729.' JB was John Baxter who came with Glas from Tealing and whose family continued in the church until almost the end. Glas and the Presbytery disagreed about whether the marriage was incestuous, and the case turns on the prohibitions of Lev 18 and 20 and the interpretations put on them by the Council of Trent and The Westminster Confession. Glas's case is that the particular circumstances of the case are not covered by Leviticus or the law of Scotland and he cites the Waldensians, 'the evangelical churches in the valleys of Piedmont' who were reported to have said 'for that which God hath not forbidden, may very well be done without his permission'. The pamphlet illustrates Glas's wide reading and his independence, even at this early stage of his career, from the received interpretation as set forth by the Presbytery. The outcome was that the case was 'called and postponed annually at the Assembly till the death of the defendant put an end to it'.[94]

Some of these teachings were weighty and others seem trivial, but it was part of the Sandemanian ethos to treat everything in Scripture, especially the New Testament, as having equal authority.

---

93. Macintosh, *Letters in Correspondence*, 47.
94. Glas, *Works*, 2:470–98.

3

The Development of the Church

WHILE MOST OF THE distinctive features of the movement can be found in the many works of John Glas, a great impetus to its development came from the writings and personality of his son-in-law, Robert Sandeman. He was born on 29 April, 1718, the eldest of five surviving sons of David Sandeman who came from Alyth to Perth in 1708 and set up a linen manufacturing business. In this he prospered, becoming a Merchant Bailie in 1735/6, and being joined in the trade by his sons. Linen making had been encouraged in Scotland by the establishment of the Board of Trustees for Manufactures, which distributed money from funds promised to Scotland under the Act of Union, which began to be released in 1727. This was the foundation of the Sandeman mercantile empire, which branched out in several directions over the generations, the most well-known being the Port and Sherry business still associated with the name.

After an apprenticeship in the family business Robert went to study in Edinburgh, either for the ministry of the Church of Scotland or for a career in medicine. The family already had contact with the Glasite Church in Perth, established in 1733, and it is probable that Robert met Glas in Edinburgh in 1734 when he was persuaded to abandon his studies and further the Glasite movement. He returned to Perth, to become an apprentice weaver, married Katherine Glas in 1737, and was ordained an elder of the Church in Perth in 1744. He moved to Edinburgh in 1756 and to London in 1760, where he was instrumental in setting up the church. In 1764 he and James Cargill set out for New England, where he gathered a small following, was involved in many disputations, suffered as a Loyalist, and died on 2 April 1771, his wife having predeceased him in March 1764 shortly before he left London.[1] Their marriage was childless, and the many Sandemans in the churches were descended from one or other of his brothers. *The Sandeman Genealogy* which was revised and published by Gerard Lionel Sandeman in 1950[2] is based on a manuscript by David Peat that had been extended and published by John Glas Sandeman in 1895 and it contains extensive evidence of the interlocking families. The best known Sandemans may have been those involved in the wine trade, especially with Portugal, but the church annals mention many more.

That is the outline of Robert Sandeman's life. He was an elder and preacher in the movement, but his greatest impact was through his writings. The earliest seems to have been a letter to William Wilson, the third minister of Perth, and a future Seceder, along with the Erskines, who was still in his post in 1738. He signed the letter along with George Miller, the town clerk of Perth and a prominent Glasite, on 24 December 1737. The scripture text at the heading is a foretaste of the flavor of the letter: 2 Tim 3:6, 'of this sort are they which creep into houses and lead captive silly women'. A maidservant in Perth had joined the Glasite church and Wilson is accused of seeking to seduce her back into his church. The letter confirms other stories about the strenuous opposition met by the Glasite church in Perth, despite its quite distinguished following. The writers attack the worldliness of the clergy, and their love of position and money, making them no better than their Roman predecessors. It strikes a familiar note when they allude to the 'ancient days of the covenants which were a delicious and happy time for the clergy'. 'When the Sectaries (so called in their honour) first came to the town, you told the overseers that they were intruding upon your charge'.[3] This is already an example of Sandeman's harsh use of language and the sharp edge of his invective, for which he was often blamed in later years.

There is a remarkable letter from Palaemon (Sandeman's nom de plume) to his father written in June 1745 and republished by the *Dundee Chronicle Office* in 1835. He begins by thanking his father for his fatherly care and so forth, but then begins to upbraid him for his wavering allegiance to the church. He is worried about his father's

> well-being in that eternal state when you leave this body. I am very sorry to say, dear father, that I am often in pain about you in this respect. You are influenced more by the authority and esteem

1. Macintosh. *Letters in Correspondence*, 119–20.

2. Sandeman, *Sandeman Genealogy*. This contains, besides an elaborate series of family trees, the picture and explanation of the Sandeman coat of arms.

3. R. Sandeman, *Letters*, "Letter to Mr Wilson."

of such as you think to be truly serious and godly, than by the authority and approbation of the living God in the Scriptures.

There is a prevailing notion among the people whom you value as good Christians that practical religion consists in carefully hearing sermons and in meditating upon and talking seriously with one another upon them. This may gain a name for godliness among men, very agreeable to the taste of the covetous Pharisee, but at the same time most abominable in the sight of God.

He accuses his father of leaving the true church and again being admitted as formerly to take his place in the Kirk Session as a ruling elder. Furthermore:

One main spring of your apostasy is giving more ear to my mother than to the voice of the Son of God in the scriptures. Our mother was never well affected to the TRUTH which we profess. This is not the first time you have apostatized from the Christian profession.

This is surely a very strange letter from a comparatively young man to his father in an era when respect to elders was more evident than it is now! It does give a flavor of the exclusiveness that developed in the early years of the movement, when 'false charity' was denounced, and it points to the supreme place given to the Scriptures, the only source of truth about Christ. The disparaging reference to his mother is even more disturbing but may reflect conflicts in families confronted with a new and demanding, even 'cultish' form of the Christian religion. It is even stranger that the letter was kept in print almost a hundred years later.[4]

Sandeman's most influential work was his *Letters on Theron and Aspasio* which was first published in 1757 and republished at least six times in the coming years. It was his response to the rather flowery *Dialogues between Theron and Aspasio*[5] which was published in 1755 by James Hervey, a series of interactions between a man of morality and a Christian, spelling out the conventional evangelical doctrine on original sin and on the imputed righteousness of Christ, which gives us salvation. John Wesley as an Arminian took exception to this writing of a former member of the Holy Club at Oxford, and considered it to be unscriptural, unnecessary, and misleading, implying that sinners were, by a sort of legal fiction, clothed by the

---

4. Morison, *Supplementary Letters*, appendix, xxiv. Also copy of "Letter from Palemon [*sic*] to His Father," written in June 1745, 3–17.

5. For a brief and lucid account of Hervey's work, see Rivers, *Shaftesburian Enthusiasm*, 36–39; and Hindmarsh, *Spirit of Early Evangelicalism*, 253–54.

protective righteousness of Christ while they were still sinners, and as we have seen he took even more exception to Sandeman's letters. Most Calvinists saw such imputation as a safeguard against trust in one's own goodness.

Sandeman attacked the thesis of the *Dialogues* from a different angle. He saw in it another way by which those seeking to be Christians trusted to their own merits, and he could not find imputation in a rational reading of scripture. In his *Letters* Sandeman develops his characteristic view of faith as belief based on a testimony, and in particular belief in the resurrection of Jesus Christ. Any searching for evidences or emotions was a way of seeking one's own righteousness, of adding to the work of Christ in the Great Atonement. Sandeman is quite severe in rebuking those whom he calls the 'popular preachers' of his day. Those who listen to the Erskines, Boston, Marshall, Guthrie, Flavell and others are on 'a devout road to Hell'. These writers were the evangelical heroes of eighteenth-century pious Scots, and also of English Evangelicals.

As Hornsby remarks, 'Sandeman's book fell like a bombshell into the evangelical camp and caused a great commotion in religious circles on both sides of the border. It was not long before a stream of controversial literature began to pour from the press'. This was a time when there was lively debate among evangelical and nonconformist theologians on predestination, the place of intellect and emotion and pastoral matters.[6] The harshness, of which his critics complain, is certainly very evident in his condemnation of the great majority of evangelical preachers, but Sandeman can also write with warmth. In his discourse on John 3:16 he speaks with passion.

> When God adopts the sinful children of men into his family, when he takes the children of wrath from the depth of disgrace they are involved in, by their slavery to sin and Satan, and exalts them to the unspeakable dignity of children in his family, he honours them in the sight of all the sons of God, of all the heavenly host, by marking them out as his favourites; and this he does by bestowing such a gift upon them as raises the astonishment and admiration of angels, as he lays open to them the manifold grace of God in a manner surpassing everything they had an idea of before.[7]

In the same discourse he also writes:

> Much have the perverters of the gospel been engaged in urging upon men the most fruitless and impious, as well as painful

---

6. See for example the arguments between Hervey and Wesley in the 1750s, in Rack, *Reasonable Enthusiast*, 452–54.

7. Macintosh, *Letters in Correspondence*, 195.

self-righteous labour, from such expressions as these, 'whosoever believeth shall be saved,' making believing to import a labour and exercise equal to that of keeping the divine law, so establishing a human righteousness to the neglect and contempt of that perfect work which Jesus wrought, which so pleased the Righteous Father. At the same time, nothing can be clearer from the Scriptures than that believing, agreeable to the common sense of the word, stands in direct opposition to all working whatsoever.[8]

While much of Sandeman's rhetoric in the *Letters* is directed at theologians, he also shows an interest in current philosophy, and particularly criticizes David Hume, well-known as a sceptic in religion, and also the author of *Essays on the Principles of Morality and Natural Religion*. This work by Henry Home, Lord Kames, an elder of the Kirk, was published anonymously in 1752, and led to the denunciation of Kames in pamphlets and in the General Assembly. He was accused by members of the 'Popular Party' of necessitarianism and other deviations from Calvinist orthodoxy, but the accusation was allowed to die away. Sandeman, in a section of the *Letters on Reason*, wrote:

> Though I am not fond of claiming any kindred to philosophers; yet I shall here quote a passage from the well-known Essays on Morality and Natural Religion and the rather as they have in Scotland lately obtained a considerable share of the public attention, 'for reasoning is our own work, and There is merit and acuteness and penetration; and we are better pleased to assume merit to ourselves than humbly to acknowledge that, to the most important discoveries, we are led by the hand of the Almighty.'

It is interesting to reflect that in the culture of the Enlightenment and the rise of the Moderate Party in the Church of Scotland, Sandeman is eagerly reading and occasionally agreeing with the foremost philosophers. Later in the same section he wrote:

> Paschal [sic], whom I mentioned as a person respected by philosophers for his uncommon abilities, could observe the original dignity of human nature, like that of a decayed palace, from the greatness of its ruins. . . . [H]ence I wonder that mankind are not seized with despair every time they reflect on the wretchedness of their condition.

8. Macintosh, *Letters in Correspondence*, 197.

He quoted the rejoinder by Voltaire, 'I see no cause to plunge into the despair mentioned by Paschal'.[9] In footnotes to several pages he quotes Hume's *Natural History of Religion* with some approbation. Sandeman's work was not wholly destructive, nor was his reading wholly theological!

It is difficult in our very different theological world to grasp just how passionate was this whole emphasis of Glas and Sandeman upon the simplicity of bare belief, but it struck a chord with many who had been 'going about to establish their own righteousness' and offered a clear and unfussy approach to the Christian faith, which is echoed by the Scotch Baptist McLean, and also by Alexander Campbell. Splitting Calvinistic hairs has not ceased and as we have seen there are those who believe that Sandemanianism is a great danger to the evangelical church today.[10]

But to return to Sandeman's life and interest we may look at his correspondence with several Independent ministers and the establishment of the Church in London. One of the ablest correspondents was William Cudworth of Margaret Street Chapel off Oxford Street. He was a friend of Hervey, and in 1757 initiated a correspondence with Sandeman, which was conducted with great courtesy, but which left the opponents just where they were, and Sandeman admits at last that he is wearied of the contest. In 1760 he wrote to George Glas:

> Last week I received a long letter from Mr Cudworth, of nearly 16 quarto pages, closely written, wherein he shows his disaffection to our creed in a more disguised manner than formerly. . . . [H]e tells me likewise that he is soon to shew me more of his mind in print, in defense of Theron and Aspasio.[11]

Samuel Pike was the pastor of a Congregational/Independent Church meeting in Thames Street and the author of a volume of casuistry, that is, statements answering queries on spiritual and ethical difficulties. One example from the book asks, 'How far may a person judge of the strength or weakness of his faith by the brightness or darkness of his frames?'[12] which suggests that the whole question of the nature of faith was much in the minds of Christians of this time. Another of his books is entitled *Philosophia Sacra or the Principles of Natural Philosophy extracted from Divine*

---

9. Sandeman, *Letters*, 4:155ff.

10. See, for example, Gay, *Secret Stifler*. This book was published in 2016, and has a preface by Professor Michael Haykin, of the Southern Baptist Theological Seminary, who has written on Andrew Fuller and Sandemanianism.

11. Jones, *Sandeman-Cudworth Correspondence*.

12. Pike, *Some Important Cases of Conscience*, 48 (Case 5).

Revelation, a book expounding Hutchinsonian philosophy.[13] He deals with such matters as creation, spirit, light, fire, elasticity, gravitation, magnetism, and electricity, and seems to foreshadow some of the work of Faraday. He also compiled a Hebrew dictionary.[14]

Members of his congregation had drawn his attention to Sandeman's *Letters* and he read them with mixed pleasure and dissatisfaction. To clear up disputed points he entered a correspondence with Sandeman, thanking him for an 'elaborate and ingenious performance', but taking exception to the spirit, style, and language which he describes as 'peculiarly severe and satirical', and ventures to offer some criticism. In the subsequent letters, which were published, we can see Pike's objections gradually being overcome, until at length, in 1765 he joined the young church in London. There was a flurry of pamphlets by various members of Thames Street, but Pike had finally made up his mind. He was subsequently an elder of the Sandemanian Church in Trowbridge and he wrote the standard account of the polity of the church, *A Plain and Full Account of the Christian Practices Observed by the Church in St Martin's-le-Grand, London, and other churches (commonly called Sandemanian) in Fellowship with them, in a Letter to a Friend.* There are many editions, the last being in 1906.

Other London Independent ministers were drawn into the church. The most notable was John Barnard, who writing to Robert Sandeman on 9 July 1759 said:

> I had a careful serious and (what is called) judicious though not learned education and was brought up to a trade by which I lived reputably until less than four years ago, when I was called upon by the Independent Church of which I was a member to give myself to the ministry of the word, with which I complied (though not quitting my trade.)

He goes on to say that he was perplexed about the meaning of faith, then found Sandeman's *Letters*, suspected at first that Sandeman was an Antinomian but finally found peace. He reveals something of the theological ferment in London Dissent when he confesses that 'before I appeared in public I was much employed about Hebrew criticism and in the Hutchinsonian way, which is quite as unpopular as what is here called Sandemanianism, so I was never much perturbed about your severity against popular preachers'.[15] On 19 July Sandeman replied in a warm and welcoming let-

---

13. For Hutchinsonian tenets see White, "Hutchinsonianism in Eighteenth Century Scotland," 157–69; and Nockles, *Oxford Movement in Context*, 208–9.

14. *Philosophia Sacra*, 1755.

15. Morison, *Supplementary Letters*, 19.

ter, commending Glas's *Pure and Undefiled Religion*.[16] Barnard was very attracted to Sandeman's teaching but in January 1760 he still had questions.

> Do you admit any persons to occasional communion who are not members of one or another of the churches in fellowship with you, and if they do, in what names? With what confession? Or is it without any? Especially do you admit Antipaedobaptists to your fellowship?[17]

In February Sandeman replied in the negative to all the questions, adding:

> Real events or cases of particular persons actually under our cognisance will be found attended by such circumstances as to leave a society influenced by the truth seldom at a loss in judging who are of the truth and who not.[18]

In July 1760 Barnard writes that he has fellowship with fourteen people but that

> about six of our number, whose profession of love to and zeal for the truth I cannot doubt are Anabaptists, and it doth not appear we can have fellowship with them and yet keep the unity of spirit and the bond of peace.

So, Barnard was left with eight believers, who were eventually part of the Sandemanian Church in the Meeting House at Bull-and-Mouth Street.[19] Barnard's later career is interesting. We have already seen how his book, *The Nature and Government of the Christian Church*, can be taken as an authoritative account of Sandemanian ecclesiology. It was reprinted in Perth in 1855 and we are told Mr Sandeman had thought highly of it. Barnard continued to correspond with Sandeman when the latter was in New England and in June 1766, he informed him that 'Messrs Pike and Chater are both Elders with us. Our number in town is 106 besides several about the country. We have a church at Banham in Norfolk where Boosey and Christie are Elders, and it is now 37 in number'.[20] In June 1768 he reports '19 men and 17 women added and there are 149 members besides out parties'. There are six members in Nottingham, and six at Wethersfield with a very eager hearing. The church at Trowbridge has been squabbling about

16. Morison, *Supplementary Letters*, 20.
17. Morison, *Supplementary Letters*, 40.
18. Morison, *Supplementary Letters*, 47.
19. Morison, *Supplementary Letters*, 52.
20. Morison, *Supplementary Letters*, 64.

diversions. There are three at Salisbury and Huddleston at Whitehaven has joined with his people. Later in the same year he reports seventeen at Liverpool, thirty-seven at Colne, and eighteen at Nottingham, besides churches at Wooler and Newcastle.[21] This may well represent the greatest spread of the churches in England. But all was not well with John Barnard. In September 1771 Robert Lyon, Glas's nephew wrote to William Sandeman from Dundee that Barnard had been excommunicated while in the pulpit! Lyon remarks that Barnard 'had never been tried for covetousness before'. Edward Wilson, elder at Kirkby Lonsdale, suggests that Barnard had 'entertained too exalted notions of his preaching abilities'. However, adds Wilson, he continued to attend the church until his death in 1810.[22] Certainly, the Barnard family continued in the London Church and Faraday married his great niece. The last deaconess at the dissolution of the Edinburgh church in 1989 was Mrs Barnard née Sandeman.

John Chater, who is occasionally mentioned as an elder in London and elsewhere is the subject of an interesting article by Alan Sell,[23] who remarks that 'he is, to put it mildly, elusive'. What has been discovered is worth noting, if only to show the diversity of the eldership in the churches. Chater was received as a church member by the famous London Independent pastor Thomas Bradbury, who also had dealings with Barnard. He studied for the ministry with Rev Zephaniah Marryatt, like Bradbury an eminent orthodox minister. On 2 April 1752 he was admitted to the list of ministers of the London Congregational Board and the following year he was called to Newport, Isle of Wight, where he remained until 1758. In 1759 he became minister of Silver Street in London, which he tried without success to remodel on Sandemanian lines. By the end of 1765 he had left Silver Street and, like Pike, joined the church meeting at Bull-and-Mouth Street. He then kept a bookshop, first on Ludgate Hill and then in Cheapside. In 1767 he published a pamphlet under the name 'Ignotus,' entitled *Another high road to Hell. An essay on the pernicious and destructive Effects of the Modern Entertainments from the PULPIT*. In this Chater attacks the theatre of his day as a sink of iniquity and goes on to claim that the immoral player is as nothing compared to the immoral preacher. He says that there is a devout as well as a profane way of going to hell and that the popular preachers only commend a sober life, not the true gospel faith and hope. The main theme is like Sandeman's teaching, but he is the only Sandemanian writer I have

21. Morison, *Supplementary Letters*, 65.

22. Morison, *Supplementary Letters*, 107.

23. Sell, "John Chater," 100–117. This article is a very useful and accurate introduction to the whole subject of Sandemanianism.

found who condemns the theatre. Archibald McLean, the Scotch Baptist, criticized the Sandemanians for their attendance at worldly entertainments. The other publication Chater produced was a three-volume novel, *The History of Tom Rigby* which appeared in 1773, a book which Sell characterizes as sentimental and improving. 'The sense of natural order which pervades the novel rebukes the disorder of religious enthusiasm', writes Sell after giving a synopsis of the moral story, and he points out how eighteenth century and cerebral Sandemanianism is and how it predated romanticism.[24]

Thomas Boosey appears as an educated London minister, caring for and living among a rustic flock at Old Buckenham. Later he is found in London and becomes an importer of sheet music, and founder of a firm which still exists as Boosey and Hawkes. A later Thomas Boosey was a friend and fellow elder of Faraday. As in Scotland a few ministers were drawn into the movement in its early days, but there is no record of accessions after the pioneering days.

Glasite Churches in Scotland

1. Dundee

The Church at Dundee was the 'mother' church of the Glasite connection, not only because it was where John Glas spent many years as an elder, but because it became the largest, although not the longest lasting, church. It dated its origin to 1730, in 1754 entered a Meeting House in the Seagate[25] and around 1777 moved into its remarkable octagonal meeting house which is now the Hall of the adjacent St Andrews Parish Church. There exist two identical copies of a list of the members of the ecclesiola at Tealing, dated 13 July 1725, containing seventy-two names, twenty-eight men and forty-four women, arranged by district or farmtoun, and in the short account which follows there is the record of a few more being added to the group and a few excluded, either because they have moved to other parishes, or because they have been brought under discipline. The record ceases in October 1727.[26]

When Glas moved to Dundee in 1730 and set up a church there, several of his Tealing flock followed him, and others, some of whom had previously travelled the five miles or so to Tealing, joined them. The first list of the Dundee church is dated December 1746, and records only names and not

24. Sell, "John Chater," 117.

25. Scott, *Notebook*, 58.

26. Scott, *Notebook*, 152–53. This list of participants is in the appendix of Murray, "Social and Religious Origins."

occupations, although a later list, of 20 September 1771 has occupations of many members and helps to fill in some of the details. In the 1746 list there are forty-eight men, four of whom have already appeared in the Tealing list. These are John Glas, described as 'teaching Elder', and John Baxter, founder of the well-known textile firm later known as Baxter Brothers, whose family maintained connections with the churches until the late twentieth century. The others were John Fleeming and Robert Owen, who had been Clerk to the Session at Tealing. Of the sixty-two women's names eight can be traced to the Tealing list, and two others were added to the society in 1726. In the 1771 list occur two other names from Tealing. The names of the women in the 1746 list include Kathleen Black, who was John Glas's wife, Grisel Smith, who came from Kirkton of Tealing and may have been servant at the manse, Margaret Murdoch, deaconess, who had been under discipline in her Tealing days for 'meddling', Margaret Butcher, wife of John Fleeming, and Euphemia Davidson, noted in the Tealing account as having gone to Dundee and returned to Tealing in 1726.[27]

From this tantalizing material only tentative conclusions can be drawn. The church grew with some rapidity. There are 110 names on the 1746 roll and only a few came from Tealing, although those were the leading folk in the Church. Notes in James Scott's *Notebook* state that on 'September 19th, 1749 Mrs Glas died between 5 and 6 a.m. very bold, and on September 14th, 1753 Lady Tealing died, bold in the faith'.[28] Dundee was at the beginning of a period of growth and development and John Baxter was one of the pioneers of the city's textile manufacture. The list of 1771 gives the occupations of the male members and does allow some conclusions to be drawn about the social structure of the congregation at the period of its greatest strength. There were five elders: John Glas, who died on 22 November 1773; William Morrison, thread manufacturer; William Lyon, writer[29]; Robert Lyon, merchant, who went to London in 1771 to serve as an elder there; and David Reid, bleacher, and there were seven deacons: Andrew Proctor, glover; Alexander Boyd, servant to Mr Morrison; George Boyd, manufacturer; Alexander Morrison, son to Mr Morrison; James Reid, heckler; John Baxter junior, manufacturer; and James Scott, merchant's clerk (compiler of the notebook which contained these lists.) The seventy-four other men

27. Scott, *Notebook*, 92, 93.

28. Scott, *Notebook*, 58. Lady Tealing was Jean Duncan, daughter of Alexander Duncan of Lundie and aunt of Admiral Viscount Duncan, the vicar of Camperdown, who was influential in the upbringing of his nephews, James and Robert Haldane, the evangelists. I am grateful to Henry Steuart Fothringham, Esq. for this information about his ancestress.

29. Lawyer.

included John Baxter senior, manufacturer; John Wemyss, thread manufacturer; Charles Peat, manufacturer; Thomas Baxter; manufacturer, all
presumably men of some substance, and several shopkeepers. Thirteen men
are listed as servants, that is employees of Mr Morrison, and there are eighteen weavers, two warpers, four tailors, two shoemakers, one bleacher, three
hecklers, three smiths, two chapmen, one gardener, one tanner, two wrights,
and three with no occupation mentioned. There were one hundred and five
women on the roll, eighteen of whom were widows, including Agnes Glas,
i.e., 'old Mrs Lyon', deaconess, and Jean Glas, widow of Thomas Glas, sixty-
seven married women, mostly with husbands in the church, twelve unmarried women, and seven without description.[30]

Another list for 1774 also gives occupations. There were four elders,
Robert Ferrier, late of Balchrystie and Glasgow, William Morrison, William Lyon, and David Reid. There were 150 members in all. In his report
on the churches in 1782 Robert Ferrier states that there were 205 members
who gathered in a meeting house with seven hundred seats that was almost always full. A roll of 1784 gives a total membership of 239, 118 men
and 121 women, a remarkable balance for any church.[31] We can draw some
conclusions from these lists. At the time of its greatest growth the Dundee
church chose its elders from the educated class, Glas and Ferrier, and the
comparatively wealthy, Morrison, Baxter, Lyon. The diaconate comprised
both younger members of leading families, who may have been seen as future elders, and a minority of men who were employees, sometimes of the
elders. The remainder of the male membership is largely connected with the
textile trade.

This was the high-water mark of the church. The Baxter family continued in some of its branches to be leaders in the church, and it remained
a strong force in Dundee. According to the *Old Statistical Account* of 1792
there were 1,160 Glasites in the city. As the nearest roll to that date counts
239 members, the others must have been members of church families, and
hearers, or auditory, as the Glasites call those who attended but did not
assume the serious commitment of membership. This means that one in
twenty of the population had some kind of meaningful relationship to the
Glasite church. Dr Robert Small, author of the report, has interesting comments on the Independents or Glasites. 'Their preachers are distinguished
in the congregation by the names of bishops or elders'.

> This congregation affords decisive proof of the importance of
> early marriage to the population. It was formed by Mr. Glas

30. MS list.
31. MS list.

about the year 1732 [*sic*] and at that time consisted of not more than 71 members, men and women. It has now collected 1160 and the increase is much more the effect of an indispensable law of the society enjoining early marriages, than of any new accession of proselytes. Besides the importance of the law to the population it appears, from this experiment, that it is also of the utmost consequence to prevent licentiousness and to promote early industry. The usual objections of its tendency to produce a debilitated race, and to increase the number of the poor, appear to be in a great measure frivolous; for in consequence of the regulations of the society, very few of the poor have hitherto been burdensome to others, and their young people do not seem to be inferior, in health and vigour to the ordinary natives of the town.[32]

In James Scott's *Notebook* there is an undated but intriguing note of Church expenditure around this time: '£1 3s 6d to 10 persons; to Montrose 3s6d; to Mr G. 10s; to wine 6 bottles, 7s6d; to bread, 6d'.[33]

After the so-called Perth heresy (see chapter 5) there is some evidence from the early 1800s of a few persons in Dundee continuing in communion with Perth, Arbroath and Kirkby Lonsdale.

In 1834, when Nathaniel Bishop visited the church, there were still six hundred at the afternoon service. The church did not give evidence to the Commissioners of Religious Instruction in 1837 although the elders are named as William Gavin and George Baxter. According to Archibald Sandeman, a Glasgow elder writing in his diary for 1890, and noting the death of Miss Crichton who was ninety-one and had been twenty-five years in the church, there were 136 members in 1843, in 1873 only sixty-seven, and in 1890 it was still further reduced.[34] By that time the church, which had joined with the London church in taking a strict line in the blood-eating controversy, had divided, and some former members were now in fellowship with Edinburgh. The large church was empty, and the remaining people met in the sealed off gallery. The Methodist Local Preacher H. F. Fallow visited the church in 1922 and found twenty-two present, all women except the elders, John Sandeman who conducted the service and Alex Moir who preached. Fallow had attended services in Newcastle as a child, and later a few times in Dundee.[35]

---

32. Sinclair, *Old Statistical Account*, 8:232.
33. Scott, *Notebook*, 20.
34. A. Sandeman, *Diary*, 16.
35. Fallow, "Two Johns, Wesley and Glas," 86.

There is one story of a late addition to the Church which is worth noting. Mr John Duff wrote to the Dundee elders from Savannah, Georgia, USA, on 6 April 1882. He has heard of the Glasites and is interested in learning more. He presents a highly Calvinistic statement of his faith and defends himself against charges of antinomianism and licentiousness. He attacks his former congregation and the church in general as worldly, giving deference to rich men. 'Carnal policy directs religious proceedings'. He objects to college trained ministers and has been accused of Plymouthism and Sandemanianism, 'and I know not what other "ism"'. He knows the New Testament states that the church should have a plurality of elders, chosen by the church from among its members. 'I have nothing to do with Plymouthism, so believes (signed) John Duff'. The next letter to the Dundee elders is dated 5 June 1891 and by now he is in Chester working as an engineer. He mentions that he has read Glas's *Testimony*, and desires to be admitted as a member: 'My mother frequently attended the meeting in Dundee about 70 years ago but was not a member'. Alex Moir, the Dundee elder, replied on 8 June 1891. 'I have to inform you that the only bodies now in connection with us in England are one in Newcastle and one in London, both without a presbytery'.[36] He mentions the division, half and half, in London five years before.

> Our friends built a Meeting House in Albion Road, London. We are the only true Church of the Gentiles [*sic*]. I suppose your parents had been Scots. In 1834 one of our elders was John Duff, and there was Alexander Duff in Aberdeen. Are you related? Now there is no church in Aberdeen, Montrose, or Perth. There is a body in Perth who call themselves Glasites, but they are descended from a body from which all the churches withdrew in the end of the last century. The body in Edinburgh who are called by the same name is one from whom all the churches withdrew in 1855.

Duff is asked for a statement of faith and acceptance of the kiss of charity, feast of charity, and abstinence for eating of blood and things strangled. Moir concludes, 'I may mention that we have seven or eight women in America with whom our friends in England and Scotland keep up a correspondence'.

Duff replied on 14 June 1891 bewailing his lonely state in Lancashire, where he had now moved. 'There are believers, but they practice a false charity under the painted name of love, peace and unity'. He accepts the kiss of charity etc., but has never had much contact with the churches and has given his Glas's *Works* to a friend. But he has visited the London and

---

36. That is, without at least two elders.

Edinburgh Meeting Houses and an Edinburgh lady asked if he was Mr Baxter from Dundee. He is willing to go to Glasgow, London, or Dundee to be received. Moir replied on 22 June 1891 that he was satisfied with Duff's statements which were read to the church. 'Please come to Dundee'. And there the correspondence ends, but in the items from the Edinburgh records extracted by Isobel Punton, daughter of the third last elder, George Punton, it is stated, 'December 24th, 1893 John Duff, a stranger from Atherton near Manchester confessed the faith and was received into the Church'. Sadly, on 13 June 1897, the entry is 'John Duff separated from the Church.' This story leaves some puzzles. While the Edinburgh records mention additions and deaths in other churches these are only the meetings in fellowship with Edinburgh, that is Galashiels, London, and a group in Dundee. So, did Mr Duff join in Dundee and then cross the boundary to Edinburgh, or was this so unusual an event that the news of it was noted, although there was no fellowship between Edinburgh and the main church in Dundee as Mr Moir makes abundantly clear?[37]

The Dundee church closed in the 1920s, and for many years the octagonal building was used as a furniture store. In recent years it has been fittingly rehabilitated as the Hall of the adjoining St Andrews Church of Scotland and there was until recently a small exhibition of Glasite memorabilia, plate, communion cup, collection ladles, a pitch pipe, books, photographs, and a model of the three-decker pulpit, with the top seat for the elders, the middle one for the deacons, and the lower one used to serve communion.[38]

2. The Perth Church

This was the second church to be founded and it is closely associated with several families, Morisons, Waterstons, Sandemans, and Bells, all inter-related over the years. Perth was another growing town, with many commercial links with Dundee. Like Dundee it was on the navigable River Tay, and it had had an almost identical percentage increase in population as its neighbor. In 1755 the population was 9,019, and in the 1790s about 19,871. Dundee in the same period had grown from 12,477 to 23,500. Many of the new inhabitants had come from country parishes where the church discipline could be strict, and in the larger urban areas there was much more freedom to find dissenting places of worship. In and around Perth the flax-bleaching industry was very important, and bleachfields were set up around the town. The Sandeman family and Hector Turnbull, also a Glasite, had

37. Macintosh, *Letters in Correspondence*; MS 364/3/15.
38. At present housed in Dundee Museum.

bleachfields at Luncarty where in 1790 eight hundred thousand yards of linen were processed, and at Tulloch where three hundred thousand yards of cheaper material were produced. More of the church members were in the learned professions and fewer in the textile industries than in Dundee, but the overall pattern is similar.

The church was formed by Glas himself and there are stories of vocal oppositions by the townsfolk to this newcomer to the town. The earliest list is dated December 1751 and does not give occupations. In that year James Cant and Robert Miller were elders. Miller had long been a friend of Glas and was the lawyer who represented him at his appeal to the presbytery in 1728. He was town clerk of Perth and served the church until at least 1762. James Cant was a correspondent of Robert Sandeman and a well-known antiquary, surveyor of customs in Perth and well-read in the Greek and Latin classics. He was an elder in Perth for forty years and towards the end of his life he served the Dunkeld church, where he carried on the business of a bookbinder and glazier.[39] The deacons were Samuel Pickering and Robert Morison. Morison founded the printing and publishing firm, which published many Glasite works and also editions of the classics. He appears in later Perth lists as Postmaster and Stationer. Smith states that he was the son of Francis Morison, glazier, and burgess, who was also a bookbinder, and Elizabeth Mitchell. Robert lived from 1722 until 1791. He married Margaret Russel, granddaughter of Principal Tullideph of the University of St Andrews. She appears in the 1751 list, next to Elizabeth Tullidaff, presumably a relative, and the same person as Elizabeth Tullideph who appears as the wife of James Cant in a list of 1772. We see here a well-marked feature of inter-marriage which has always characterized the Glasites. Robert Morison was also a bookbinder with a branch business in Dunkeld which Cant took over when as an elderly man he went to be elder there. In 1773 he added printing to his concerns.[40] There were seventeen other male members including Robert Sandeman's three brothers, David, William, and George, and Patrick Miller who later succeeded his father both as town clerk and elder. There is a list of those who had 'died in the church' including Thomas Sandeman, a fourth brother. Twenty-seven female members are named, making a total of forty-eight in all.

Dr Charles Waterston in his fascinating book, *Perth Entrepreneurs, the Sandemans of Springland*,[41] notes that when the Jacobite forces occupied Perth in 1745, James Crie and other magistrates, including George Miller,

---

39. Smith, *Historians of Perth*, 59.
40. Perth lists.
41. Waterston, *Perth Entrepreneurs*, 19.

the town clerk, and Robert Morison, the postmaster of Perth, responsible for government funds, fled to Edinburgh. Miller hid the keys of the town hall in Methven Woods. After a week Prince Charles Edward and his army resumed their march on 11 September 1745 accompanied by several hostages, including former provost Patrick Crie and Bailie David Sandeman's son David. After the Battle of Culloden in 1746 the town council of Perth was anxious to affirm its loyalty to the Hanoverians and sent a loyal address to King George. Almost all those named were Glasites, as well as being leading townsmen, and their loyalty to the legitimate government was no doubt inspired by their belief that it was their duty as Glasites to uphold civil authority, a belief that led to trouble for Robert Sandeman during his stay in New England.

The next list, also without occupations, is appended to a letter dated March 1903 from Robert Morison, a great-grandson of his eighteenth-century namesake, to an unnamed cousin in the Edinburgh church, and is a copy of an original list dated 17 April 1763. The elders were James Cant, George Miller, Robert Morison, and William Sandeman. The deacons were David Sandeman and Robert Rattray, and thirty-nine other men were named, including five other Sandemans, George Glas, the sea-going son of John Glas and Patrick Miller. The list of 1774 gives occupations. The elders were James Cant, Robert Morison, postmaster and stationer, Patrick Thomson, merchant, David Robertson, clerk to the bank, and Patrick Miller, writer. There were seven deacons and fifty-three men, weavers, bookbinders, tailors, and apprentices to various firms. There were also two aged men upon bounty, one of whom was the former deacon Robert Rattray. Presumably the bounty was the support of the church for members who needed financial aid. There were fifty women, two of whom were deaconesses, giving a total of one hundred and three members. In 1782 Robert Ferrier gives the number of Perth members as one hundred and twenty, and the meeting house seating five hundred is constantly full.[42] There is one other list, of 20 March 1804. There were thirty-two men, and thirty-four women. No less than nine of the men had been disqualified from the elder's office by a second marriage. One of these was a natural leader, James Morison, who was a prolific author on biblical subjects, and a collector and publisher of Glasite material. In a rare reference to marriage procedure, Smith states that he married his first wife, Margaret Mitchell, at the age of nineteen in the Glasite church. He was married to his second wife, Grace Lindsay, also in the Glasite church, by Patrick Miller, the town clerk, in 1789.[43] By the

42. Mackintosh, *Letters in Correspondence*, 126.
43. Smith, *Historians of Perth*, 88, 89.

time this list was drawn up, the church had started to decline, both numeri-cally and socially and the controversy over assurance linked to the demand for unanimity in the church had contributed to this decline. There were now two Glasite churches in the town. According to Archibald McWhirter 'in 1845 the larger party met at 267 High Street, and the smaller portion, known as the doon-bye meeting, was at 232 High Street'.[44] On 22 October 1846 David Lindsay died while preaching in the church. There is an inter-esting comment about Glas Sandeman, born in 1793, who was 'named after his maternal grandfather, John Glas'.

> For ten years before he died Glas Sandeman's mind had become much imbued with the love of scripture. He sought for the books his mother had studied and revered especially the name of the man after whom she had called him, and sometimes far into the night he took from the shelves the old volumes of Glas and Sandeman and read them and above all the scriptures with his younger two boys. In the afternoon [sc. of Sunday] the three might be seen entering the Glasite meeting House to listen to the expositions of Mr James Morison.[45]

The Perth Church did give evidence to the Commissioners in 1837. The Glasites met in a Meeting House in Perth East Parish, which had been built between 1760 and 1770, and its cost was not known, although there was a debt of one hundred pounds on the building. There were three lay pastors and the average attendance was one hundred and twenty to one hundred and thirty with forty to fifty communicants. Most of the people were poor and working class, and all lived within two miles of the Meeting House. Ordinary collections were applied to the poor of the congregation and the proceeds of a monthly collection were applied 'to the relief of stranger poor'. The attendance at a local census on 11 December 1881 was fifty-two.[46]

Another family that became associated with the church in the nine-teenth century was that of the well-known distillers Arthur Bell and Sons. Arthur Bell's grandfather William Bell joined the Dundee Glasite Church in 1793. He went to London in 1799 on a disastrous business venture, and after sequestration was in debt for the rest of his life. He died in 1834, leaving nothing for his sons to inherit. His eldest son, Robert Fitzroy Bell, born in 1790, joined the Glasite Church in Edinburgh where he was a merchant. Af-ter various successes and setbacks in business he died in 1867. His seventh child, Arthur, was then taken on as a traveler by a firm of wine merchants

44. McWhirter, "Kail Kirk."

45. Barbour, *Memoir of Mrs Stewart Sandeman*, 175.

46. *Report by the Commissioners of Religious Instruction*, appendix, 6:148.

in Perth who were also associated with the Glasite Church, and from that beginning he built up the successful firm of Arthur Bell and Sons. His portrait still adorns the bottles of Bell's Whisky. In later life he retired to Scone, where he attended the Parish Church. In his tribute after Bell's death in 1900 the Scone parish minister said, 'brought up in a smaller communion [sc. Glasite], he had latterly come to feel at home in the establishment . . . he rejoiced that the church was now becoming more active in all good works'. Certainly Bell was one of the noted philanthropists of his day, and the Gannochy Trust founded by his son, who married a Sandeman, continues to do good work today. He was not the only prosperous man of Glasite heritage who found his final spiritual home in the National Church without forgetting his origins and his early study of the Bible.[47]

The original church gradually diminished in numbers and renewed fellowship with the Edinburgh church in June 1896. It was known in Perth for its generosity to public charities. For many years it gave proportionately the largest sum of any city church to the Perth Infirmary. In 1912 the elders were James Fairweather, ordained in 1878, who died in 1928, and James Gardiner, ordained in 1882, who lived until 1933. The deacons were David and Thomas Gorrie. After Fairweather's death the church of approximately twelve members closed on 14 November 1928 when eleven members, and one each from London and Dundee were present. Its assets were shared by town charities including the Hospital, and other surviving Glasite churches. Some of the Fairweather family occasionally travelled to Edinburgh to worship, and F. A. Fairweather (presumably the son of the late elder) took part in the ordination of Gerard Sandeman to the elder's office in 1964.[48]

3. The Glasgow Church

The church in Glasgow which was erected, to use the phrase in the records, on 1 May 1762, and which was put into some disarray by the resignation of McLean and Carmichael, was never strong either in numbers or influence in the earlier years of the movement. There is a list in a manuscript letter to Robert Boswell in Edinburgh dated 7 September 1770. James Smith is the sole elder, and no deacons are mentioned. The other men are John Leighton, Alexander Gillies, Robert Malloch, and David Scott, shoemakers, John Cree, schoolmaster, and three more unspecified. There were fourteen women making twenty-five members in all. The next list is in James Scott's *Scrapbook*, and is dated 1772. Now James Smith has been joined by Daniel

---

47. Waterston, *Perth Entrepreneurs*, 131.
48. Ordination of Gerard Sandeman, 1964.

Malloch as an elder. He is mentioned in the Aberdeen list of 1751 as an elder there and in the scrapbook as having been ordained elder by James Cargill and Robert Sandeman at Dunkeld on 21 July 1746. Another list for 1 January 1782 gives James Smith and Moses Miller, formerly of the Paisley church, as elders, and eleven other men, including Daniel Malloch, received in July who has either been disciplined or has been serving elsewhere as an elder. There were twenty women. In 1782 Robert Ferrier gives the membership as twenty-nine and hardly any auditory.[49] The early story of the Glasgow church was not a happy one. It seems to have been dominated by shoemakers, who shared with weavers an aptitude for controversy, and were able, as Malloch's sketchily known career suggests, to be mobile in the service of the church. That they were reasonably prosperous men is shown by the fact that John Leighton and Daniel Malloch were admitted as Burgesses and Guild Brethren of Glasgow by purchase, in 1785 and 1776 respectively.[50] None of the other members appear among the Burgesses and Guild Brethren and it may be assumed that in the tiny society in Glasgow the same tendency occurs as in Dundee and Perth. It is those men who have made some mark in trade who are given the offices in the church.

When Bishop visited the church in 1834 it is obviously in a much healthier condition, with three elders and two deacons, but in 1837 only one elder is mentioned, Archibald Warden, presumably the man who entertained the Bishops. He declined to give evidence to the Commissioners. The church met in the Old Grammar School in St Paul's Outer High Parish.[51] In 1860, according to James Brown, there was one elder, Mr Moyer, (Moir,) about two hundred of an audience though only forty-two members.[52] Around 1841 the Glasites had purchased a chapel in George Street from a Scotch Baptist congregation which had amalgamated with another church of the same order.[53]

We have some information from Glasgow at the end of the nineteenth century in the diaries of an elder, Archibald Sandeman. Many entries deal with the arrangements for elders to travel to Dundee, Newcastle, and London to constitute a presbytery, and there are also notes of a close correspondence among the churches. On Sabbath 19 October 1890 he records that Mrs Baxter has been at Danbury, met Mrs Baldwin, who corresponded

---

49. Mackintosh, *Letters in Correspondence*, 126.

50. Anderson, *Burgesses and Guild Brethren of Glasgow*, 193.

51. *Report by the Commissioners of Religious Instruction*, appendix, 2:12.

52. Brown, *Religious Denominations of Glasgow*, 18.

53. Yuille, *History of the Baptists in Scotland*, 180.

with Dr Rorie of Dundee, and enjoyed the company of the sisters there.[54] He also mentions a 1786 letter sent to Halifax, written by a servant girl in the family of Mrs Bell, Dundee, explaining the faith. 'It's like a voice from former generations speaking to a succeeding one. (Psalm 78 verses 1–8)'.[55] Sandeman was also sent a narrative by Ezra Styles of Robert Sandeman's appearance and proceedings during his visit to America with views on the doctrine he taught. Noting a death in the fellowship he writes, 'We are left to see in the low state of the churches one of the evidences of the last time'.[56] However, the next entry announces the baptism of Mrs Boswell Sandeman's baby at Lenzie (John Charles).

On 2 August Henry and Edward Young were chosen as elders in London, and Sandeman was present. On the Monday the church met fasting and the service concluded around 11.45 a.m. 'The auditors were invited to breakfast, and about 63 sat down'. He was still there on 13 September when Mr Leighton, a member of an important London family,

> took offence at remarks made about him by several brethren concerning his qualifications for the Elder's office. He declined to take the steps set out in Matthew 18,[57] and withdrew. It was pointed out what a mistaken view he took of the matter, but he refused to listen to the brethren and re-affirmed his withdrawal in very emphatic terms. The church had to confirm his separation.[58]

On Sabbath, 24 January 1892, came the news of the death of James Warden Blair in Rio de Janeiro. His middle name links him with the elder who entertained Nathaniel Bishop.

On Sabbath 27 October 1893 a letter was read from Lucy Ely of Danbury acknowledging a contribution from the fellowship of the churches in Britain to the brethren in America, and on Sabbath 29 September 1895 a letter from Miss Piers of Halifax telling of the death of Miss Prior in Montreal.[59] On Sabbath 14 March 1897 'Mrs Cree, aged 76 and my son Archie and his wife made profession of faith'. Mrs Archie Sandeman who had not been baptised in infancy was baptised on her confession, and on 25 April 1897 two additions in Newcastle were noted. One was Mrs Thomas Proctor, from

54. A. Sandeman, *Diary*, 9.

55. A. Sandeman, *Diary*, 10

56. A. Sandeman, *Diary*, 14.

57. Matthew 18 verses 15–17. First a personal meeting, then with one or two more, then tell it to the church. Glasites took this sequence of interviews very seriously.

58. A. Sandeman, *Diary*, 18–19.

59. A. Sandeman, *Diary*, 32.

a leading family in the tiny Newcastle fellowship whose Meeting House was shortly, in 1899, to be acquired by the railway company. The other was 'Miss Embleton, whose father, an aged doctor, had long considered the doctrine, and she had observed Mr Deacon, when dining at her father's table, always refused to partake of game'. At last she asked the reason and he told her of scriptural objections to blood and she further enquired concerning the church.[60]

On Sabbath 30 July 1899 the church met after the Love Feast to consider new office-bearers. After prayer and scripture 'the roll was called, and the church was of one mind in calling Archie and Patrick Sandeman to the office of deacon, and Mrs Cree to that of deaconess or ministering widow'.[61] These very ordinary diary entries do give us a flavor of the life of the Glasgow Church at the end of the nineteenth century. There is a scrupulosity about the church 'going about the ways of the Lord', and there is also a sense of being an intimate part of a fellowship of churches, for mutual aid and encouragement in a time of decline. The strength of family connection with the church is typical of all the fellowships, as indeed is the important role of the Sandeman family in its many branches. It is also interesting that news from Danbury comes reasonably frequently, the last announcing the deaths of Mrs Baldwin and Lucy Ely, daughter of the last American elder.

From a small account book which mostly contains detailed account of housekeeping and travel, the same elder notes deaths and visits. On 29 January 1904 there was a church party, at the cost of two pounds.[62] And in May when Miss Vincent, presumably of the London family, was in Glasgow a small party went to the theatre. In 1915 Miss Scott gave up charge of the Meeting House. In 1933, Nora Blair, née Sandeman and Rhoda Philip joined the church. London friends were present as were sisters from Dundee.

The Glasgow church continued to meet until sometime in the 1950s, and its last address was in Ashley Street in the University area of the city.[63] Earlier there was a Meeting House, presumably the one purchased from the Scotch Baptists, at 136 George Street, in the City Centre.

60. A. Sandeman, *Diary*, 37.

61. A. Sandeman, *Diary*, 32.

62. Add. MS 409/1/8, n.p.

63. Thomson and Patterson, *Scottish Churches' Handbook*, 28; Hornsby, "John Glas, (1695–1773)."

4. The Paisley Church

The town of Paisley was famous for religious and political radicals, many of whom were weavers, who, according to local memory, could finish enough cloth or thread in four days to make a living, and had the rest of the week to discuss and argue. Baptists and Independents were strong there, and there is a wonderfully evocative account of an independent meeting known locally as the Pen Folk, which flourished for some decades around the end of the eighteenth century.[64] The Glasite Church, which was erected on 3 October 1767, seems to have been small, and by 1834 Bishop notes that the members regularly joined with the Glasgow members for worship. There is a list of 1772. One of the elders, Thomas Palmer, went to Liverpool in 1773. His co-elder was William McAlpine. Moses Miller, later of Glasgow, heads the list of men with the note that he was made elder in October 1773. There were thirteen other men and eighteen women, making thirty-two in all and this is the number, with a considerable auditory, that Ferrier records in 1782.[65] The list for 1774 gives occupations. William McAlpine was a weaver, Moses Miller a tailor. No occupation is given for Archibald Dove, the deacon. Of the other fourteen men, ten were weavers, two manufacturers, and two wrights.[66] The church seems to have ceased in the middle of the nineteenth century.

5. The Church at Kippielaw/Galashiels

This church began in a village in the parish of Bowden, near Melrose, and appears in Glasite correspondence variously as Kippielaw and Darnick. It was founded by the former minister of St Boswells, George Byres, who, having served as an elder in Edinburgh from 1738–1740, acted as elder in Kippielaw until his death in 1773.[67] Robert Ferrier reported the Galashiels church, as it had become in the 1770s, as having twenty-six members and a considerable auditory in 1782.[68] The only list headed Darnock [*sic*] is dated 1772 and there is one from Galashiels dated July 1775. These contain several names in common and we may assume that the church moved to the larger weaving town of Galashiels after Byres' death. James Craw, a shoemaker, was sent as an elder from Arbroath in 1784 to take Byres' place and there is no occupation given for his fellow elder William White, nor for the deacons,

64. Gilmour, *Reminiscences of the Pen' Folk.*

65. Mackintosh, *Letters in Correspondence*, 126.

66. Church list.

67. *Fasti Ecclesiae Scoticanae*, 2:192.

68. Mackintosh, *Letters in Correspondence*, 126.

Hugh Sanderson, James Clark, and Henry Watson. Eighteen married men are listed, most with occupations. There were three weavers, three tailors, a clothier, a skinner, a grocer, a mason, a day laborer, two servants and a shoemaker. There were four unmarried men and twenty-three women. A Church of fifty was a reasonable number in a small town, but it must have gone through a difficult time, with many erasures in the list, because there were only twenty-nine members in 1782.[69] By the end of the nineteenth century Galashiels members were included with Edinburgh statistics.

The building, now in a poor state of repair, is in Botany Lane, and consists of a meeting room and an adjoining house which may have been a home for the housekeeper, who cared for the Hall and cooked the Sunday meal.[70] It replaced a building of 1775, which was their home when they moved from Darnick.

6. The Dunkeld Church

Dunkeld, a small city with a medieval cathedral, lies about twelve miles north of Perth. A Glasite church met there for almost a century. A glover and merchant named James Cargill (ca. 1705–1779) was ordained an elder in the Dundee meeting on Whitsunday 1730, where he was a colleague to Glas. He was the first elder of the church who had not been ordained in the Church of Scotland, after the church had decided that ruling elders and teaching elders were the same office according to Paul's letters. In 1735 Cargill moved to Dunkeld, where he was postmaster until his death in 1779. In 1746 Daniel Malloch was ordained to the eldership by James Cargill and Robert Sandeman. When Sandeman accepted an invitation to visit New England, in 1764, Cargill accompanied him, and shared some of the opposition that Sandeman encountered for his loyalist views. He returned to Scotland in July 1766, and his second son was ordained as a deacon in 1773, but subsequently declined to accept nomination as an elder. Cargill senior died in 1779, and James Scott, a Dundee elder wrote an elegy on him. As an example of this verse form here is a quotation. Palemon was Robert Sandeman's nom-de plume in his *Letters*, and the verses commemorate the journey the two men shared.

---

69. Church lists.

70. In Cruft et al., *Buildings of Scotland, Borders*, 296, there is a description of the building, but the statement that the adjoining building was the minister's house seems to be inaccurate.

He with the dear Palemon went
unto Earth's remotest ends.
And there the tidings glad that God was pleased
with boldness they did both declare.
They there endured reproaches great,
Palemon there slept in his Lord,
and both until life's final close,
held fast the true, the faithful Word.[71]

Robert Duff, shoemaker in Dunkeld who had been made a deacon in the Perth church in 1767, became an elder in Dunkeld in 1779, and shared leadership with James Cant, also from Perth. In 1785 there were negotiations about a new meeting house, and Cant advised against acquiring the Independent chapel in case of resentment in the town, and another building, not so convenient, was chosen. In 1789 James Gemill, an elder of the Glasgow church, offered to release his fellow elder Alexander Boyd to go to Dunkeld and supply the vacancy. In 1796 Peter Scott was made an elder at Dunkeld according to James Scott's Scrapbook.[72] Cantor states that the Dunkeld Meeting House was closed before 1821,[73] and in 1837 the church, of ten members and an attendance of around thirty, met in the upper floor of a flat rented at ten pounds per annum. The *Old Statistical Account* mentions fifty Independents who follow the teaching of John Glas. The *New Statistical Account* of 1843 mentions only four or five Glasites still resident. When Bishop visited the remnant at Perth in 1834, he records three men and six women in Dunkeld, who presumably were in fellowship with the 'orthodox' church. McWhirter, in his article 'The Kail Kirk', tells of the last member, Alexander Connacher, who,

> ... for many years prior to his death in 1849 walked each Sunday to Perth accompanied by his daughter. They left in the early hours and reached Perth in time for the morning service, and after staying overnight with friends in the city, commenced their long return journey at dawn on Monday. A member of the same family, Margaret Connacher, who died at the age of 104 in 1923, had been at the time of her death associated with the Perth church for 87 years and was a regular attender at the age of 100.[74]

71. Scott, *Notebook*, 193–94.
72. Scott, *Notebook*, 67.
73. Cantor, *Faraday*, 26.
74. McWhirter, "Kail Kirk."

7. The Aberdeen Church

The Glasite church in Aberdeen was set in order on 16 June 1750. The *Old Statistical Account* for Aberdeen notes its number of 'examinable persons' from 1758 to 1770. In 1758 there were forty-five such persons, in 1760, fifty-seven, and thereafter the numbers decrease, until in 1770 there were twenty-seven members.[75] In that time the population of Aberdeen increased from 8,460 to 11,198. In 1772 David Lindsay and Patrick Leighton were elders. After a hopeful start the Aberdeen church did not attain any growth and in Ferrier's list there are 'only eighteen members, with two elders, no deacon and almost no auditory, for there seems to be no attention whatever paid to the doctrine in that town, and (which has surprised me exceedingly) for these six years past they have neither received nor put away a single person. This is our utmost limits to the north, except a single woman in Buchan, one of the wildest places in all the Highlands of Scotland'.[76] When the Bishops visited, there were nineteen members.

In the *New Statistical Account* of 1843, the contributor for Aberdeen notes 'small numbers of Friends, Glasites, Irvingites and Unitarians'. In his chapter on the 1851 Census of Religious Worship for Aberdeen, MacLaren notes that 'the Glasites were the smallest religious group included in the census for Aberdeen. Their inclusion is no doubt related to their fairly long history and to the fact that they were considered to be "an old and respectable body"'.[77] On Census Sunday the Glasites, with sittings for one hundred had thirty attenders in the morning and twenty-two in the afternoon, 0.02 percent of the total church attendance on 30 March 1851. Alexander Gammie in his comprehensive volume *The Churches of Aberdeen*, published in 1909, includes the Glasites in his chapter on 'some forgotten Sects'. 'They, a respectable body, met in St Andrew Street', he writes and 'their chapel was known as the "Broth Kirk" because of a notion, supposed to be partly correct, that there was a kind of mess after the forenoon service'.[78] The chapel in St Andrew Street disappears from the *Aberdeen Directory* in 1870/71. Archibald Sandeman's diary mentions James Marshall from Aberdeen attending the services on Sabbath 12 January 1890, a reminder that scattered brethren continued to worship with constituted churches whenever possible. Presumably this is the same James Marshall who entertained the Young brothers on their tour in 1881 where he is associated with the Broadford

75. Sinclair, *Old Statistical Account*, 19:180.

76. Mackintosh, *Letters in Correspondence*, 125–26.

77. MacLaren, *Religion and Social Class*, 41–42.

78. Gammie, *Churches of Aberdeen*, 376.

Works, a large linen manufactory near the centre of the city, which was closed in the 1990s.

8. The Arbroath Church.

This church represents the followers of Francis Archibald, who adhered to him when he resigned from the parish of Guthrie in 1730. It moved to Arbroath in 1742, and when Ferrier sent his statistics to E. Foster in Nova Scotia in July 1782 it had fifty-two members, with two elders and two deacons, and a large auditory. In 1764 the Church at Perth called John Glas to the eldership there and the churches at Dundee and Arbroath were reluctant to let this happen. Thomas Palmer and James Scrymsour wrote to him on behalf of the church pointing out that Dundee was 'the most centrical place for you, where you may see your friends at Perth and Edinburgh at any time; and the churches in the North when needful, as it cannot be expected but that they will need and love your visit, although you were come that length that you could only say, "children, love one another"'. In the division of 1798 it allied itself with Perth, and with the church at Kirkby Lonsdale, which had originated from those associated with James Allen and the church at Gayle.

In the early nineteenth century we learn something of the church from the correspondence of Edward Wilson, elder at Kirkby Lonsdale, with Patrick Cochrane (1771–1837), elder at Arbroath and a printer and publisher. Cochran was related to the Gorries of Perth, and the Rories of Dundee. His grandson married Margaret Allen, a descendant of James Allen of Gayle. Wilson has an interest in what is happening in other fellowships. On 18 April 1811 he writes, 'The new Baptists at Kendal seem to be verging very fast towards Unitarianism'.[79] He had heard a very eccentric character preach in Manchester called William Gadsby. 'His expressions are sometimes very coarse and even indelicate'.[80] In a letter of 27 July 1811, he writes, 'Are the brethren at Arbroath more unanimous yet about the necessity for a Presbytery, and what is Haldane and his friends now doing in religious matters?''' There seem to have been questions even at this late date about the need for more than one elder to be appointed before a church could carry out discipline and the Lord's Supper. In 1810 and 1834 the Scotch Baptist churches split over this matter. There are other letters between John Howe

---

79. MS 9/4/3, 16.

80. Gadsby, a leader in what came to be known as the Gospel Standard Strict Baptists, was troubled by some of his followers developing Sandemanian tendencies and wrote 'What is Faith, or the Faith of the Sandemanians found wanting,' Gadsby, *Works*, 1:280–307.

of Halifax and Cochrane which refer amongst other matters to correspondence with Walker of Dublin, on assurance.

> I trust that the manner in which he speaks will relieve the minds of some in Perth, whom I have heard express themselves as not understanding him on Assurance. There is a difference betwixt knowing assuredly that that same Jesus who was crucified is both Lord and Christ and trusting or boasting in the assurance of our believing.[81]

There is also a letter of 5 November 1831 from Robert Morison of Perth to Patrick Cochrane giving extracts of a communication from Octavius Mitchell in Matanzas (Cuba): after congratulating Morison on his long life and health, Mitchell describes his life on horseback, and 'on Sabbaths when he peruses those books which formed our earliest associations: the bible in four languages, together with Bibliotheca Sacra, Morison's Key to the First Four Books of Moses, Sandeman's Letters, Jones on the Trinity, Coles on God's Sovereignty, Pascal's Thoughts, etc.' Far travelled Glasites did not forget their roots![82]

Wilson also tells the story of a young man of eighteen whom they put away.

> He joined the Baptists at Kendal, then took a meeting house here and commenced preaching—one simple man joined him—they celebrated the Lord's Supper but soon differed. The youth went to Kendal and preached among the Wesleyans, then became a proselyte of a flaming minister of the Establishment. He now wants to go to college and be ordained. Then the young man came back to the Church at Kirkby Lonsdale as he could get no money. He applied to return to membership with eloquence and tears, but only his parents supported him, claiming he was 'of late a different character.[83]

Wilson also comments on Mr Walker of Dublin who finds fault with the constitution of all other Churches but his own as not following the apostolic plan. 'He is a very extraordinary man. I should like to meet him.'[84] Wilson alludes in his letters to publications and writings of his own including a chart of Christian Church beginning with Revelation. He reads William Jones's *Journals* and his *History of the Waldensians* and mentions in 1807

81. MS 9/3/23.
82. MS 9/3/21.
83. MS 9/4/3, 19–20.
84. MS 9/4/3, 19–20.

a breach in the Arbroath Church which had been healed and of which he heard from Dundee.

The Arbroath church, whose meeting house built in 1783 and demolished in 1909, seems to have died before the Bishops' tour of 1834, although the *New Statistical Account* of the Burgh gives an 1823 figure of Glasites as one hundred and thirty-four, ninety-nine in Arbroath, and thirty-five in the neighboring parish of St Vigean's.[85] In 1833 there were sixty-nine in attendance of whom twenty-seven were communicants. The report to the Commissioners tells in 1837 of an Old Scots Independent Church which had been until eight or nine years before known as 'the Glasite Independent church'. It had twenty-nine communicants and an attendance between forty and fifty.[86] One 'eminent Arbroathian' associated with the church was James Chalmers who was credited with the invention of the adhesive postage stamp. His father was a member of the Church.[87]

9 The Montrose Church

This Church was set up in the very early years of the Glasite movement. In 1782 it had twenty-eight members, two elders and one deacon, with a neat small meeting house and a considerable auditory.[88] A possible reason for its relatively small size is that in 1770

> a small society in Montrose unanimously adopted the Scripture view of Baptism, but most of them having been connected with the Glasites, were tenacious of some of their peculiarities, with which they understood the Baptists did not agree. They wrote to Archibald McLean on these particulars, and after several letters had passed between them, they yielded the points in dispute and requested him to come and baptize them.[89]

He did this, but the church did not prosper.

This was the church where David Buchanan the publisher was an elder, whose teaching so disturbed the Perth Church, and it adhered to the majority at the division of 1798. When Nathaniel Bishop visited in 1834 there were two elders and twenty-five members, in a neat two-storey Meeting

---

85. Sinclair, *New Statistical Account*.

86. *Report by the Commissioners of Religious Instruction*, 6:56.

87. McBain, *Eminent Arbroathians*, 275.

88. Mackintosh, *Letters in Correspondence*, 125.

89. Rippon, *Baptist Annual Register, 1795*, 363.

House. He mentioned the poverty of the church and gave a donation from the American churches.

10. The Leith Church

The Church in Leith, the seaport of Edinburgh, was set up in 1763, and in 1772 the elders were Thomas Walker and David Chisholm. Apart from some correspondence involving an anonymous 'young and inexperienced boy' as he describes himself in 1814, calling for renewed unity between Perth and the other churches, there is little evidence for the life of the church. In 1782, Ferrier reports, 'one mile from Edinburgh, on the sea-shore is Leith, having a church of twenty-five members, including two Elders and two deacons, and a very small auditory'.[90] James Scott Marshall, the historian of Leith, writes, 'The Glasites had a meeting house in the later 18th century in Mason Court Lodge, off St Andrew Street. This body, with their all-day Sunday services, which always included a "Love Feast", remained in the port for half a century, but faded from the scene in the 1820's'.[91]

A few Glasites met in Cupar, Fife, until the early nineteenth century, and there were groups in Leslie and Kirkcaldy, also in Fife. A Church in Newburgh, between Dundee and Perth on the north side of the Tay and a hotbed of radical sects, was formed on 13 June, 1767. On 19 September 1770 Dr William Carmichael, elder of the church at Newburgh died. He was the brother of Robert Carmichael, briefly a member of the Glasgow church. Another dissenter, Alexander Pirie, who died in Newburgh in 1804, was something of an irritant in the Secession churches. He taught the philosophy class in the Burgher Seminary in Abernethy, near Newburgh from 1760–762, then was ordained in the Burgher Church in Newburgh, charged with a Christological heresy, and although the charge was dropped in 1770, he accepted a call from the Relief Congregation at Blairlogie near Stirling, against the wishes of the Presbytery there. The church in Blairlogie was independent until Pirie left in 1778. He returned to Newburgh where he gathered an Independent congregation which is sometimes referred to as Glasite. This was the church which Hall the traveler encountered, although he says that Pirie was a Berean. Pirie published several controversial works including a *Dissertation on the Hebrew Roots*,[92] a copy of which was in the Edinburgh Meeting House, and a *Dissertation upon Baptism*, which was described as showing mental vigor and acuteness. As an appendix to that work he adds a *Treatise on the Eating of*

90. Mackintosh, *Letters in Correspondence*, 126.
91. Marshall, *Life and Times of Leith*, 163.
92. Pirie, *Dissertation on the Hebrew Roots*.

Blood, a practice which he strongly condemns on biblical grounds. Wilson of Kirkby Lonsdale valued *Pirie's Works*.

11. The Edinburgh Church

The Edinburgh Church, while not the largest in Scotland, played an important part in the story of the churches and attracted to its membership several notable people. The Meeting House in Barony Street, built in 1835–36, on the eastern edge of the New Town, closed in 1989, and services continued to be held in the home of Gerard Sandeman, the last elder, until almost the end of the century.[93] The building was given by its trustees to the Cockburn Society, who in turn conveyed it to the Scottish Architectural Heritage Society. This was a disappointment for the Society of St Pius X who had been interested in acquiring the church.[94] In 2018 the pews and pulpit were removed and taken into storage. The cupola was restored and the whole worship area refurbished as an art gallery. 'The Ingleby Gallery whilst recognising that John Glas himself might not fully approve, is very glad to bring this extraordinary building back into public use.'[95] Many Sandeman men appear on the lists of elders and deacons, and the other leading family, the Waterstons, provided leadership into the twentieth century and members until almost the end. Other names that recur include the Dickson family who were gunsmiths in Edinburgh, and no doubt provided the guns which shot the birds which caused the great dispute about draining the blood. The firm still exists, with a gun-making branch in Dunkeld. William Ferguson, the elder who died in 1985 was the son of an elder, and Gerard Sandeman was one of four brothers, sons of an elder, all of whom were deacons.

Robert Ferrier, in his letter to Edward Foster states that the Edinburgh Church had seventy-five members, four elders and four deacons and that the meeting house was commonly full.[96] The further story of this church is largely told in other chapters, but the Waterston family may be described here. They were the dominant family in the late nineteenth and early twentieth century, but their connection began much earlier. In his book, Perth Entrepreneurs, Dr Charles Waterston traces the Sandeman family and his own Waterston ancestors through several generations. His great-great-great grandmother, born Catherine Sandeman in 1755, married William Waterston in 1776. His first wife had died in the year previous and he himself

93. Personal knowledge.
94. Acc M/409, 10/679.
95. Text from Ingleby Gallery leaflet, 2018.
96. Mackintosh, *Letters in Correspondence*, 126.

was born in Spott, East Lothian, in 1729. He was a schoolmaster in Dunbar before moving to Edinburgh in 1751 where he was employed by James Lorimer, dealer in torches and flambeaux. Lorimer became bankrupt in 1752 and Waterston opened his own business as a wax chandler in 1752, prospering and building a house with garden and workshops in Dunbar's Close off the Lawnmarket (near Edinburgh Castle and where the Headquarters of the Bank of Scotland now stands). By this time William, like his new bride Catherine, was an active Glasite in the Edinburgh Church, the author of several of the Church's hymns and an accomplished violinist. He died suddenly in 1780 and Catherine, by now mother of three young sons, decided to carry on her husband's business.[97] She is mentioned in Elizabeth Sanderson's monograph *Women and Work in Eighteenth Century Edinburgh* as 'Mrs Waterston, Candlemaker 1783; W[idow]. Wm. Waterston, wax chandler, Old Greyfriars Parish; advertised in *Edinburgh Advertiser*, 1 December 1783 selling candles "at her warehouse".'[98]

In 1786 she married Robert Ferrier, whom we have previously noticed as a leader first in the Old Scots Independents and then as a Glasite elder in Dundee. He was a widower and on his second marriage he was required to lay down his elder's office. He joined his wife in her business, now known as Ferrier and Waterston, but had no good reputation as a businessman. The family moved to St John's Hill, to one of the first houses to be built outside the city wall, and their neighbor was the eminent geologist, James Hutton. Ferrier withdrew from the business and became a classics tutor at the university. He died in 1795.[99] The St John's Hill house became the home of the next four generations of Waterstons. Catherine, with the help of her son George, carried on the business until her death in 1832. She invested in property and became famous for her hospitality. Some of her family remained in the Glasite Church until the second half of the twentieth century. A succession of George Waterstons were elders and occasional writers of Glasite tracts, while expanding the business, latterly known as George Waterston & Sons Ltd, with members of the family on the board of directors at the time of the firm's two hundred and fiftieth anniversary in 2002.[100] From the manufacture of flambeaux and sealing wax the company expanded into printing including the production of bank notes for the Bank of Scotland and formed a London branch.

97. Waterston, *Perth Entrepreneurs*, 100.

98. Sanderson, *Women and Work*, 211.

99. Sanderson, *Women and Work*, 102.

100. Watson, *Seal of Success*, 57.

Among notable members of the family was John James Waterston, (1811–1883) a scientist who worked with the Admiralty and then with the East India Company in Bombay. Before his return to Edinburgh in 1857 he had written a work on the physiology of the central nervous system, and a later one on the kinetic theory of gases. These were not well received in his lifetime, but his biographer, J. B. S. Haldane, wrote in 1928 that 'he was one of a brilliant group of physicists turned out in the early part of last century by the Scottish universities'. Papers that were rejected or neglected were 'foundation stones of a new branch of scientific knowledge, molecular physics, as Waterston called it, or physical chemistry or thermodynamics as it is now called'.[101]

More recently George (fifth) Waterston, after a few years as a director of the business, became one of Britain's best-known ornithologists, and like his brothers, Robert Ferrier, and Sandy, was brought up in the church.[102] After the Second World War few members of the core families joined the church, and it slowly shrank until it closed in 1989.

It is worth noting that there were no churches in the Gaelic-speaking Highlands, and that only Perth and Dunkeld were on the fringe of the Highland area. Glasites were essentially lowland people and many of their early churches were in weaving centers such as Dundee, Arbroath, and Montrose, which were linked by sea routes.

The Churches in England

1. The London Church

The largest church was in London, founded by Robert Sandeman and drawing several ministers of Independent Churches into its fellowship. It will be forever associated with the remarkable Michael Faraday, and some of its story will be told when he becomes the focus of our attention. Like most churches it consisted largely of interlocking families, and the appendices to Cantor's book give interesting lists. In the great disruption over the eating of blood the London people took a leading part and that story is told elsewhere. The Church in fellowship with Glasgow and Dundee closed after the death of its last elder, Henry Young, in 1939 and the other church closed in 1985.

---

101. Quoted in Watson, *Seal of Success*, 11–12.

102. Robert Ferrier Waterston was the veterinary surgeon who cared for our dog when we lived in Kirkcaldy around 1970, which made for interesting conversations in the surgery. He died in July 2018.

2. The Church in Norfolk

In the 1760s there was a Church in the Norfolk village of Banham which was cut off due to 'lack of brotherly love and discipline'. Some members formed a church at nearby Old Buckenham which had twenty-two members in 1808 and thirty-two members in 1838, mostly farmers and mostly poor and Thomas Boosey, father of the music publisher, was praised for being 'a refined gentleman who worked a small farm and looked after poor peasants'. Later it had strong links with the London Church whose elders and deacons visited regularly. Faraday's niece, Caroline Reid, who accompanied him on a visit in 1842 described the Meeting House as 'a very pleasant cheerful room, could hold about a hundred, sloping roof, seats comfortable—sort of forms with a little raised desk'. Her uncle preached and 'the meeting house was quite full'.[103] The last members, the Lovedays, joined the London Church around 1900, when we can presume the little village cause died. The Church at Wethersfield in Essex was halfway between London and Norfolk, but it soon disappeared from the records.

3. The Church in Newcastle

This seems to have been for some time a thriving community also visited by Faraday. According to Mackenzie's[104] history of the city it was founded around 1757, and in 1827 met in a commodious meeting house in Forster Street. Its Elder Mr Leighton, surgeon, had recently died and the current elder was Jeremiah Spence, 'a man of distinguished worth'. His father had come from Aberdeen around 1739 and his brother, Thomas Spence was the author of the Spencean scheme, a radical political and philosophical movement. Despite E. P. Thompson's[105] comment, that he had been brought up in a Sandemanian household, Thomas had no commitment to the Church.

William Paradise, a London elder, moved there in 1843, and the fellowship moved into a new Meeting House in Picton Terrace, and after the Wednesday meeting in 1861, when Faraday was visiting, 'we had a merry party', a sort of house warming. In 1881 Henry and Edward Young, future elders of the London Church, visited Newcastle on their way to Scotland, and called on several of the members, enjoying music in Edward Reid's house after a very small Wednesday evening meeting—'distance is a problem'. By the end of the century the church was without a presbytery and it

103. Cantor, *Faraday*, 67.
104. Mackenzie, *Historical Account of Newcastle-on-Tyne*, 399.
105. Thompson, *Making of the English Working Class*, 39.

was one of Archibald Sandeman's tasks from time to time to arrange elders' visits either from his church in Glasgow or from Dundee. Proctors, Reids and Deacons were the main families, and the names of Reid and Deacon are prominent also in London membership lists. This was a closely intermarried and interlinked church. On 25 April 1897 Archibald Sandeman records that there were two additions at Newcastle.

4. The Church at Wooler, Northumberland

This church, which was an early foundation, depended much on John Handasyde, who moved as an elder to London, somewhat to Glas's displeasure, around 1764. It does not seem to have long survived the loss.

5. The Church in Liverpool

The Liverpool Church was founded in 1767 and occupied a former synagogue in Matthew Street from around 1780 until 1821 when it moved to a new Chapel in Gill Street, which was seated for one hundred and ninety persons. That chapel seems to have closed around 1840. John Walker, who is very ambivalent about the Glasites, as he calls them, does admit to meeting a very pleasant older man, an elder in Liverpool, who did not seem to be so bound as others by the system.

6. Other Churches

The Church at Nottingham set in order by Barnard and Pike in 1768, after a start marred by controversy, disciplinary problems, and local opposition seems to have thrived in the early nineteenth century. There was also a strong Scotch Baptist community in Nottingham and out of it came a following for the Campbellites in the 1830s.[106] John Morley from London moved to Trowbridge in 1768. Barnard and another elder called Davies visited in 1771 and Samuel Pike served as an elder until his death in 1773, after which it fades from the story as does the church at Chesterfield. The church at Kirkby Lonsdale and a small company at Kendal allied themselves with the Perth 'heretics' and maintained correspondence for some years with Perth and Arbroath.

---

106. Thompson, *Let Sects and Parties Fall*, 20–22.

The Churches in Wales

As in other places Sandemanianism entered Wales through the writings of
Glas and Sandeman. On 9 December 1766 John Popkin, a well-to-do Calvinistic Methodist preacher wrote to Glas to tell him of his gradual acceptance of the 'new doctrines'. He had been an enthusiastic reader of Hervey,
Boston, Erskine, and the Puritans, and had borrowed Sandeman's *Letters*
from a parish clergyman. 'I could not tell what to think of him. Sometimes
I thought he was a bold and faithful friend of the truth; and other times I
thought he was an enemy, a scoffer, a derider of all true religion'. Popkin
then acquired Glas's *Works* and other Glasite writings and had them translated into Welsh. (This was the only account of translation I have found.)
Popkin immediately ran into controversy with the evangelical leaders in
Wales, but when Barnard and other London leaders visited Wales, some
converts were made, and a meeting began at Swansea, with Popkin as an
elder. Other smaller groups met, and some notable converts were made.[107]
Fairly soon however the opposition of the evangelical churches proved too
strong for the movement and it faded away.

Christmas Evans, (1766–1838) was one of the great Welsh preachers of
his generation. In the 1790s the works of Glas, Sandeman and particularly
Archibald McLean, the Scotch Baptist were circulating in North Wales, and
an influential Baptist preacher John R. Jones of Ramoth adopted what were
virtually Sandemanian views of faith, which led him to oppose the emo-
tionalism of the evangelical preachers. The Baptist community divided and
there are still a few congregations of Scotch Baptists in Wales. Evans was for
a time captivated by Sandeman's doctrines and claims to have lost his desire
for aggressive evangelism for some time until he read Fuller's *Strictures* and
returned to a warmer faith.[108]

There are two allusions to imperfect attempts to form a Sandemanian
Church, one in Dublin and the other in Bristol. John Barnard, writing to
William Sandeman in 1768, has heard of one Stafford, who was put away
from the Anabaptist Church in Whitehaven for Arianism and settled in
Dublin where he has a colleague and thirty followers and all the observances
in the church. 'They absurdly agree with us in all things except the character
of the Son of God, and the subjects of his Kingdom, which they appear to
call little matters'.[109] In another letter to William Sandeman in 1766 Barnard
wrote about Hart, of Bristol, a beneficed clergyman, 'overtaken with our

107. Mackintosh, *Letters in Correspondence*, 29.
108. Gay, *Secret Stifler*, 41–19.
109. Morison, *Supplementary Letters*, 67.

doctrine by reading the *Letters*, who, to ease his conscience and keep his living formed a society of such as agreed with him, about 16, and among these he is an Elder, and every sabbath evening they pretend to the Lord's Supper, the feast of charity and all the Gospel order. I was led to inveigh very strongly against Mr Hart's way of doing'.[110] Sandemanians by this time had to be all or nothing, but Mr Hart's activities remind us of the situation in Tealing while Glas was still the parish minister.

James Allen and the Churches of the Northwest of England

James Allen led the church at Gayle near Hawes in Wensleydale until his death in 1804, and members of his family were associated with it until at least the late nineteenth century. The story begins with John Wesley's friend and sometime fellow worker, Benjamin Ingham, who was born in Ossett, Yorkshire on 11 June 1712. He was influenced by the 'Holy Club' while a student at Oxford and ordained in the Church of England by the bishop of Oxford, John Potter, in 1735. Like John Wesley, his brother Charles and George Whitefield he went to the colony of Georgia for a brief period, and there was assured in his faith partly by his contact with the Moravian missionaries. On his return he preached around his home district with such effect that he was prohibited from preaching in the Diocese of York. Thereafter he conducted services in his mother's church and anywhere else in the neighborhood where he was welcomed, building a connexion of at least sixty meetings by 1740. He invited help from the Moravians, but soon parted company from them. Until 1760 Ingham, ably assisted by his followers William Batty and James Allen, succeeded in extending his group of churches, forming his converts into societies, which were similar to Methodist class meetings.[111] He was not as interested in church order as Wesley and the churches formed a very loose connection, mainly in the northwest of England, where the church at Wheatley Lane near Burnley still meets, the sole survivor of the Inghamite group. The churches were registered as dissenting places of worship by 1754, and in September 1756 Allen and Batty were ordained as 'General Elders' to assist the General Overseer, Ingham himself. So far the loosely knit group of believers, meeting often in homes and in a few church buildings seemed on a prosperous path. But then, in the early 1760s the whole connection unraveled and, according to one estimate, eighty groups of followers were reduced to thirteen.

110. Morison, *Supplementary Letters*, 61.
111. Rack, *Reasonable Enthusiast*, 217.

There were several reasons for the break-up of Ingham's churches, but the most notable was the 'horrid blast from the North'.[112] There had been many discussions about church order and the use of the lot in choosing elders for the meetings, and sometime in the late 1750s Ingham read Glas's *Testimony of the King of Martyrs* and Sandeman's *Letters on Theron and Aspasio* and as a result he wished to discover more about this Scottish church, its close attention to scripture and its organisation. He sent his two closest co-workers, William Batty and James Allen, to meet Sandeman in Edinburgh in late summer 1761. Both these men belonged to minor land-owning families in the Dales. Allen, who had studied at St John's College, Cambridge, and having been destined for the church had heard Whitefield preach in Haworth in 1750 and was often entertained by Grimshaw, the evangelical rector of Haworth with

> great cheerfulness and hospitality. Many of the most sensible and knowing of his people turned Baptist to his great grief and mortification. I afterwards heard Whitefield frequently and rather admired his popular talent to rouse and affect, than his aptness to teach by opening the scriptures to instruct, inform and edify. His charity was truly antinomian for he was a Presbyterian in Scotland, an Episcopalian in England, and an Independent in America.[113]

In 1749 James's uncle Richard had brought Methodist and Moravian preachers to Wensleydale, and raised questions about the nature of faith, imputed righteousness and the sufferings of Christ. When Ingham came to Gayle Allen had a 'manifestation of Christ crucified'.[114] In 1761, while still an Inghamite he became involved in discussions about the divinity of Christ. He was a man searching for assurance and truth and was ripe to be influenced by the Glasite teaching and practice. Batty had also been influenced by the Evangelical revival and from 1760 until his death in 1787 was an elder of the Inghamite chapel at Wheatley Lane.

It was William Romaine, the evangelical Anglican and friend of the Countess of Huntingdon (whose sister-in-law had married Ingham), who used the phrase 'the horrid blast from the North', in a conversation around 1780. 'If ever there was a church of Christ upon earth, that was one. I paid them a visit and had a great mind to join them. That was a blessed work of

---

112. *Evangelical Magazine*, August 1814, 308, quoted in Shenton, *Romaine*, 177n35. See also Pickles, *Benjamin Ingham*, passim.

113. Allen, *Letters of James Allen*, 99–101.

114. Allen, *Letters*, 103.

God among that people'.[115] But the Glasite doctrine 'destroyed all'. So what was this blast? Writing to Mr S. Churchill in London, on 7 September 1761 Sandeman says:

> The Yorkshiremen, who were both preachers of long standing, staid with us more than eight days. I went with them to Perth, Dunkeld and Dundee, and the longer we were acquainted the fonder we were of each other. Mr Glas was much pleased with them. They brought a very affectionate letter, with five guineas, from Mr Ingham who is their chief leader in raising the profession of faith in Yorkshire and in the neighboring counties. Scattered in a circuit of about 500 miles, they have about 1500 people, who appear to love their doctrine and have separated themselves from the Church of England. They have formed three churches; they have Elders, they receive members by the laying on of hands; they have the kiss of charity and the feast of charity; they have the Lord's Supper once a month or so, but Mr Ingham has been pressing to have it every Lord's day.[116]

James Allen in particular seems to have been impressed with the arguments advanced by Glas and Sandeman and to have decided that their ideas on church order were superior to Ingham's. Such was the alarm among the followers of Ingham that a conference was called in 1761 to meet at Thin Oaks on Newby Moor near the home of William Batty. Far from uniting the churches it produced a confrontation between Ingham and Allen. The result was a schism, and the subsequent decline of Ingham's following.[117] By the end of the decade there were six or seven little churches of the Allen faction. In an undated letter, written perhaps in 1763, John Glas writes to Edward Gorrell, an early associate of Allen:

> I suppose Mr Allen has a little church at Gayle, whereof he and his wife are members, and that the church assembles constantly to observe all the ordinances except the breaking of bread, with binding and loosing, which cannot be regularly done without bishops, two at least making a presbytery. When any of your Newby church come there they are received and act as members of that sister church while there, by virtue of the communion of churches; and even so one of the Newby presbyters being at Gayle, assembling as a church acts as a presbyter, and with Mr Allen makes a presbytery, to bind and loose and to break

115. Quoted in Shenton, *Romaine*, 177.
116. Mackintosh, *Letters in Correspondence*, 65–66.
117. Cantor, *Faraday*, 56.

bread. Thus our churches from the first helped one another in this same necessity. . . . One indeed, may baptize, that is doing nothing to the church.[118]

In July 1763 James Allen gave an account of his friends as follows: 'At Kirby-Stevin 10 men, 13 women; Newby 15 men and women; Gayle 4 men and 4 women. At Kirby-Lonsdale is the prospect of a little church'. On the second of August he writes from Newby:

> 16 are united at Kirby-Lonsdale. 3 more are added here, and seven at Kirby-Stevin. Mr Gorrell lately a preacher with Mr Ingham, now joined with Mr Allen. Kirby-Stevin 30; Newby 24; and Gayle 8; Kirby-Lonsdale 16-in whole 78.[119]

In the circumstances these numbers denote reasonable growth, but with growth came dissension. Relations with the Scottish churches cooled and Allen, having left the Inghamite connexion, now found himself in conflict with Glas. In late 1763 there were complex questions about a matter that is made to sound like a breach of promise of marriage, and although Glas (having expressed a wish to visit to 'you in these parts; but my age and circumstances deprive me of that pleasure') signs a letter to Allen in December 1763, 'I am, very dear brother, yours affectionately', and at the end of the year receives a reply from Allen concerning the case, also signed, 'yours affectionately',[120] it is evident from a letter from Glas to Edward Gorrell in February 1764 that his patience with Allen and the troubles in the churches in the north of England is wearing thin. Allen finds that he has escaped from the overpowering influence of Ingham only to find that Glas is quite as interfering, accusing Allen and his followers of being too fond of sermons and not careful enough about the order of the church. In a letter to R[obert] F[errier] in April 1767, Allen makes this quite clear.

> I left Ingham because of the authority he assumed and the unscriptural usuages [sic] he introduced into the order of his churches. When we joined the Glassite [sic] churches we presumed we were now at liberty from every human yoke and might indulge the spirit of free enquiry into the mind of God in the scriptures. How great then was our disappointment!

One Robert Gordon, perhaps an envoy from Scotland, visited Allen and said, more than once, 'I mind the churches did so and so'. Allen found

---

118. Mackintosh, *Letters in Correspondence*, 47.
119. Mackintosh, *Letters in Correspondence*, 47, 48.
120. Mackintosh, *Letters in Correspondence*, 46.

that the appeal to the scriptures was opposed by 'what will Mr Glas and the churches of the North say to this?'[121] He discovered that in the Glasite churches the influence of tradition overruled Scripture.

Allen then, in his letters, gives instances of his disagreement with the tradition. These were 'laying down of an Elder's office in consequence of a second marriage. Does this honour marriage? Does it vindicate the holiness of the marriage bed?' He points out that it is a custom in the Greek church. The prohibition in 1 Timothy was only valid in the early Jewish and pagan world, where digamy and polygamy were tolerated. Then there is the refusal of admittance to the fellowship after the second excommunication 'which seems to want a scriptural prescription for its support'. This he sees as a custom introduced because of a serial offender and repenter of drunkenness, and not as a law of Christ. He quotes 1 Cor 5 as the only account of an excommunication and tells the sad story of 'some twice excluded' who 'wait at the posts of the door of the church with total resignation and patience and are treated with friendly regard'.[122]

Another tenet of the developed Glasite churches was that those who aspired to the elder's office should have faithful children. The churches held this to mean that the mature children should be able to profess their faith, but, writes Allen, 'God brings his elect to the knowledge of the truth in his own time. If it is insisted that children be in the faith this is a human tradition and a new law'. Then there was the issue of a church having to be fully set up with a presbytery[123] before a new member can join. Allen mentions a person from York, one of his churches, who had to travel to Nottingham to find a fully organized church where he could receive the laying on of hands of the presbytery. 'Mr Sandeman was not at liberty to restrict the "two or three" to the presbytery'.[124] Later, in October 1785 when he was almost alone in his tiny group of churches Allen wrote to his son, Oswald, a doctor in York, about

> the honouring and maintenance of ministers. The anti-Christian clergy have convinced themselves of the plea of living by the gospel to the aggrandisement of their families and themselves. Dissenting ministers in general, to the utmost of their power, have followed the footsteps of the established church. 'He that commences minister commences gentleman in figure

---

121. Allen, *Letters*, 2.

122. Allen, *Letters*, 7–11.

123. Presbytery refers to the body of at least two elders necessary for communion and discipline.

124. Allen, *Letters*, 21.

and appearance. In true churches Elders and them that labour in word and doctrine must be honoured.' A tent-making clergyman would make an awkward figure in the Establishment, and Dissenters in general would blush at the sight.[125]

Although born into a reasonably affluent family, settled for many generations on farms near Hawes, Allen worked as a stocking weaver. 'After I was driven from the churches I supported my family in a plain way through the good economy of my beloved helpmate, my business and the continuance of my father's allowance'.[126]

Allen wrote *Observations on the Book of Psalms in General*, particularly the eighteenth, republished in Dundee in 1836 in which he 'considers the Lord Jesus Christ as the chief speaker, David as a prophet, and an eminent type of Christ', and commentaries on most of the New Testament, some of which were republished by the Glasites in 1924.[127] His *Treatise on Redemption* was republished in Edinburgh in 1927. *The Dangers of Philosophy* was republished in 1852 by James Everson of Beverley, the Scotch Baptist pastor and editor.[128] The Church at Kirkby Lonsdale was carrying on a lively correspondence with Patrick Cochrane, printer and elder in Arbroath in the early nineteenth century, the Arbroath church being in fellowship with the majority party in Perth. Copies of a previous edition of the *Dangers of Philosophy* had been presented to the London Church early in the nineteenth century but since 'Allen had died excommunicate the Elders had condemned it without explaining their reasons', wrote Edward Wilson, an elder at Kirkby Lonsdale, who may have been a relative of Allen's wife, to Patrick Cochran. He also remarked, in a phrase that illumines some of the disputes between churches, 'ignorance is the mother of unanimity'. Allen wrote sixty-four hymns in the original edition of the *Kendal Hymnbook* used by the Inghamite churches. The one hymn that seems to have received wider acceptance is 'Sweet the moments, rich in blessing', which, modified by Walter Shirley, is in several twentieth-century hymnbooks. An edition of his hymns, published in 1761, is entitled *Hymns for the use of those who seek and those that have found redemption in the blood of Christ*. He must have been a difficult colleague, as were so many in this wider movement, but it is a tribute to his work and character that there was still a remnant known to

125. Allen, *Letters*, 36.

126. Allen, *Letters*, 43.

127. Allen, *Notes on Mark, Luke, and John.* Edited by A. F. Sandeman, Edinburgh.

128. Morison, *Supplementary Letters*, preface.

the Perth church in 1889.[129] The chapel in Gayle is said to have been used for
Christian worship until the early years of the twentieth century.

In 1810 Wilson of Kirkby Lonsdale wrote to Cochrane of Arbroath
that he had 'received a few lines from Hawes, (the Allenites) requesting my
views on two subjects, (suppose law and assurance) which their minds appear in difficulty about. I declined this and offered a personal interview'.[130]
In 1821 John Allen, possibly a son of James, wrote to Cochrane about
threats of division in Hawes, Kirkby Lonsdale, and Kendal, but also of the
addition of new members including a woman from Keighley who 'resides
40 miles distant but has been at Gayle'. In a later letter he refers to correspondence with America. 'There is something in the way they handle
the doctrine of assurance which sounds a little strange, though in the end
they seem to be clear of building upon any other foundation, perhaps,
than that which has been laid in Zion—it is a dangerous subject to meddle
with'. Oswald Allen (1816–1878), a banker in Kirkby Lonsdale and probably a grandson of James, published *One hundred and fourty-eight hymns
in Hymns of Christian Life* in 1861. One stray reference may be mentioned.
Sometime in the late nineteenth century, according to Dr Rorie, David Gorrie junior of the Perth church married, by special license, Margaret Allen,
daughter of Edward Allen at Askrigg, Yorkshire, which is very near Gayle.
Presumably she was a member of James Allen's extended family.[131] It should
be noted that Oswald, (1767–1848) the eldest son of James, and Matthew,
(1783–1845) his youngest were connected with apothecaries in York. They
had a strained relationship, and Matthew was for some time involved with
the Sandemanian fellowship in London, where he studied as an alienist and
a phrenologist. Faithfull, from whose thesis more can be learned about the
Allen family, finds that Samuel Pike had a part in James Allen's exclusion
form the Sandemanian fellowship.[132] Rather implausibly she maintains that
Pike remained a Hutchinsonian.[133]

But the main interest of these little churches is that the Faraday family
were early converts of Ingham, and followed Allen at the breach, worship-
ping in the chapel at Wenning Bank, Clapham, where the leader was Edward
Gorrell of Hazelhall. Michael Faraday's grandparents Robert and Elizabeth
lived at Clapham Wood Hall and their second son, John, was a deacon at
the Clapham meeting house. Their third son, James, became an apprentice

129. Perth MS Letters.

130. MS 9/4/3, 12.

131. MS 318/4/1, Gorrie, *Genealogy*.

132. See Faithfull, "Evaluation of an Eccentric," 12–14.

133. Faithfull, "Evaluation," 14.

blacksmith and moved to Kirkby Stephen where he became a member of the Sandemanian Church before 1790. In that year he and his family moved to London where he was hired by James Boyd, a Sandemanian who had moved south many years before from Dundee and who had a flourishing smithy and ironworks. James joined the London Church, which was then at Paul's Alley in the Barbican on 20 February 1791, and on 22 September 1791 his third child, Michael, was born.[134]

---

134. Cantor, *Faraday*, 58.

4

Divisions and Reunions

Disagreements

'The Perth Heresy'

IN AN ARTICLE IN the *Perthshire Advertiser* in 1949 Archibald McWhirter wrote, 'In the early years of last century the Church in Perth became divided for doctrinal reasons not now ascertainable and the smaller portion were known as "the bread and cheese Kirk". In 1845 the larger party met at 267 High Street while the others known as 'the Doon-bye Meeting' met at 232 High Street.'[1] McWhirter's date for the division is a little late, and the doctrinal reasons, although they may seem microscopic, are ascertainable. The comments on the two churches need to be explained and expanded.

When the Bishops on their tour of British Sandemanian Churches visited Perth they found only a small and poor congregation which represented those who adhered to the majority of the churches in the movement.[2] The greater part of the strong and well-resourced church had broken away in 1798–1799 over what Dr Rorie, at the end of the nineteenth century, called 'almost metaphysical' theological differences.[3] These obscure differences were nevertheless very real. The churches at Perth, the majority of the Church at Arbroath, a few in Dundee, and the church at Kirkby Lonsdale in Cumbria were effectively separated from all the other churches for almost a century. Only at the end of the nineteenth was the remnant of the

1. McWhirter, "Kail Kirk."
2. See chapter 6.
3. MSS 9/4/1, 26.

Perth Church reunited with Edinburgh. Pamphlets in the National Library of Scotland tell something of the story. The first is a *Statement of the Differences which unhappily subsist between the congregational churches of Perth and Arbroath and those with whom they were formerly connected.* This was published in Perth by R. Morison in 1799. Two New Testament texts head the work: 1 Cor 1:10: 'I beseech you . . . that ye speak the same thing and that there be no divisions among you', and Rom 16:20: 'and the God of peace shall bruise Satan under your feet shortly'. The second pamphlet supplementing this is entitled *A short but exact account of the Difference and Awful Division that took place at Perth among those called in common Glassites, which ended in their separation (and a few in Arbroath who took part with them from their sister churches in Scotland and England)* reprinted Perth, 1833.

By combining these sources, the rather sad story can be reconstructed. The Perth Church stated its leading tenets as follows:

1. Holding fast the form of sound words concerning justification by the blood of Christ <u>alone</u> in opposition to any species of self-righteousness.

2. Subjection to no human authority in matters of conscience.

3. Self-denying obedience to the 'ALL Things' which Christ has commanded and especially his new commandment to love one another by which all men shall know his disciples.

Together these are 'The One Thing Needful.'[4]

> While it was constantly maintained that the precious blood of Christ was that which alone purges the guilty conscience, . . . the more orthodox, Calvinistic, or as they are called Evangelical class of the religious world, approved. But when it was asserted that the Gospel knows no distinction in the human character— vile and respectable alike—, the religious world, whether moralists or Calvinists joined in arms against it. And when it was taught that in the latest hour of their lives they stand as much in need of mercy as when they first heard it . . . it was everywhere spoken against.[5]

The Perth church was 'very wary of talk of assurance of faith and hope because of the continual deceitfulness of the heart and the danger of Pharisaism'.[6] Second Peter 1:10 is quoted, 'Give diligence to make your calling and election sure; for if ye do these things, ye shall never fail'.

---

4. Anon., *Statement of the Differences*, 1.

5. Anon., *Statement of the Differences*, 1.

6. Anon., *Statement of the Differences*, 12.

The common interpretation that by doing these things our salvation is assured is confused. This would be a very dangerous
doctrine, and very inconsistent with revelation. Can calling and
predestination be made sure by our doing? Calling and election
refers here to Old Testament history and the great and precious
promises should be kept in mind.[7]

This somewhat obscure exegesis is the basis of the Perth brethren's attitude to assurance. They were anxious to preserve divine sovereignty and
human fallibility, and to avoid presumption. It seemed dangerous to them
that other Glasites were talking of assurance in a much more positive way.
The immediate cause of their alarm was a visit made to the Montrose Church
by two members of the Perth Church. They heard David Buchanan speak
publicly and found fault with his doctrine, so the Perth church made an
investigation. Both parties were called to Dundee so that the church there
could judge between Montrose and Perth. Thereafter the Perth Church sent
a statement to all the churches in Scotland and England, and the 'whole, with
one voice (except for a few at Arbroath and four or five in Dundee) declared
their opposition to the Perth doctrine as a doctrine calculated to draw men's
minds from that activity which is called for in the Christian warfare'.

The doctrines held by Buchanan in his correspondence with the Perth
Church were stated to be:

1. That truth is a living principle in the hearts of men that are taught of
   God to know it and believe it, powerfully and irresistibly leading or
   constraining them to abound in the work of faith, the labour of love
   and the patience of hope in our Lord Jesus Christ.

2. Joy in believing is not the joy of the hypocrite but the beginning of
   eternal life.

3. Believers can receive a foretaste of eternal life, an experimental knowledge and confirmation of that truth which they already have believed
   on the evidence of divine testimony.[8]

In a letter quoted in the tract the Perth church condemns the church
at Montrose for holding that the guilty sinner may, by continuing in the
profession and the self-denied obedience of the Gospel, attain to some assurance of his being a believer. Perth considers this to be a corruption of the
Gospel of Christ. They quote a letter from the Nottingham church which

---

7. Anon., *Statement of the Differences*, 23.
8. Anon., *Short but Exact Account*, 3, 6, 7.

objects to Perth's 'unbounded self-sufficiency' and accuses the church of 'darkening clear scripture'.[9]

The issue is that of the possibility of assurance. Could a believer claim to be sure of salvation or was this, as Perth asserted, presumption and possibly hypocrisy? Some in Perth went even further and implied that hypocrisy was inevitable, given the deceitfulness of the human heart.

> A man speaking to the Church in view of fellowship confessed his iniquity in hope of mercy. As he came from a sect which maintains the doctrine of Assurance pretty strongly, one of the elders asked him whether he had not cause to fear lest the profession he was making should be in hypocrisy. He said he had the greatest cause to fear. One of these brethren (who said there was nothing in the heart of man save hypocrisy and deceit) spoke to the following effect. 'Have you not only cause to fear, but are you not convicted, that not only what you are now saying but what you ever will say will be in hypocrisy?'

This brother had gone too far even for the Perth church, and was spoken to. He and others pursuing this *reductio ad absurdum* went on to claim there was no need for self-examination, for only unbelief would be found. The Perth elders commented that 'the profession of faith seemed now to be the profession of unbelief'. The extremists, who soon left the church and formed a separate meeting elsewhere in Perth, also maintained 'that to pray that any of the effects of the gospel might be produced is self-righteous and profane, and that to exhort one another to any of the self-denied effects of the Gospel could only serve the purpose of gratifying self-righteous pride'.[10]

In a letter from an old manuscript belonging to Patrick Cochrane of Arbroath there are further elucidations. The Dundee brethren maintain

> that a guilty sinner after making the confession of the faith may by continuing in that profession and in the self-denied obedience of the Gospel attain to some assurance of his being a believer and that he may arrive at some evidence and satisfy his own mind that the joy he had upon his first believing was not the joy of the hypocrite, and that this evidence it is his duty to seek after. That in this exercise Christians arrive at an experimental knowledge of what at first they believed on testimony and experience some additional work of the Spirit as the Comforter distinct from that which teaches to call Jesus Lord.

9. Anon., *Short but Exact Account*, 21.

10. Anon., *Statement of the Differences*, 28.

In Perth on the other hand the brethren think that

> they are bound by the Word of God to resist this as a corruption of the Gospel of Christ. Faith produces fruits, but the daily experience of the believer is of hypocrisy, unbelief, and every fruit of a deceitful and desperately wicked heart. The work of the Spirit as comforter is first and last to convince of sin, giving hope in despair. There is a danger of using assurance to consider themselves rich and increased with goods.[11]

Perhaps Dr Rorie was too optimistic in his characterization of the differences as 'almost metaphysical'.

The division seemed complete. But there were efforts to heal the breach. In the autumn of 1814 letters were exchanged seeking reconciliation or at least explanations. An anonymous letter from Perth, apparently sent to the Leith church by a 'young inexperienced boy', asked:

> Are we of one mind as to our hope before our Maker? This, sir, I am persuaded will never be ascertained until we leave Glas, Sandeman, Young and Morison out of the question. Let the church at E. draw up a simple statement of their profession of faith and hope and of how they adhere to all the things Christ commanded, and avoid the writings and opinions of any man, and lay it before the church at Perth and its connections and vice-versa.[12]

The reply from Leith did have a statement of faith—'we are saved by the free sovereign gift of God and this faith uniformly (in all who have obtained it by lot) works by love to all who are of the truth for its sake only'.[13] The vexed question of the necessity of an elder being the husband of one wife is raised in the next letter from Perth, and it is remarked that the most distressing circumstance is that each side acted unwarrantably at the time of the separation. 'Which party is at fault and needs to repent?'

> The churches at Edinburgh and the others have always considered the Perth church as denying the necessity of the work of faith and the labour of love, and the operation of the Holy Spirit, while the latter consider that the former build their hope before their Maker upon that work of faith. There is misunderstanding on both sides.[14]

11. MS 9/4, 1, 171.
12. MS 9/4, 2.
13. MS 9/4, 4.
14. MS 9/4, 18.

In November 1814 there is a report of an abortive conference between representatives of the Perth and Edinburgh churches. Edinburgh insisted that reconciliation should be one by one, not by churches, and put all the blame on Perth.[15] More questions arose. Can a church receive a member who has been put away twice? Should a member eat with excommunicants? Should a member be connected to Friendly Societies? Should Bible Societies be supported? May a member go repeatedly to other places of worship on a Sunday evening? These questions arise from time to time, reminding us that the Glasite communion was not, at least in those days, monolithic, and the references to human authors emphasize the recurring theme of going only to the Scriptures. The issue of discipline being applied to churches as well as individuals is at the root of many of the Glasite divisions and was never quite resolved.[16]

In Patrick Cochrane's correspondence for August 1832 he refers to a letter from John Howe of Halifax, which he had shown to friends in Arbroath, Kirkby Lonsdale, Perth, and Aberdeen. He mentions a letter from Mr Walker:

> I trust that the manner in which he speaks of the Bereans will relieve the minds of some in Perth who I have heard express themselves as not understanding him on Assurance. There is a difference betwixt knowing assuredly that that same Jesus who was crucified is both Lord and Christ and trusting or boasting in the assurance of our believing. There is a contrast between John 6 verse 69 and John 16 verses 24–32.

The letter from Howe refers to his correspondence with John Walker of Trinity College Dublin, who alludes to the controversy regarding personal assurance. When he 'attempted to read it to the brethren and compared it with Sandeman's teaching several who had been acquainted with Sandeman objected'.[17] James Morison in a letter of December 1830 remarks on changes in Europe and Great Britain, remarkable doings. 'In all that is going forward I hope the Brethren in both England and Scotland will be found taking no part but watching and keeping their garments pure and rendering unto Caesar the things that are his'. Gloomily Cochrane asserts that 'laxity of principle in US also applies to Great Britain and Europe. There is a near approach to that condition when the flood was brought upon the earth'. Equally gloomily he says that the union of churches (sc. Glasite) has

15. MS 9/4, 22.
16. MS 9/4, 39.
17. MS 9/3/23.

repeatedly been tried but in vain.[18] So abstruse discussions about assurance are discussed side by side with notice of the revolutionary changes in Europe and the many reforms in Britain.

The Divisions over the Eating of Blood

Disagreements and divisions over this other somewhat arcane issue seriously weakened the Glasite churches during and beyond the nineteenth century. To explain why when only four churches remained in the first half of the twentieth century, the church in Edinburgh being in fellowship with one church in London and the church in Glasgow with the other, there was such a continuing division and why a Glasgow elder replying to a correspondent who was considering joining the body could in 1891 refer to the church in Edinburgh as a body who are called by the same name (i.e., Glasite) but one from whom all the other churches withdrew in 1855, we must look at Glas's teaching and the interpretation of it, or rather of the relevant Scriptures.[19]

In 1743 Glas published a work entitled *The Unlawfulness of Blood-Eating shewed from a view of the Tenure by which the Christian Gentiles from the Beginning held their Liberty in Christ from the Yoke of the Law of Moses.* His main texts are Acts 15:19–21, and Acts 21:18–25, which show that both at the so-called Council of Jerusalem and in later teaching, there was no necessity for Gentiles to be circumcised, but that laws concerning sexual purity and the objection to eating blood were still binding on all Christians. Meat sacrificed to idols (idolothytes,) things strangled and blood were forbidden then and, Glas maintained, always, for Christians.

> The first Christians (who were not the worst of the kind,) knowing the import of the precept concerning blood, observed it most religiously. And although questions arose amongst them, about idolothytes and fornication, yet we never read of any of them who had the confidence to say anything in favour of eating blood, or to move any objection against the obligation of the precept, in any case.

Glas quotes Tertullian, Minucius Felix and one of the martyrs of Vienne and Lyons as testifying that Christians did not eat blood. This was a defense against the slander that Christians ate human flesh and blood. At the end of the work Glas refers almost as an afterthought to an idea which was much used in the later controversy 'that it could not appear so ridiculous to

18. MS 9/3/20.
19. MS 364/3/15.

them as it may do now in the Christian world, to forbear the blood of beasts out of respect to the atonement in the blood of Jesus Christ'.[20]

James Allen, in his *Commentary on the Acts of the Apostles*, written in the second half of the eighteenth century, is quite specific about the eating of blood. On Acts 15:29 he says, 'Gentiles who believe must abstain' from

1. Things offered to idols. This abstinence was a term of Church communion;

2. Fornication, which Allen interprets as 'every method of satisfying the natural propensity of the sexes except the marriage bed, and in this place, perhaps, fornication hath a particular respect to false worship'.

3. Things strangled and from blood, i.e., flesh with the blood in it and blood separated from the flesh.

The Gentiles were bound to abstain from things strangled and from blood on the same footing that they were bound to keep themselves from idolothytes and fornication. 'Blood' was never allowed to man for food, for in the grant of food to Noah, the blood is reserved. So it was under the law, Lev 17, and so it is here again under first part of the New Testament revelation. The use of blood for food is prohibited, because 'it is the life of the creature, and because it maketh atonement for the soul. To eat it therefore is both brutal and irreligious. It is a practical disregard to that blood by which the Church is purchased. Who are we to withstand God?'[21]

Presumably all Glas's followers agreed on the principle of abstinence from the eating of blood for the first century of the church's life and development. It seems that the controversy on the issue began in the 1820s. In a letter of 1854 there is a reference to a previous raising of the question in 1822 when Mr Neilson, as elder from Glasgow, being in London, objected to the practice of the London brothers and sisters freely partaking of game. A correspondence between the churches took place, and Mr Leighton, a London elder, came to Scotland and convinced Glasgow and Edinburgh that the London church conformed to the rules about blood-eating.[22]

It was in 1854/5 that a permanent breach between Edinburgh and Galashiels on the one side, and all the other churches was made, to the sadness of many and the breaking up of families and friendships. The major question discussed in the London Meeting House was whether the blood had to be drained immediately after the animal's death or whether time

20. Glas, *Works*, 2:171–72.

21. Allen, *Notes on the Acts and the Epistles*, 29.

22. Add. MSS 11/9, "Letter from Edinburgh to London," November 1854.

could elapse and there was then the possibility that some blood might seep into the animal's flesh, from where it could not be effectively removed. Miss J. Hornblower, a school teacher who was a member of the London Church and who had been on holiday in the Scottish Highlands, wrote to Mrs Blair, a friend in the Dunkeld church.

> I did not scruple to eat game—I then explained to you that I considered when the birds were shot they must bleed so as to render them fit for a Christian's table, although I should certainly avoid partaking of them if not in a condition to be freed from the blood. . . . [T]he dark colour of the (? gamebirds') flesh arises from the nature of their food and not from the suffusion of blood in its substance.[23]

There was considerable difficulty obtaining consensus on the matter in the London meeting house. Michael Faraday, an elder in the Church, 'appears to have suggested that, since Scripture does not specify when and how the blood should be drained, a test should be held to find out whether blood could be cleaned effectively some time after the animal's death'.[24] Despite this pragmatic suggestion, the London and Dundee Churches agreed on

> the clear meaning of the Scriptural prohibition on the eating of blood, declaring that it is contrary to the divine law to eat an animal unless the blood has been drained at the time of its death, otherwise some of the blood is bound to remain in the animal's flesh.

So strongly did the London churches hold to their interpretation of the scriptures concerning the eating of blood that they were willing to consign the Edinburgh and Galashiels churches to the status of heretics. Perhaps the issue was complicated by the social customs of the middle-class members of the Edinburgh church. The elders were men of note in the city. William Buchanan was a prominent lawyer, George Waterston a manufacturer and printer, and most significantly, William Dickson was a gunsmith. Gentlemen shot gamebirds, and possibly deer, and the question of the drainage of blood was more than theoretical.

There were several different strands in the controversy. On 7 November 1854 Thomas Boosey, a London elder, along with others, wrote to the church at Dundee, acknowledging London's error,

---

23. Add. MSS 11/9, "Letter from Miss J. Hornblower to Mrs Blair, Dunkeld," 12 October 1854.

24. Cantor, *Faraday*, 69.

concerning the light manner in which we held the commandment to all believers in Jesus Christ to abstain from blood
and things strangled with the evident reference that the commandment has to the blood of the Great Atonement, without
the shedding of which there could have been no remission of
sins. (Romans 14:1–4 and 1 Timothy 4: 4 do not apply to the
prohibition.)

In January 1855 the same elder wrote to the Edinburgh church:

We do not consider by this that we are in any way brought under the Levitical law or that we are prohibited from eating the
flesh of any animal whatever, if it has been bled at the time of its
death. I strongly disagree with the Edinburgh position that food
is lawful if the blood is afterwards cleansed. This may be im-
possible—but we regard such flesh as 'flesh with the life thereof
which is the blood thereof' and therefore a forbidden thing by
God's command to Noah and all mankind.[25]

There are at least two important theological themes here. The Edinburgh church considered that the other churches were in danger of Old
Testament legalism, and of overemphasizing the Noahic covenant, and this
is discussed at length, and the blood of animals is closely connected with the
shed blood in the death of Christ and thus becomes central in the soteriol-
ogy of the movement.

George Baxter of the Dundee church wrote to Miss Hornblower in
November 1854:

It seems of the same nature of that command given to our first
parents respecting the tree in the midst of the garden, only as
that declared their dependence on God as the Author and Lord
of their life of which their disobedience deprived them, this
declares the guilty sinners' dependence on the Lord God, the
sovereign Author of the redemption by blood and disobedience
to it imports disregard to that Blood.[26]

We can see in these abstruse comments how Miranda Seymour, in her
description of the Glasite families whom Mary Shelley visited in Dundee
might describe the Glasites as practicing a 'mild form of Vegetarianism'.[27]

The disagreements took an inexorable course. Despite many protesta-
tions of a desire for unity, the battle lines had been drawn. In November

25. Add. MSS 11/9. And Faraday, "Letter 2918," in *Correspondence* 4.
26. Add MSS 11/9.
27. Seymour, *Mary Shelley*, 75.

1854 the elders of the Dundee church wrote to William Buchanan in Edinburgh stating their case. After the church had met and discussed the question the Edinburgh leaders replied 'the length to which you appear to carry your views are not supported by the authors of the scriptures and would surely result in a new commandment not warranted by the divine word. The commandment is not to eat things strangled, but game is not strangled but shot'. Sisters, both servants and mistresses spoke at the meeting of their methods of preparing game, an unusual reference to female participation in important doctrinal discussions.[28]

In November 1854 a letter signed by four London elders, four deacons, and four other members was sent to Edinburgh, expressing their dissatisfaction with the 'lax' Edinburgh position, and the next month a four-man deputation from Dundee visited Edinburgh to resolve the matter. They were joined by Mr Vincent and Mr Leighton, elders from London, whose presence was both a surprise and an annoyance to the Edinburgh elders. Far from achieving unity the meeting broke up in discord. Alexander Moir, a Dundee elder, wrote:

> We then went home to our lodging and felt much shocked at the arbitrary manner in which the discipline had been conducted and grieved to see a whole Church resisting the Divine Word for the gratification of their own lusts.

More letters passed between the churches and on 31 January 1855 the London church in a letter signed by Michael Faraday amongst others terminated relations between London and its allies and Edinburgh. This entailed the breaking of friendships such as that of Faraday with Buchanan and the severing of family ties in this closely interrelated fellowship. As Cantor remarks, 'The discipline of the Church of Christ was considered of greater importance than personal friendships'.[29]

Although we hear of individuals in such churches as Glasgow coming under 'the influence of false doctrine' it seems that the lead of Dundee and London was largely followed. 'We have learned', wrote the London Church 'that our friends in Dunkeld, Perth, Montrose, Aberdeen and Fife are all heartily joined in the same mind', and the Glasgow Church added the brethren in Norfolk, Chesterfield, and the Church at Newcastle to the agreed position. In May 1855 a long letter from Danbury signified the agreement

28. Add MSS 11/9.
29. Cantor, *Faraday*, 70.

of the American churches with 'Dundee etc. which left Edinburgh and the remnant in Galashiels isolated'.[30]

And so, the division remained for thirty years, no doubt being one of the factors in the decline of the churches. Then, on 31 October 1884 Thomas Vincent, elder in London who had been moved by a sister's approach to George Waterston in Edinburgh regarding reunion wrote to Charles Philip and Alexander Moir in Dundee with a view to reconciliation. The letter fell on stony ground indeed. The Dundee reply spoke of 'the alarming nature of your communication and the great error of entering into correspondence with George Waterston on the subject of the separation which took place 30 years ago. After patient dealings the Edinburgh church stood as excommunicants and this action was considered a deed of love. Edinburgh has not repented'.[31] Mrs Young, who was probably the person who approached her brother-in-law, George Waterston, in Edinburgh, was 'put away' by the London Church for her action, and Benjamin Vincent, London elder and assistant secretary and librarian of the Royal Institution, answered some questions from the Dundee Church in an uncompromising manner:

> I reminded the Church of the chief object of the foundation of the churches above 100 years ago—viz-.-the revival of the unreasoning obedience to the commands of Christ, based upon Charity—the love of the Truth—and the danger of these being obscured by false Charity or superseded by Brotherly Love—its accompaniment. It is very strange that the Edinburgh people should have attempted to set aside the Old Testament as our guide over a portion of the law left as a burden in the New Testament.[32]

But all was not peaceful in London. On 6 November 1884 the Edinburgh Church sent a statement by George Waterston to the churches at Glasgow and Dundee stating, amongst other things, that the London Church does not consider that game as ordinarily sold is in a proper condition for food. The Edinburgh elders admit that this could be the case and that in a case of doubt the brethren must abstain. The practice in Edinburgh is to refrain from partaking of game in the house of strangers as there is apt to be a want of due supervision in respect of blood.[33]

On 11 November 1884 D. Blaikley, a London elder, wrote to C. Philip, elder in Dundee, suggesting that 'excommunication' of Edinburgh was a too

30. Add MSS 11/9.

31. Add MSS 11/9.

32. MSS 9/1/2. "Letter from B. Vincent to C. Philip," 30 April 1885.

33. MSS 9/1/2. "Statement by G[eorge] W[aterston]" sent to Glasgow and Dundee, 6th November 1884.

harsh an expression. Rather they should speak of withdrawing from Edin-burgh, and he refers to John Glas's *Treatise on the Lord's Supper* chapter 5, section 6, that 'the binding or loosing of a complete church belongs to him who walks in the midst of the Golden Candlesticks'.[34] On 19 February 1885 George Waterston wrote to Alex Moir in Dundee, 'We fear our invariably careful practice in regard to shot animals was not sufficiently considered in 1855. We were principally occupied in resisting the Law of Moses being placed as our sole law in this matter. We observe the decree in the light of the New Covenant'. This was not taken as repentance by the church at Dundee, but in London there were signs of disagreement and a softening of attitudes, especially among the younger brethren.[35]

On the second and third of September 1885 meetings were held in the Meeting House at Barnsbury, London, to clear the whole matter, as during the disputes the Lord's Supper could not be eaten by the London church. On 2 September in the deacons' seat were T. Vincent and D. Blaikley, London elders, C. Philip and D. Philip, Dundee elders, and A. Moir and A. Sande-man, Glasgow elders. Also present were several London deacons, a deacon from Dundee and one from Glasgow, and a member from Newcastle. The meeting began with a solemn prayer led by T. Vincent, quoting Zeph 1:12, 'And it shall come to pass at that time, that I will search Jerusalem with candles, and punish the men that are settled on their lees; that say in their hearts, The Lord will not do good, neither will he do evil'. In the discussion the actions of the churches towards Perth in 1798 was taken as a precedent. The central matter of disagreement seems to have been whether one church could discipline another, and whether a church, like an individual, could be considered beyond reconciliation after two excommunications. Blaikley ap-pealed to John Glas and his statement that a church is subject to no judica-tory under heaven, and Sandeman pointed out that the statement had been written before the churches were formed in the manner in which they after-ward came into existence. A. B. 'rather excitedly' charged Dundee friends with advising study of Glas yet now departing from his views. After all the discussions the roll was called of both male and female members and the church was nearly equally divided. As it was late another meeting was called at 7 p.m. on the following day when the Dundee, Glasgow and Newcastle brethren adjourned to a separate room and constituted themselves along with the London members who agreed with them as churches following the true discipline. T. Vincent said there was no obstacle to this but that the church would assemble as usual on the next Sabbath. Thereafter one London

---

34. MSS 9/1/2, "Letter from London Elders to C. Philip, Dundee."
35. MSS 9/1/2, "Letter from G. Waterston to A. Moir, Dundee."

church was in fellowship with Edinburgh and the other with Glasgow, most of Dundee and the remnant at Newcastle. Seventy-three members of the London church divided almost equally, one church comprising thirty-three members and the other forty. There were only fourteen men and they were divided equally, seven in each church.[36]

Dr James Rorie, the Dundee Glasite who withdrew from the Dundee church in a letter of 8 September 1885 addressed to C. Philip, the Dundee elder, and who was in fellowship with Edinburgh after the split, continued to address the question of the eating of blood and in his diary records some of his thoughts on the matter. He looks at various texts in the Pentateuch, beginning with the Noahic covenant in Gen 9:3–4, and in Lev 17:10–14, especially the ban on Israelites and strangers among them eating blood, and the command to cover the poured-out blood with dust, verse 13. 'The life of the flesh is in the blood'. Unlike others he does not here refer to the blood of the atonement. In a letter to an anonymous correspondent he elaborates on the matter.

> You appear to put the question on a new footing. I always understood the question to be whether it was possible to remove the blood from the body of the animal whose blood had not been shed when it was killed. You put the question thus: 'A affirms that matters forbidden are blood and things strangled, while B affirms they are blood and things strangled and otherwise killed without their blood being shed.' I rather incline to B's position. Acts 15 must be seen in the light of the Old Testament. What is known as science must be carefully excluded—unaided human reason always leads to results directly opposed to the Word of God, e.g. Geology shows the world was not created in six days and human philosophy shows that man was not made in God's image. We must endeavour to interpret scripture by scripture. In Genesis 9 flesh and blood refer to flesh and blood used in sacrificial purposes.

Here the letter unfortunately seems to end, with a reference to shooting animals. 'In shooting animals their blood is not shed, and they are equally forbidden.'[37] In a letter of 11 September 1886 to Mrs Baldwin in Danbury, Dr Rorie, having outlined a Glasite view of church history and mentioned the dispute of 1820 on blood-eating and at the same time on baptism, remarked, 'If in stating that shot and unblooded animals were the

36. "Notes, partly from memory of the occurrences at the meetings on 2nd and 3rd September 1885 at Barnsbury, London which resulted in the division and separation in the Church there." And see Cantor, *Faraday*, 41.

37. Rorie, *On the Sinfulness of Eating Blood*. Add MSS, 318/4/6.

same as strangled, the Dundee and Glasgow elders meant they were in the same physical condition then they certainly stated what pathologically is not the case and in insisting that the ceremonial law in Leviticus must be imposed they certainly went beyond what is literally decreed in Acts 15'. Rorie was writing in the seventies and eighties of the nineteenth century and his usually eirenic or even 'liberal' ideas are nevertheless constrained by the biblicism of the Church. 'The history of the Glasite churches is a sad and melancholy narrative', he wrote to Margaret Baldwin, one of the last of the American believers.[38]

Attempts at Reunion

In a collection of manuscript letters we can follow an attempt to bring the divided churches together. This follows a plea from the Perth elders, James Gardner, and J. Fairweather, dated 13 May 1888. The preamble is worth noting: 'Note of the results arrived at in a meeting of the Elders and deacons of the Church of Perth on the subject of the possibility of the churches and scattered brethren in this country known as Glasites or Sandemanians walking together in the fear of the Lord as having the same Faith and Hope and minding the same things'.[39]

Although the Perth church had been isolated for a hundred years, the leaders there were obviously still in touch with their former brethren, and felt it was their duty to seek to make peace. The elders pointed out that they had not been

> concerned in the matters which have troubled the other churches at various times and especially in 1808, 1855 and 1885, and believing that now no such difference exists which led to the separation of the Perth church from the others in the end of last century have been led to consider whether the known differences between the various churches are such as ought to prevent our acknowledging each other as companions in the Faith and Hope of the Gospel.

> The one matter that stands in the way of union is the application of our Lord's law in Matthew 18 verse 15 to any other than offences between brethren who are members of the same church.

38. MSS 9/4/1, "Letter from James Rorie to Mrs Baldwin," 11 April 1886. Nothing I have found refers to blood transfusion, the matter that has so disturbed the Jehovah's Witnesses.

39. MS letter, 1.

'If thy brother shall trespass against thee' is so very simple and
plain a command that to say a word upon it apart from each
separate church in its own discipline and among its own members seems certain to lead to confusion and distress.

They go on to say that applying this command to members of different
churches or to differences between churches has resulted in dissension and
separation in the past 'and we fear would so result again'. It is very important
that brethren of different churches and scattered brethren should be united,
and the Perth church appealed to the other churches to follow the things
which make for peace. They conclude, 'consider of it, take advice and speak
your minds'.[40]

The appeal was addressed to the church assembling in Glasgow,
through Archibald Sandeman; the church in London through J. Blaikley;
the church in Edinburgh through George Waterston; the church in Dundee
through Mr Philip; the brethren assembling in Newcastle through T. Deacon; the church in Dundee through Dr Rorie, (that was the dissident church
which held fellowship with Edinburgh); the other church in London meeting in Albion Road through Benjamin Vincent; and the remnant meeting
with Mr Allen in Gayle.

Replies were soon received. George Waterston laid it before the church
for consideration and promised that the brethren would give their opinion on
the following sabbath. Dr Rorie, who had received the letter from Mr Morison
of Perth said that he, Dr Miller, and Mr Duncan had been in Edinburgh when
the letter was discussed, and they were in entire agreement with the Edinburgh Church, and much gratified with the Perth initiative. A very different
response came from the main Dundee church. David Philip replied that the
elders did not think it proper to lay the letter before the church.

Firstly, because any reconciliation between brethren and those
who have been separated from them can only be brought about
by those who have been separated coming before us making
confession of repentance of their error and desiring fellowship,
and secondly because we already have the mind of the church in
regard to the application of our Lord's law of discipline.[41]

Both the London churches seemed to believe that the verses in Matt
18 apply both to individuals and to churches, but asked for further explanations, and in a letter to an unspecified London church on the 28 May
the Perth church sought to clarify its position. George Waterston consulted

40. MS letter, 1.
41. MS letter, 5a.

writings of John Barnard, and of his great-uncle James Morison, who in a paper of 1855 who had 'a very clear view of the evils of churches taking action one against another'. In the very full letter from the Edinburgh Church (scattered brethren from Dundee, Galashiels and Newcastle having expressed their full concurrence), noted with great pleasure that the church in Perth believes that the points of difference no longer exist which separated the church in Perth in 1798 and would assure the church in Perth that 'no effort shall be wanting in their part to come to one mind as it is quite possible that some of those points of difference may have been overstrained'. The rest of the letter seeks to clarify the law in Matt 18, and broadly agrees with Perth.[42] The Glasites in Newcastle seem to be divided, as a member was present at Edinburgh and Thomas Proctor aligned himself with the Glasgow position, which is outlined in a letter of 7 June 1888 addressed to 'my dear cousin', a reminder of the interrelations that crossed the lines drawn by doctrine and biblical interpretation. Archibald Sandeman regretfully writes that differences may be necessary however much there is a human desire for reconciliation, and even if the true church is reduced to a remnant.[43] This refusal to accept the Perth proposal is much less abrasive than the response of the Dundee church. There are other shorter letters, and it appears that the only outcome of Perth's appeal was the reunion, in 1896, of the Perth church with the Edinburgh brethren.

Even this was hard to achieve. In March 1896, responding to overtures from Edinburgh for reunion John Gorrie, a Perth elder, seems to be in favor but the elders wrote to George Waterston:

> We should have preferred that the divisions in London and Dundee should have been healed because communion on our part with Edinburgh and the churches in London and Dundee who are agreed would seem to widen the breach between them and the Glasgow Church and the churches in Dundee and London who are still separated.

Perth held that the words of Matt 18 are only binding on members and that an elder or a deacon of one church cannot exercise their duties in another church. Waterston thinks that Edinburgh and Perth should remain apart from the 'Glasgow, Dundee and London combination'. In June 1896 the Edinburgh church records, 'The Church in Perth united with us in brotherly friendship'.[44]

---

42. MS letter, 15–21.
43. MS letter, 6.
44. Edinburgh MS notes.

The letter addressed to the remnant at Gayle[45] does not seem to have elicited a reply. The Meeting House (now in other use) and the little Sandemanian graveyard at Gayle near Hawes in Wensleydale are still there, a monument to the work of the first leader of the church, James Allen, and his family.

45. See chapter 5a

6

Michael Faraday and Some Less Famous Sandemanians

SINCE MICHAEL FARADAY IS quite the most famous person to be identified, during his whole life, with the Sandemanians, he is also the one who has had most attention paid to him and his relationship with the church. Geoffrey Cantor's excellent book says all we need to know about him and the London church, and indeed much more about the general ethos and life of the Glasite/Sandemanian churches.[1] There were others who in their time and place are worthy of notice, so before we turn to look at Faraday's life and faith we may look at some interesting members and associates of the churches.

The Boswell Family

James Boswell, besides writing the biography of Samuel Johnson, was an inveterate diarist, and the many volumes of his diary afford wonderful glimpses, not only of his intriguing character, but also of the ecclesiastical life of his time. His uncle, Dr John Boswell, (1710–1780) was a noted physician, who had studied in Edinburgh and then under Boerhaave, the famous teacher of botany, medicine, and chemistry at Leiden in the Netherlands. He was president of the Royal College of Physicians of Edinburgh from 1770–1772 and lived on the south side of the Meadows in that city. He became a member of the Glasite Church in the city on 18 April 1762. Dr Johnson, having heard Boswell talk about his uncle's Museum, asked why he had quitted practice. 'I said because his whimsical change of religion

1. Cantor, *Faraday*, passim.

had made people distrustful of him as a physician, which I thought unreasonable as religion was unconnected with medical skill.' Johnson then remarked on 'crazy piety.'[2] 'On the road he (Dr Boswell) disputed warmly for his particular tenets as to the Christian religion: salvation by faith alone, etc. I felt some pain when I found how ill I could argue on the most important of all subjects, and cold clouds of doubt went athwart my mind.'[3] According to his nephew the doctor then distinguished himself by twice being excommunicated. Here is James's account.

> I found my uncle the Doctor was at present excommunicated by his CHURCH for whoring. I never before was certain that he indulged himself in it, but Robert [his son] told me that they had sufficient evidence and that he had confessed with all appearance of deep contrition; but that they were not sure if they were warranted to receive him again into their society, as he had before been put out from among them (for something else I believe) yet after receiving again had been so wicked. Robert was amongst the most forward to put out from among them his father, with the utmost indignation, that God might be merciful to him, but that the church must have much difficulty to be satisfied of his sincerity.[4]

The account in James Scott's scrapbook is slightly different. 'Saturday 17th May 1772, Dr Boswell cut off for drunkenness and swearing.'[5] As we shall see with Faraday, the fear of a second separation from the church and therefore theoretically final exclusion was very real. On 9 October 1775 James Boswell's son was baptised, apparently at home, and Robert 'came in after the ceremony, which as an Independent he did not like to attend.'[6]

In his entry for Sunday 21 May 1780, James writes:

> I had long intended to go to the Glassite Meeting-house and hear Robert Boswell preach. I chose this day, as I fancied there might perhaps be something of a funeral sermon on Dr Boswell. Grange went with me. Mr Lawrie showed us to the gallery. He sat in view. Grange and I were concealed. It is, I believe, more than twenty years since I was in this meeting- house, when my mind was tender and sore with religious terrors. I was pleased to find that they were not in the slightest degree renewed today. We

2. Milne, *Boswell's Edinburgh Journals, 1767–1786*, 236n27.

3. Milne, *Boswell's Edinburgh Journals*, "19 September 1774," 153.

4. Pottle and McWeiss, *Boswell in Extremes*, 110.

5. Scott, *Notebook*, 19.

6. Milne, *Boswell's Edinburgh Journals*, "11 October 1775," 198.

were disappointed, for Robert did not preach. . . . John Young preached. The latter harangued with a clear, strong voice and a fluency of words. But he uttered strange doctrine. He in explicit terms asserted predestination and election and inculcated that his hearers should not only not imagine that anything they could do to distinguish them from the most profligate had the least influence in obtaining their salvation, but if they had even a wish to be better, that they might recommend themselves to GOD, they were departing from the Christian faith.

James professes himself horrified with this doctrine, which of course echoes Sandeman's *Letters*, but he is able to commend 'very fine singing in parts. It reminded me of a choir of monks or nuns.' In the afternoon James went to hear Dr Blair preach 'beautifully and rationally.'[7] On Sunday 2 September 1781, as Dr Blair's Church was closed for painting, the intrepid James went to the Berean Chapel at the foot of Carrubber's Close, off the High Street opposite St Giles, and heard Mr Barclay pray and lecture 'drearily and wildly. He differed little from the Glassites [*sic*].' Barclay was the leader of the Bereans.[8]

In April 1777 James and his cousin Robert were on a journey for family business in the north of England and they improved the time by theological discussion.

> After dining at Kelso, we got into a conversation on religion in the fly, and a keen dispute we had. Robert maintained that everything concerning our salvation was done by Christ. I maintained that after Adam's fall the gate of heaven was shut; that although we might climb up the hill of virtue, it could not avail us till the gate was opened. This all human power or merit could not effectuate. Christ came nobly forth as our saviour and opened the Kingdom of Heaven to all believers, and now all who fear God and work righteousness, all who climb up the hill by the aid of divine grace can have entrance into that glorious state where they forever adore their benefactor. . . . I led him calmly to give me an account of his sect, of its principles and practices and I found something very pretty in it; only I thought it not consistent with the state of society in the world. He said it was not, and that Christians were and ever would be but a few.

7. Milne, *Boswell's Edinburgh Journals*, 396.

8. ODNB. For a good account of the Bereans see Hastings, *Encyclopaedia of Religion and Ethics*, 2:520, A. Miller. See also Campbell, "Berean Church."

Later he comments that although the Independents or Glasites do not admit any efficacy in morality in working out our salvation, 'they are very strict in enforcing it.'[9] Robert 'scrupled to spend Sunday in travelling.'

Robert, of whom James was very fond, and who was his agent and solicitor in Edinburgh,[10] was a remarkable man. He was a Writer to the Signet and served as Lyon Clerk in the Court of the Lord Lyon, the arbiter of Scottish Heraldry, from 1770 until his death in 1804. He was acting Lord Lyon King of Arms from 1795–1796. As a Glasite elder he translated the Psalms from the 'original tongues' and based on Kennicot's edition of the Hebrew Bible. This version was used thereafter in all the churches, with emendations from time to time, indicated by small strips of paper over the changed wording. He frequently preached in various Glasite churches and in the London church, on 1 April 1804, while preaching on the text 'all flesh is as grass,' he collapsed and died in the pulpit.[11] He had married Sibella, daughter of William Sandeman of Perth and therefore a niece of Robert Sandeman and had a large family. His daughter Elizabeth who married John Anderson, and in her widowhood became a deaconess in the Edinburgh church, where her kindliness was much appreciated. Of her four daughters the eldest, Sibella was an Episcopalian, and the other three, Mary Anne, Elizabeth and Catherine were Glasites. They lived in the fashionable George Square and their parties were attended by the young people of the Glasite church. There was music and dancing, always ending with 'Sir Roger de Coverley' and they had romantic Jacobite sympathies, and possessed several relics of Bonnie Prince Charlie. One of the daughters, Elizabeth Carre Anderson, was a poet whose devotional verse was read at the Wednesday meetings of the Church. The three Glasite sisters died within the same month in 1878, and the poems were published as a slim volume in 1903.[12]

William Godwin

William Godwin (1756–1836) is well known as a novelist and radical political philosopher. He came of dissenting stock. His grandfather studied at Philip Doddridge's Academy and became an Independent Minister as did Godwin's father. The succession almost continued for another generation as William showed an interest in ministry from an early age. After attending a school for the children of dissenters in Kent he was sent to study with the

---

9. Pottle and McWeiss, *Boswell in Extremes*, 109–10.

10. Walker, *Private Papers of James Boswell, Correspondence* 1:320n1.

11. Cole, *General Correspondence of James Boswell*, 1:2n5.

12. Elizabeth Carre Anderson, *Songs and Verses*, privately published.

Independent minister Samuel Newton in Norwich, where he was unhappy under the strict discipline. In accounts of Godwin Newton is referred to as a Sandemanian, but this is scarcely accurate. Rather he was influenced by Sandeman's views on faith but there is no evidence that he followed the customs of the Sandemanian churches. So, when Godwin was turned down by Homerton College in London on suspicion of Sandemanianism, it was surely because of his expressed views of faith as bare belief. He was welcomed at Hoxton College, also in London, which under the teaching of Andrew Kippis and Abraham Rees had a reputation for Arminianism and worse, Kippis being a Socinian and Rees an Arian.[13] But Godwin claimed to have kept his stubborn Sandemanianism untouched, although he supplemented it 'with a creed upon materialism and immaterialism, liberty, and necessity, on which no subsequent improvement of my understanding has been able to produce any variation.'[14]

After a series of short pastorates in Independent churches Godwin finally seems to have lost his faith and ceased to practise any form of Christianity. Yet Middleton Murry commented 'Godwinism is secular Sandemanism [*sic*] and the much-derided perfectibility of man is no more and no less than the re-assertion is secular terms of the possibility of regeneration.'[15]

But Godwin kept his friends in the Church, and when his daughter Mary in her teens contracted an infection in an arm, sometimes specified as eczema,[16] she was sent first to Ramsgate and then in May 1814 to the family of William Thomas Baxter at 'The Cottage' on South Baffin Street, on the outskirts of Dundee. Baxter was the third son of Thomas Baxter, and a great-grandson of the John Baxter who left Tealing with John Glas in the earliest days of the church.[17] He had met Godwin in London in 1801, and his son-in-law David Booth,[18] brewer, schoolmaster and lexicographer, a quite remarkable man who lived at the time in the little weaving town of Newburgh, where Glasites, Bereans, Scotch Baptists and others found a home, also influenced Mary. Booth had been corresponding with Godwin since 1802. Godwin hoped to stimulate Mary's interest in politics, as

13. One who denied that Christ was equal to God the Father.

14. ODNB, "William Godwin."

15. Middleton Murry, *Heaven—and Earth*, 261.

16. Mary Shelley's recent biographers note the Glasite episode, with varying degrees of puzzlement! Seymour, *Mary Shelley*, 73–86; Gordon, *Romantic Outlaws*, 49–60; and Sampson, *In Search of Mary Shelley*, 66–70.

17. MS 318/4/1, Rorie, *Baxter Genealogy*.

18. Conolly, *Eminent Men of Fife*, 70. Both DNB and ODNB add little to Conolly's account, which lists his numerous publications, except the claim that Booth was only five feet tall.

Dundee had been in the 1790's a nerve-centre for radical discussion and both Baxter and Booth were still, in 1812, stout Jacobins.[19] Isabella Baxter, Mary's favorite among the Baxter daughters, knew the events of the French Revolution so well that 'she almost seemed to inhabit the past.' But there were other influences in Dundee. Ghost stories, and tales brought back by fishermen and whalers may well have had their part in her famous story of Frankenstein. Victor Frankenstein travelled north via Cupar, St Andrews and the Tay shore on his way to Orkney.[20] It certainly seems possible that a stay in a Glasite household in Dundee had some part in the imagining of that remarkable story.

Mary stayed in Dundee for less than a year, and with Isabella visited Booth in Newburgh. In 1814 Booth visited London, probably to see Godwin and possibly to ask permission to marry Mary. This is speculation, as there is doubt about the precise date of the death of Booth's wife Margaret, but if that was the case his suit was rejected and instead he married Isabella. To marry one's deceased wife's sister was not allowed by church law in Scotland at that time and certainly was deemed wrong by the Glasites, who excommunicated both Booth and Baxter.[21] The later history of Mary and Isabella is scarcely relevant to our story but can be found in Miranda Seymour's biography of Mary Shelley. The ODNB entry for David Booth asserts that as an elderly man he was a sceptic.[22]

William Archer

Archer (1856–1924) was a leading theatre critic in London for many years. He was a friend of George Bernard Shaw, A. A .Milne, Edmund Gosse, and other authors and playwrights and is often referred to in their biographies as a wise and confident guide. He was one of those responsible for bringing the works of Ibsen to Britain. He came from a rather unlikely background. His grandfather owned a firm of timber merchants which went bankrupt in 1823. He moved to Norway, and his sons emigrated to Australia and California, where Thomas became a sheep farmer. Later Thomas also moved to Australia and then when his wife Grace Morison became unwell he returned to Perth and took rooms above a shop in the High Street. The Archer family

19. Seymour, *Mary Shelley*, 74. This is an unusual stance for the usually conservative and royalist Glasites. It may indicate a greater diversity in political thought than we would expect.

20. Shelley, *Frankenstein*, chapter 19.

21. Seymour, *Mary Shelley*, 85.

22. ODNB, "David Booth."

were followers of John Walker the Separatist,[23] and Grace was the daughter of James Morison of the publishing and printing firm J. and R. Morison, for generations faithful members and leaders of the Perth Glasite church. 'The Glasites', writes his biographer, 'were Sabbatarians and the Walkerites argued that every day was equal in holiness.'[24] In Norway the Archers had held worship in their own home, and in Perth they attended the Glasite church where Thomas was willing to conform to that church. His wife, according to an earlier biographer,

> though not a professing member of the Glasite Church, held Glasite views and conformed to their observances; while Thomas Archer was in general sympathy with the very similar views of the Walkerite or Separatist Church to which most of his brothers and sisters belonged.[25]

When William was a student at the University of Edinburgh he was expected to keep up attending both the Glasite meeting house and private family meetings.

> Their meticulous devotion to these observances instilled in him a fierce hostility towards religion and religious practice which he never lost. It became a vital component of a view of the world in which everything was subject to the test of reason.

He is said to have trained himself to sleep with a finger in the Bible, and wake up at the end of the sermon, and he carried this trick over into dull theatrical performances.[26] The entry in ODNB is a little unfair on the Glasites when it claims they were anti-theatre!

The Buchanan Family

David Buchanan, whose preaching so disturbed the Perth elders who had visited Montrose, precipitating the 'Perth schism', was born in Montrose in 1745, and, intending to enter the ministry of the Established Church, he graduated M.A. in Aberdeen. He was reputed to be an accomplished classical scholar. He joined the Glasite Church in Montrose and became an enterprising publisher. He produced editions of Johnson's *Dictionary* and other important works. He also published in 1790 works by William

---

23. Whitebrook, *William Archer, a Biography*, 35.
24. Whitebrook, *William Archer, a Biography*, 36.
25. Archer, *William Archer, Life, Work*, 85.
26. Archer, *William Archer, Life, Work*, 87.

and Alexander Christie, members of a distinguished Montrose family, who founded the first Unitarian Church in Scotland.[27] He had three sons, the eldest of whom, William (1781–1863,) studied law in Edinburgh and was called to the Bar in 1806, where he had a notable career, becoming Queen's Advocate and Solicitor of Teinds, or Tithes, on which subject he was the acknowledged expert. He married Elizabeth, daughter of Rev James Gregory of Banchory, and after his father's death he turned his thoughts to religion, becoming an elder of the Edinburgh Glasite church in 1823 and serving until his death. An obituarist remarked:

> There was nothing to be gained in a worldly point of view by being associated with a small sect, while there was a good deal to be lost from the ridicule and distrust that follows strong religious convictions on trivial matters, that the majority of mankind reckon matters of utter indifference. He sought no personal advantages from political connections, and for many years he had ceased to take any interest in party struggles.[28]

He was a friend and correspondent of Faraday.

Some Eminent Dundonians

Dr James Crichton

The obituary of Dr James Crichton marks the life of a distinguished member of the Dundee Church. He was born in 1772, presumably into a Glasite family, and when a medical student aged eighteen he married the nineteen-year-old Elizabeth Gorrell Baxter, sister of that most prosperous Baxter, William of Ellangowan. 'I married the object of my desire whilst still a stripling—considered by my friends an act of extreme folly.' But early marriages were encouraged in Glasite circles. The couple had eight children. Dr Crichton pioneered operations for the removal of the stone, and he is described as a lithotomist. He was a Town Councilor in Dundee, and 'in religion a Dissenter, he remained during his long life, (he died in 1860) faithful to the principles of the Glassite communion.' His faith is summed up in a way that illuminates the simple but powerful creed of the Glasites, 'he put his trust in the GREAT ATONEMENT that had been made for the chief of sinners and

---

27. Short, "William Christie and the First Unitarian Church," 26n26.
28. Obituary of William Buchanan. MS 9/4/2, 55.

strong in faith and strong in hope he trusted that the divine mercy would be extended to him, not as a profitable servant but as a pardoned sinner.'[29]

Dr James Rorie

Dr James Rorie (1838–1911) was for many years the Superintendent of the Royal Dundee Lunatic Asylum, and author of its *History*, published post-humously in 1912. He was an indefatigable collector of Glasite letters and other documents and much of the *Archive* in Dundee University was gath-ered by him. He was a genealogist, detailing the Baxter family, a diarist who noted the weather in Dundee from day to day, a Bible student, compiling in 1864 *Notes on the New Testament*, in which he examined, for example, Matt 26 verses 45 and 46, comparing translations in Latin, Greek, German, and French, concluding that there is difficulty in reconciling the two verses. He wrote also *On the Sinfulness of Eating Blood*,[30] and remarked, while asserting his agreement with the general Glasite teaching, that

> what is known as science must be carefully excluded—unaided human reason always leads to results directly opposed to the Word of God e.g. geology shows the world was not created in six days, human philosophy shows that man was not made in God's image. We must endeavour to interpret scripture by scripture.[31]

In 1885 Rorie sought to act as a peacemaker in the blood-eating dispute.

> Divisions have arisen from overzealous endeavour to secure oneness of mind and of judgement on matters however large and important they might seem during the excitement and heat of controversy, are but small when compared with the great truths concerning salvation as revealed in the Divine Word. . .The original principles were laid down in Glas's *Works*, not that I attach any importance to J. G's exposition beyond the fact that his views have always seemed to me of all others most in accordance with revealed truth.[32]

He referred to a dispute in 1820 about blood-eating, which was less noticed because of a contemporary difference on the subject of baptism.[33]

29. Obituary of James Crichton MS 9/4/2, 30.
30. MS 318/4/1.
31. MS 318/4/1.
32. MS 9/4/1, 28.
33. MS 9/4/1, 105.

Rorie's questioning mind eventually led him to secede, on 8 September, 1885, in a letter to the Dundee elder Charles Philip. Along with Dr Miller and a few others, he allied himself with the marginally more liberal Church in Edinburgh.[34]

Daniel Macintosh

Daniel Macintosh came from Atholl on the edge of the Highlands to Perth in 1788 and to Dundee in 1793. He was a student in Haldane's Seminary in that city from 1802–1805 but left the 'New Independents' in 1807 and opened a school. He had been married by Haldane's associate, William Innes, in 1802 and had a large family. He joined the Glasite church and from 1807 was an elder for a few years, left the church and returned a year later as a private member. 'He was a beautiful reader in the assemblies of the Word of God.' In 1851 he edited *Letters in Correspondence* and died in 1860.[35]

The Baxter Family

John Baxter,[36] a handloom weaver, left Tealing with John Glas, and his eldest son, also John, is described in the lists as Manufacturer. One of the latter's sons, William, always designated as of Ellangowan, the name of his house, founded the firm of Baxter Brothers in 1822, having made a fortune supplying sailcloth to the Royal Navy during the Napoleonic Wars. He married Elizabeth Gorrell, presumably a relative of the Gorrells of Newby near Allen's church in Gayle. His daughter Mary Ann died in 1884. She was a member of Panmure Street Congregational Church, and was very generous to smaller churches, provided they did not use bazaars as a fund-raising method.[37] She gave endowments to the Congregational College, and in her will left money to it and the London Missionary Society, amongst other good causes. She was also the largest donor at the foundation of Dundee University College, at that time part of St Andrews University, and she is commemorated in a window in St Salvator's Residence in St Andrews along with the medieval bishops who founded the other colleges. In the next generation William's son David was awarded a baronetcy in 1863 and gave

---

34. MS 9/4/1, 41.

35. MS 9/4/2.

36. Gauldie, *Dundee Textile Industry*, xvi.

37. McNaughton, *Early Congregational Independency*, 1:167.

'munificent gifts' to his native city, including Baxter Park.[38] Mary Godwin's host was a son of John Baxter the second. Baxters continued in the churches until almost the end.

Henry James Senior

Henry James senior, father of the psychologist William James and the novelist Henry James, was a correspondent of Faraday in the late 1830s.[39] According to his biographer Austin Warren,

> what Henry James saw and experienced during this sojourn in England we do not know, no record remains but its intellectual consequence—the espousal of the Sandemanian Gospel. Mr Robert Sandeman, 'that respectable sectary,' had died at the Connecticut village of Danbury more than 60 years before, but his sect continued in existence; and among them Mr James found an adumbration of views which were beginning to take shape in his own mind. He desired to return to the simplicity of the early church, to put brotherly love and the fellowship of believers before doctrinal quibbles and dogmatic professions, and the 'Christian Socialism' he perceived among the Sandemanians attracted him as did their view of faith as belief, and their insistence that the Deity had no respect of persons.[40]

So much was James impressed that he published an edition of Sandeman's *Letters* in 1838. But the 'espousal' did not last for long and James thereafter pursued the teachings of Swedenborg.[41]

James Tytler

James Tytler (1745–1804) was the fourth child of George Tytler, minister of Fern in Angus, a well-connected upholder of patronage in the Church.[42] James studied both at Aberdeen and Edinburgh, possibly for the church, but his first employment was as surgeon on a whaling ship. He discovered a talent for writing and summarizing, and his greatest achievement was to write most of the second edition of the *Encyclopaedia Britannica* in 1776.

38. MS 318/4/1. Rorie, *Baxter Genealogy*.
39. Faraday, *Correspondence*, letter 1112, 9 October 1838, 2:521–22.
40. Warren, *Elder Henry James*, 34.
41. Emanuel Swedenborg (1688–1772), scientist and speculative philosopher.
42. Whitley, *Great Grievance*, 225n13.

He attended the Glasite Church in Edinburgh, and married Elizabeth, the orphan daughter of James Rattray, a solicitor according to ODNB, which suggests he left the church after he and his wife had parted.[43] He set up an apothecary's business in Leith which was patronized by the Glasite members, but he gradually moved in his religious thinking to a form of Deism and was never again connected to any particular church, although he published, on his own printing press and while he was in the debtors' sanctuary at Holyrood in 1774, a polemical essay aimed at John Barclay, the leader of the Berean church.

In 1784 he made the first balloon flight in Britain, but others such as Vincent Lunardi were more successful, and Tytler lived by journalistic hack work, one article of which led to his arrest for sedition in 1789, a year in which the government was especially nervous about possible insurrection.[44] He emigrated to Salem, Massachusetts, and died there in 1795. He may be typical of persons with enquiring minds who were influenced for a time by the seemingly radical tenets and the sociable nature of the Glasite faith.

Charles Ives

The American composer and insurance executive was born into a Congregationalist family in Danbury, Connecticut, in 1874. He was a great-great-grandson on his mother's side of Ebenezer White, the Congregationalist minister who welcomed Robert Sandeman on his arrival in America. It has been claimed that his thinking on congregational freedom and unanimity showed the influence of Sandemanianism. James McClendon, the Baptist theologian, also writes of Ives' views on the limitation of wealth and income. While McClendon does not cite Sandemanian influence, the subject of wealth and its limitation certainly was raised amongst the early Sandemanians of Danbury.[45]

Sandemanians in Fiction

I have found two references to Sandemanians in nineteenth-century fiction. Edward Everett Hale (1822–1909) was a Harvard trained Unitarian minister for many years pastor of the second Congregational Church in

---

43. ODNB, "James Tytler."

44. For Tytler, see Fergusson, *Balloon Tytler*.

45. Baron, "Efforts on Behalf of Democracy"; and McClendon, *Biography as Theology*, 152–56.

Boston, and Chaplain to the U.S. Senate from 1903–1909. He wrote many imaginative stories mainly based in New England, with occasional references to Sandemanians. 'The Ingham Papers, some memorials of the life of Capt. Frederic Ingham, U.S.N., sometime pastor of the First Sandemanian Church, Nagandavic,' was published in Boston in 1869, and, in a mixture of 'fun, fact and fantasy', mentions his ministry, but gives no details. Hale obviously knew of the Church but uses its name almost as a joke. Ian Maclaren, the pen name of Rev John Watson, a Scottish minister in Sefton Park, a Presbyterian Church in Liverpool, and a well-known writer of the 'Kailyard' School of sentimental stories, remarks in his story *Afterwards*, published in 1898, that Sandeman 'sold port and invented a new church.'

Michael Faraday

Undoubtedly the most well-known Sandemanian is Michael Faraday, the scientist and teacher, who served as member, deacon, and elder in the London Church, and who exercised a ministry of reconciliation and exhortation in several of the churches in England and Scotland. He has been fortunate in his biographers, of whom there are many, and he has been particularly well served by Geoffrey Cantor, whose study, *Michael Faraday, Sandemanian and Scientist* is an outstanding presentation, not only of both aspects of Faraday, but of the Sandemanian movement and of the London Church in particular. Gerard Sandeman confided to me that 'Dr Cantor has almost got us right,' which was high praise indeed. Most of this account derives from Cantor's book and articles.

   Michael Faraday was born in London on 22 September 1791 to James and Margaret Faraday, whose roots were in that part of northwest England where religious nonconformity was strong, and where Benjamin Ingham and James Allen had evangelized and built up small churches. Faraday's grandparents had been Inghamites but had followed Allen's leadership and worshipped in Edward Gorrell's Sandemanian Chapel at Clapham Wood. They moved to Kirkby Stephen where there was another Sandemanian church, and from there to London. There James Faraday was employed as a blacksmith by James Boyd, a Sandemanian from Dundee. James joined the London Church, then meeting in Paul's Alley, Barbican. Although Margaret did not become a member of the church, she and her children attended even after James died in 1810.[46]

   In 1821 Faraday married Sarah Barnard, daughter of Edward Barnard, silversmith and elder. He was a great-nephew of John Barnard, who had

46. Cantor, *Faraday*, 59.

left the Independent ministry to become a Sandemanian in the early days of the London Church. On her mother's side she was descended from the Boosey family, another leading Sandemanian family. Sarah had made her confession of faith two years earlier. Having satisfactorily responded to the questions of the elders, and after the unanimous vote of the members, Michael was admitted to the Church on 15 July 1821, saluted with a holy kiss and received a hearty welcome into the fellowship. On 1 July 1832 he was appointed a deacon undertaking to visit the sick and care for the functioning of the Meeting House, and in October 1840 he was ordained an elder. On 28 October he wrote to William Buchanan, the Edinburgh elder:

> I doubted not that it was of the Lord's doing but my utter unworthingness [sic] and unfitness made me tremble with the fear of its being to the increase of condemnation at that Day when God would judge all men by Jesus Christ, for I thought of what he said to Pharaoh 'for this cause I have raised thee up that I might show forth my power in thee' (Romans 9:17). But the love of the brethren and their consolations and above all I hope the power of God has removed much of this trouble. . . . I feel greatly like a hypocrite in all I say or do.[47]

Sandemanian teaching about the continuing unworthiness even of the elect must have contributed to this ambivalent feeling and the lack of assurance, modified by the trust that he knew was placed in him.

On 31 March 1844 Faraday was excluded from the Church. The reason given by some of his earlier biographers was that he had accepted an invitation to visit the Queen on a Sunday. This would have presented a difficult choice for Faraday as he was both a loyal citizen who would wish to obey his sovereign, and a Sandemanian elder who, with all his fellow members, was expected to attend the Sunday services. In John Gladstone's *Biography*, published in 1872, it was claimed that he defended himself, and thus put himself outside the fold. Cantor has examined the evidence closely and has not been able to find any corroboration of this story.[48] Moreover, the record shows that eighteen other members were excluded on the same day, about 20 percent of the membership. This seems to have been a difficult time for the churches. A letter from George Baxter, one of the Dundee elders at the time notes that the churches in Britain and America

> have been visited by terrible things in righteousness. The Head of the Church appearing among them as the Lord of the

47. Faraday, *Correspondence*, letter 1321, 28 October 1840, 2:704–5.
48. Cantor, "Why Was Faraday Excluded," 433–37.

conscience searching his Jerusalem with candles and punishing the men settled on their lees (Zephaniah 1 verse 12). His chastening hand has been heavy upon you and us.[49]

The point at issue seems to have been the question that troubled the churches very frequently: could the elders make decisions for the fellowship by themselves, or did they need the concurrence of all the members? This seems a more likely reason for the exclusion, which left Faraday low in health and spirits. He was restored on 5 May 1844 as a member but not until 1860 as an elder, and he demitted that office voluntarily in 5 June 1864.[50]

Sandemanians were not proselytizers, and referred enquirers to their published works, but Faraday's attachment to the Church was known. Herbert Mayo (1796–1852) the neurologist, wrote to him in March 1840:

> I return your book with many thanks and not without admiration of the fine Christian spirit that breathes in the strictness of internal discipline and judicious forbearance towards others of the body to which you have bound yourself. I shall avail myself of the permission, without offence, which I consider your note to convey to me- to visit your place of worship.[51]

Several years later in August 1854, John Barlow, Secretary of the Royal Institution, wrote in a rather different vein.

> In England nothing would induce me to associate with what is called an 'Evangelical Clergyman' or with anyone else who made a parade of religion, because I never knew any such who was not at heart an infidel, a debauchee, or a rogue or at best a tool of one of those characters. Now this does not seem to be the same in Roman Catholic countries. The discipline of the confessional must restrain breaches of the moral law. Your connection does the same thing by different machinery. Therefore, I am always disposed to think well of and to confide in a member of it.... Mrs Faraday said that 'I should find your form of worship ridiculous'. Now I cannot imagine anything less possible to deride than the simplicity and earnestness of your ritual and I am sure that must pervade the daily life of those who are exercised by it.

---

49. Quoted in Cantor, *Faraday*, 63.
50. Cantor, *Faraday*, 279.
51. Faraday, *Correspondence*, letter 1250, 10 March 1840, 2:640.

Faraday replied a few days later, 'I must pass by your observations on religion.'[52] Rev John Barlow was not only Secretary of the Royal Institution but also sometime Chaplain-in-Ordinary to Kensington House.

Despite his undoubted position of fame and influence in the scientific community and the wider world, Faraday remained devoted to his church, visiting Edinburgh and Dundee, preaching exhortations which have been carefully preserved and having a special care for the little community at Old Buckenham. His unwavering faithfulness, despite times of mental and spiritual anguish and fear of a second excommunication, is a testimony to the most attractive elements of the Sandemanian faith. Michael Faraday was a scientist and a Christian,[53] and while he was reticent about the effect of his faith on his scientific work, he could draw

> an absolute distinction between religious and ordinary belief, and argued in an address at the Royal Institution in the presence of the Prince Consort, that what we can know from religious faith is not incompatible with what we know from reason. He quoted Romans 1, verse 20, 'for the invisible things of him from the creation of the world are clearly seen, being understood by the things that are made, even his eternal power and Godhead,' and argued 'I have never seen anything incompatible between those things of man which can be known by the spirit of man, and those higher things concerning his future, which he cannot know by that spirit.[54]

For him the Book of Nature could not be in conflict with the book of Revelation.

Cantor mentions many Sandemanians who worked at the Royal Institution. Benjamin Vincent, who made his confession in 1832, and was subsequently deacon and elder of the London Church, was made assistant secretary in 1848 on Faraday's recommendation and later in the same year also librarian of the Institution. In 1887 he produced a *Dictionary of Biography*, and, a very Sandemanian task, compiled an index of people, places, and subjects cited in the Bible. In 1858 John Handasyde Buchanan, bearer of two distinguished Sandemanian names, was made assistant librarian. Many Sandemanians worked in the book trade, in Perth as well as London. The

52. Faraday, *Correspondence*, letter 2839, 22 August 1854, 4:762.

53. Latourette's suggestion that the 'staunch individualism bred in that group (the Sandemanians) presumably made no small contribution to his attainments' must be balanced by the great desire for unanimity in all things that was so strong in the church. Latourette, *History of the Expansion*, 4:169.

54. Cantor, "Reading the Book of Nature," 71.

printers and publishers Morisons of Perth were in the church for many generations and Baxters, Leightons and Barnards bound and repaired books for the Royal Institution.[55] Cantor also mentions some Sandemanian scientists, such as Samuel Pike, whose writings include *Philosophia Sacra*, an exposition of Hutchinson's natural philosophy, Dr John Crichton, John James Waterston, whose scientific papers were at first ignored and then seen as important researches into the kinetic theory of gases and Alexander Tilloch[56] who edited the *Philosophical Magazine* and whose theological writings were acceptable to the Sandemanians. He was an elder of the Old Scots Independents[57] in London.

Several years ago I was invited by Very Rev Robin Barbour, ex-Moderator of the General Assembly of the Church of Scotland, and well-known New Testament scholar, to his home at Fincastle near Pitlochry, to see the portrait of Glas Sandeman. He was the sixth child of David George Sandeman of Perth, was born in 1793 and died in France in 1855. He married Margaret Stewart of Bonskeid, and their only daughter, Margaret Fraser Sandeman, born in 1823, married George Freeland Barbour, 1810–1887, great-grandfather of Robin Barbour, who contributed a preface to Dr Waterston's book, *Perth Entrepreneurs*. Such are the wonders of genealogy, that Dr Waterston could claim Robin Barbour as his eighth cousin! There are no doubt other gems to be found in the *Sandeman Genealogy*, edited by Gerard Sandeman, not least the interpretation of the Sandeman coat of arms.[58]

---

55. Cantor, *Faraday*, 75–79. John Saumarez Smith edited letters between some who owned and worked in the fashionable West End bookshop in Curzon Street and includes many from and about Handasyde Buchanan, who at one point claimed that two of his five times great-grandfathers were Scots booksellers. This was in the 1970s. Saumarez Smith, *Spy in the Bookshop*, 164.

56. Cantor, *Faraday*, appendix 3, 303–4.

57. McGavin et al., *Historical Sketches of the Rise*, 41–42. The ODNB article gives fascinating detail of Tilloch's life and work but mistakenly claims that he was a Sandemanian, 'like Faraday.'

58. This coat of arms, registered in 1780, is illustrated in Cantor, *Faraday*, 44–45, and has references to Sandemanian theology.

7

America

THE STORY OF THE Sandemanians in New England has been very well re-
counted in several publications[1] and the following will only be an outline of
the story. The Sandemanian Church pointed enquirers to the printed word
or to personal correspondence, and in Britain did not seek converts in the
public square. It was the model of a non-aggressive Christian body. In Faraday's *Correspondence* he only reluctantly refers to his faith and his church.
Yet, on 10 August 1764, Robert Sandeman, having received invitations from
Ministers who had read and approved his *Letters* and being encouraged by
his father-in-law, set off from Scotland aboard the new ship 'George' with
James Cargill and his nephew George and arrived safely in New England,
probably in Boston, after a voyage of seven weeks.[2] Within the week that
he arrived Sandeman preached three times at the Green Dragon Tavern in
Boston.[3] This was a new departure for the church and Sandeman set out to
reach as many people as he could by preaching wherever he was allowed,
as an eighteenth-century itinerant minister. The ground had been prepared
by the reading of his *Letters* and his *Correspondence with Pike*, and his work
included visiting some who were sympathetic to his teaching and accepting
the hospitality of New England ministers.

There was nothing unusual about books crossing the Atlantic. From
the seventeenth century onwards there was much correspondence between
ministers in Scotland and those in New England, and each group influenced

---

1. Such as Walker, *Sandemanians of New England*, 133–62; Hankins, "Different
Kind of Loyalist," 223–49; and Smith, *Perfect Rule of the Christian Religion*, 92–182.

2. Macintosh, *Letters in Correspondence*, 80.

3. Stiles MSS, 340, fol.4, cited in Stanley, "Glassite-Sandemanian Movement," 136.

the other. Wodrow exchanged news with the Mathers and later the writings of Jonathan Edwards were influential in the Evangelical revival in Britain. It is not surprising that Sandeman's writings became known, especially as some of his followers were already in New England when he arrived. A great new opportunity seemed to have opened for him in a new world.

After preaching in Boston Sandeman set off for a quite extensive tour, beginning in Portsmouth, New Hampshire, where he preached in the pulpit of a Mr Bounds. In Newport he preached in a Baptist Sabbatarian Meeting where Ezra Stiles first met him and heard him preach. Stiles described Sandeman as 'of middling stature, dark complexion, a good eye, uses accurate language, but not eloquent in utterance, has not a melodious voice, his expressions governed by Sentiment, his Dialect Scotch, not graceful in his Air and Address, yet has something that deforces attention.'[4] He shared a meal with Stiles, where the discussion of his theology led Stiles to say that White, one of those who invited Sandeman to America, and his followers very much agreed in doctrinal sentiments but was hesitant about 'your new church polity.' Sandeman turned to James Cargill and said, 'we shall soon know when we come to converse with them.'[5] Sandeman and Cargill then travelled to Danbury, Connecticut, joined by Andrew Oliphant, a Glasite from Scotland, who had been in the Colonies for some time, and who had not found a church to suit his views. In Danbury they were kindly received by White, and Sandeman preached both in White's Church and in a few others for two months. However Stiles's thoughts proved prophetic. White and his people did not accept his practices and Sandeman wrote to them that he must leave.[6] He was equally unsuccessful in neighboring Newtown, where despite some agreement, the people were unwilling to give up Watts and Doddridge nor would they join in anathematizing the whole Christian world except the Sandemanian churches.

On 2 August 1765 the *New Hampshire Gazette* announced that on 28 July, in Portsmouth, Mr Robert Sandeman for the first time performed services in the newly edifice lately erected in Divinity Street (so called) by a number of well-wishers to the gospel. Lecturing on Tuesday and Thursday evenings at 6 o'clock will be constantly attended. A list of the Portsmouth Church made a year later on 4 May 1766 shows twenty-seven members, eighteen men and nine women, with three elders, Sandeman, Cargill and

4. Stiles, *Memoirs of Robert Sandeman*, 34, cited in McMillon, *Restoration Roots*, 52.

5. Stiles MSS 340, fols. 29–30, cited in Stanley, "Glassite-Sandemanian Movement," 138.

6. Macintosh, *Letters in Correspondence*, 97.

Oliphant, and two other British Sandemanians, David and Ann Mitchelson.[7] Also among the members were the merchants Nathanael Barrell and his brother Colburn, later to be correspondents of Sandeman and leaders in the churches. Danbury became the main and longest lasting of the American churches and did not die out until the beginning of the twentieth century.

The *Correspondence* between Robert Sandeman and Nathaniel Barrell gives a flavor of the early days of the church in New England. In May 1766 Sandeman in a letter to Nathaniel Barrell shows his impatience with those who listen but are unable to accept his doctrine and practice.

> I have got many entreaties to preach but have declined hearkening to any. I see no business I have to preach to people who disregard the appearance of God's Kingdom in the churches. If they will not regard the light that shines to best advantage from its proper candlestick let them stand to their hazard and follies any sort of clergy they wish.

He goes on to say that while in Boston he has received letters from Mr Pike and Mr Chater, suggesting that the doctrine and appearance of Christ's heavenly kingdom are making great inroads on the anti-Christian kingdom. 'I close all my salutations with a double buss to my special friend Queen Esther and my young fellow sufferer Sally deputing you to convey the same in the heartiest manner.'[8] In these last remarks we see a kinder, even flirtatious Sandeman, and get a glimpse of his attractiveness, that belies his sometimes angular and combative manner. In June 1766 he wrote to Nathaniel's brother Colburn 'not forgetting my jolly young friend Nancy,' but also about a new convert, Ben Cozier, who has asserted that he believes he has been freed by Christ from the obligation to obey God's laws, 'which roused me a good deal.' Antinomianism is always lying in wait for High Calvinists. In October of the same year, alluding to the mild persecution suffered by the new converts he wrote an affectionate letter to Nathaniel:

> Neither you nor Colburn have yet been confined to your lodgings two whole years as Paul was, and none of you has yet been honoured to wear a chain by way of a bracelet around his arm. Have patience, you know not what further degrees of promotion are yet awaiting you.[9]

In January 1767 Sandeman wrote to Nathaniel Barrell apologizing for a letter that

7. Macintosh, *Letters in Correspondence*, 99.

8. Robert Sandeman to Nathanael Barrell, 23 May 1766, *Sandeman-Barrell Papers*.

9. Robert Sandeman to Nathanael Barrell, 23 May 1766, *Sandeman-Barrell Papers*.

did not flow from a Christian temper, but from selfish resentment caused by unexpected reflections on my conduct. I take this opportunity to retract the bitterness of that letter. I have read your 15 discourses and am charmed with a rich vein of excellent doctrine running through them, but you are too hard on the clergy.

This is a different aspect of Sandeman who does not usually apologize for harshness, least of all about the clergy! In the same month he wrote again to Barrell to tell of receiving into the Church Mrs Stainer, a poor widow with half a dozen children. 'She has been much depressed by the influence of self-righteous doctrine and confessed the truth like a captive set at liberty.'[10]

Later letters from Sandeman to Colburn Barrell are published in *Letters in Correspondence*. He gives his advice when Barrell is 'closely beset by wicked and unreasonable men.' As in his advice earlier to Nathaniel Sandeman exhorts Colburn, 'I am fully of the mind that your truest wisdom lies in remaining as silent and quiet as possible and, as Peter speaks, to "seek peace and ensue it"'. Colburn had been attacked and provoked by a writer with the pseudonym 'Protestant' who represented those who were opposed to the Stamp Act. To both the brothers Sandeman's counsel was to restrain their righteous anger and suffer as good soldiers of Jesus Christ.[11] This quietist attitude was designed to protect the little churches from reprisals by the 'Patriots' as they were caught up in the crosscurrents of political life in these uncertain days. Sandeman himself with his nephew Bob, living in Danbury at the hospitable home of Asa Church, a blacksmith, found himself in trouble in 1770. Church was fined forty pounds 'for keeping Bob and me in his house for a fortnight.' Church appealed and Sandeman appeared before Mr Justice Benedict and defended himself 'as a harmless stranger.' In his defense he spoke of the protection 'afforded in Britain to dissenting preachers of all sorts, whether strangers in the place or not.'[12] The sentence was not carried out, but the affair demonstrates the dangers the Sandemanians ran. After Sandeman's death on 2 April 1771, the Sandemanians lacked a leader, yet they continued to meet in Boston, Danbury, and several other places. The epitaph on his tomb in Danbury must be quoted:

> Here lies until the resurrection the body of ROBERT SANDE-MAN, a native of Perth North Britain who in the face of continual opposition from all sorts of men long and boldly contended for the ancient faith; that the bare Work of Jesus Christ, without

10. Robert Sandeman to Nathanael Barrell, 23 May 1766, *Sandeman-Barrell Papers*.

11. Macintosh, *Letters in Correspondence*, 106–7.

12. McMillon, *Restoration Roots*, 57.

a thought or deed on the part of man is sufficient to present
the chief of sinners spotless before GOD; to declare this blessed
truth as testified in the Holy Scriptures he left his country- he
left his friends, and after much patient sufferings finished his
labors AT DANBURY, 2nd April 1771 aged 53 years.[13]

As in Britain, Sandeman's writing and preaching and the way of life of
his followers drew criticism and also some support. Among proponents of
his doctrines were several Yale graduates, Ebenezer White Sr and his sons
Ebenezer White Jr and Joseph Moss White. While a Sandemanian in several
facets of his theology White Sr never seems to have joined a Sandemanian
fellowship. In the disputes between Old Lights and New Lights amongst
the Congregational Churches of New England, there was space for new and
challenging ideas of the essence of the church and indeed of the Christian
faith. Sandeman's teaching on faith, his doctrine of the independence of the
local church and his insistence of what he saw as a primitive church order
led some, including the Whites, away from the orthodoxy they had previously professed. In 1764, just before Sandeman's arrival in Boston, Ebenezer
White Sr was dismissed from his pastorate in Danbury. It was from those
who left the First Church with him that the longest lasting Sandemanian
church in New England was gathered. Titus Smith and Theophilus Chamberlain had been set aside by the so-called 'Scotch Society,' the Society in
Scotland for Propagating Christian Knowledge, for missionary work among
native Americans in 1765. Sometime in the early 1770s Smith converted
to Sandemanianism and was ordained an elder in Boston and sent to serve
the church in Newhaven. He signed a document stating that his religious
faith meant that he could not participate in revolutionary activities and
he had to move eventually to Halifax, Nova Scotia, where he died in 1807.
Chamberlain resigned his missionary post in 1767, visited New York where
he purchased a volume of Sandeman's writings and was convinced that his
work as a salaried minister was sinful. Like Smith he was ordained an elder
in Boston and then moved to Danbury, making his living as a clothing re-
tailer. Also, like Smith he eventually moved to Halifax, where he served as
a government administrator until his death in 1827. These were educated
men, of some social standing and they were not the only such people. There
were never more than 100 Sandemanians in New England, but many of
these were significant in their communities.

There were notable supporters, but there were many who saw the new
churches as a danger and a challenge. There is not space here to look at
many in detail, but some must be mentioned. Samuel Langdon (1723–1797)

13. McMillon, *Restoration Roots*, 58.

was pastor of the First Church in Portsmouth, New Hampshire and he published in 1769 *An Impartial Examination of Robert Sandeman's Letters on Theron and Aspasio.* He wrote:

> The Author of the Letters on Theron and Aspasio hath but the force of his genius, which is sprightly and satirical [*sic*] to ruin the credit of the most eminent divines of the last and present age and make a general attack on Christian professors of all denominations. If we believe him, the true faith of the apostles was very near if not entirely lost out of the world after the first generation of Christianity and hath never been recovered except among a very few enlightened individuals, until he himself, with the assistance of a near friend, was so happy as to hit upon it again and begin the glorious work of reformation.

For Langdon it is the harsh language and high claims to originality at least in his own times that are attacked at some length, and his doctrine of faith that is disputed.

Isaac Backus, a notable Separate Baptist writer and theologian, who was at the time of his book living in Middleborough, wrote *True Faith Will Produce Good Works* published in Boston in 1767. It is a considered criticism of Sandeman, suggesting that his book has an Antinomian tendency.

> Since his writings have been a means of hardning [*sic*] many in iniquity and of entangling in perplexity some serious minds, I shall attempt to point out the pernicious principles which he has interspersed among many choice truths. It is readily granted that this writer has pointed out many dark strokes in the writings of our most noted divines; and if he could clear off all their mistakes he should be as welcome thereto, as any crow could be to take all the carrion out of our pleasant fields.

This is damning with faint praise indeed for to Backus Sandeman was a real threat. He believed that the minds of those who listened to Sandeman had been corrupted by his 'artful presentations that it is pharisaical pride for any to tell of inward experience, and to rejoice in what God has done for them.' Backus also objected to various facets of Sandemanian church order, notably the insistence on unanimity and such practices as foot-washing and the kiss of charity which he saw as merely peripheral to the Christian Faith. He also accused Sandeman of intellectual dishonesty, 'he is so honest that he exerts all his wit to expose the nakedness of protestant fathers, but adopts their good observations, while he conceals their names that they may pass as his own.'[14]

Another writer who criticized the customs of the church was Samuel Mather (1706–1785) of a distinguished clerical family, who published in 1768 *A modest account concerning the salutations and kissing in ancient times in a letter to a friend requesting the same, wherein Mr Sandeman's attempt to revive the holy and charitable kiss and the love feast is countered.* Mather considers the words for kiss or salutation in Hebrew, Greek and Latin showing that in the ancient world there were various forms of salutation, such as embracing, giving the right hand, and sometimes among the Jews with a kiss. Kissing, he considered, was practiced by the Persians and the Romans 'promiscuously' with good or bad sorts of people. He says that kisses in the Scripture were 'not with the mouth kissing the lips of another; which has become the custom in later ages; it is supposed Mr Sandeman and his more knowing disciples practise this.'[15] 'We are particularly to conform ourselves to the innocent custom of our own time and country, taking care to abstain from even the appearance of evil.' He also points out that there is no example in scripture of men kissing women. If it existed in the early church the custom died out 'from the prostitution of it.' Love Feasts were also open to abuse. He quotes Beza, 'whoever will now urge for this practice (i.e., Kissing) in Christian assemblies is not only foolish, but will also labour under suspicion of some base crime.'[16]

The churches in New England, never strong, gradually shrank and died out, as did the church in Halifax, Nova Scotia, whose most prominent member was John Howe, (1754–1835) loyalist printer in Boston, who migrated to Halifax during the War of Independence, becoming a magistrate of that city and continuing in the family faith, serving as an elder until his death. Stayner refers to the Sandemanians as a devout group of dignified business men.[17]

They were not forgotten in Britain, and regular correspondence and some visits were maintained for many years. We have seen how Nathaniel Bishop and his wife toured Scotland and England and made contact with almost all their co-religionists. James Rorie corresponded with Mrs Baldwin, in Danbury, and Archibald Sandeman in Glasgow was receiving news of members of the Bishop family right up to the end of the nineteenth century. The Sandemanians in New England were fiercely loyal to the British Crown

14. Backus, *True Faith Will Produce Good Works*, 9–10.

15. Mather, *Modest Account*, 12.

16. Mather, *Modest Account*, 18.

17. Stayner, "Sandemanian Loyalists," 62–123.

and suffered accordingly. In the turmoil both in the state and the churches they were able to gather a few thoughtful folk and their tenacity was quite remarkable. Mr Knapp of Danbury, probably an elder, wrote to Dr Rorie in March 1886, 'the great Head of the Church has forsaken the churches by not keeping them of the same mind and walking by the same rule.'[18] Mrs Baldwin who was one of the last members in Danbury, in one of her letters to Dr Rorie, on 26 April 1886, remembers that she 'read the scriptures, and read Mr Glas, there was the letter but for a long time I failed to see and feel the spirit. I searched Robert Sandeman's *Discourses* and Gabriel Russell's[19] *Notes on the Revelation.*' She refers to the man who must have been the last elder in Danbury as very illiterate but teachable. Contact was maintained by occasional visits from Britain to Danbury. In his *Diary* for Sabbath 19 October 1890, Archibald Sandeman of the Glasgow Church records that 'Mrs Baxter has been at Danbury, met Mrs Baldwin, and enjoyed the company of the sisters.' The diarist was sent a narrative of Ezra Stiles of 'Sandeman's appearance and preaching during his visit to America, with views of the doctrine he taught'.[20]

18. MSS 9/4/1, 134.

19. A promising elder in Dundee who died, aged thirty-six, in 1795. Macintosh, *Letters in Correspondence*, 313.

20. MSS 364/1/1, 9.

8

A Story of Slow Decline

IN 1966 I WAS commissioned to prepare a *Centenary History of the Baptist Union of Scotland*, of which I am a minister, for the event in 1969.[1] It was then, as I read about the early days of Baptists in Scotland, that I really discovered the Glasites, although I had heard of them earlier. Archibald McLean, the leading writer and elder of the Scotch Baptists in the late eighteenth century, and his fellow elder Robert Carmichael, had briefly been members of the Glasgow Glasite church, and I was curious to discover more about the possible links between Glasites and Scotch Baptists. The hints of connections in earlier publications spurred me on to look more closely at the whole question of Glasite practice and theology and its expanding influence. Towards the end of the 1960s, when I was beginning to work on my PhD thesis, I ventured into the Meeting House of the 'Church of Christ, commonly known as Glasite or Sandemanian' in Barony Street, Edinburgh, and was welcomed in the cautious way that Glasites responded to strangers, since they were naturally shy of folk wanting to write about their quaintness rather than their deeply held beliefs and customs. When I was a student in Edinburgh in the 1950s I had met a member of the Waterston family. The university chaplain Dr David Read joined a group of us in the common room and asked us which church we belonged to. Sandy Waterston said, 'I'm a Sandemanian' which stopped the conversation for a few minutes. Later I heard from one of Sandy's schoolfellows, whose family were leading members of the Open Brethren, that Sandy would visit his home and watch from

---

1. Murray, *First Hundred Years*.

afar while the other boys played Monopoly.[2] The ban on games of chance still held. Sandy had also been impressed by Billy Graham's crusade in Glasgow and had tried to persuade his wealthy Glasite aunts to contribute, but in vain. I knew there were such people and over several years, culminating in an invitation to the last service in the Meeting House in 1989, I was able to visit the church a few times and to share in their services, although not in the Love Feast which was reserved to members, and I was invited and welcomed into the homes and libraries of the two last elders, William Ferguson and Gerard Sandeman.

The Edinburgh Meeting House, the last to survive, closed when the caretaker, who had a house within the premises, retired. Thereafter the few remaining members continued to meet in the home of Gerard Sandeman until shortly before his death in 1999 at the age of ninety. Here again I have a personal note. In 1959, just after I left home, my parents moved into a bungalow on the Braid Hills, a suburb of Edinburgh, two doors away from the Sandeman home. My father told me that the man in that house was an atheist. They had been at school together, a school at which boys who were too late for prayers joined with the few Jewish lads and the even fewer Roman Catholic pupils to hear the announcements after the religious rite was over. (It was the same when I attended that school a generation later.) Gerard Sandeman, brought up in a Glasite household, was not permitted to come to prayers with those of other churches, therefore my father concluded that he was an atheist. Sadly, two Edinburgh business men, each with a remarkable knowledge of the Scriptures and a deep devotion to their respective churches, were never able to acknowledge one another as believers.

At the beginning of the twentieth century there was a church in Perth, which had reconciled with Edinburgh in 1896, and which closed in 1926. Into the 1970s remnants of the church travelled by bus to Edinburgh for services. Barony Street is conveniently near the bus station. Dundee, with its remarkable octagonal meeting house seems to have gone into a catastrophic decline by the 1920s after a division in the late nineteenth century, when Dr Rorie, Dr Miller and a few others joined the Edinburgh Church. A few continued to meet in Galashiels, Newcastle and Old Buckenham until around 1900, when the churches in New England and Nova Scotia also came to an end.

The encyclopedic *Scottish Churches' Handbook* published in 1933 has an excellent and accurate account of the Glasite Churches. It states 'there are only four congregations, and these represent two branches of the movement. The churches in Edinburgh and Glasgow are each in fellowship with a church in London.' Both Scottish churches had an elder called Sandeman.

---

2. Private information.

One of the London churches closed with the death of the last male member in 1939, and the Glasgow church closed in the 1950s.[3]

Some statistical snapshots can illustrate the life of the Edinburgh church. In 1887 there were five elders, three of whom were Waterstons, five deacons, including one in Galashiels and two in Dundee, where the church seems to have divided, probably over the blood-eating issue, and the more liberal members had joined with Edinburgh. There were also three ministering widows, or deaconesses, one of whom was in Galashiels. There were sixty-four members in all. In 1895 there were fifty-seven members, and in 1900, forty-four. In 1920 there were four elders, three deacons, seven other men and thirty-eight women. By 1943 the Sandeman family, all collateral relatives of the childless Robert Sandeman, predominated, as two of three elders, all three deacons and two of three other men belonged to the family. In 1982 Dorothy Elizabeth Barnard, née Sandeman, a widow whose surname linked her with the eighteenth-century elder, was ordained a deaconess.[4] She died in 2005 at the age of ninety-four and may have been the last member to die.

Of the three last elders, who were all in the elders' seat the first time I visited the church, George Punton died in 1980, William Ferguson in 1985, and Gerard Sandeman in 1999. At the closing of the building there was one elder, one deacon, Patrick Sandeman, who by this time had lived for many years in Perthshire and was an occasional attender, one deaconess and three women. In her *Scotsman* obituary of her father Patrick, Mary Sandeman, a well-known folk singer, wrote that his faith was sustained by a small family church. The last addition to the church was that of Isobel Punton, daughter of the elder, and she was also the last to be married, not in the church, but in Trinity Lodge, Wardie, Edinburgh in 1977. Gerard Sandeman had to register as a 'temporary minister' for this event.[5] William Ferguson's daughter Joan, like her mother, did not join the church but attended regularly. She was secretary of the Scottish Genealogical Society and Librarian of the Royal College of Physicians of Edinburgh, where the portrait of James Boswell's Glasite uncle, Dr John Boswell, hangs on the wall.

Some extracts from the books of the Edinburgh congregation, of which I have a photocopy, give a little more insight into the life of the congregation, and its close interest in the other remaining churches, particularly that in London.

3. Thomson and Patterson, *Scottish Churches' Handbook*, 27–28.
4. Add. MSS 409, Box 5.
5. Add. MSS. 409/6/34.

1890: March 2nd, John Loveday of Old Buckenham joined the church in London.

1890: March 16th. Mrs Loveday, wife of John Loveday, also joined the church in London. (The Lovedays had been the main family in the church in Old Buckenham, Norfolk, which had closed about this time)

June 1st. elegy sung for Mrs Chisholm, who confessed the faith a few hours before death.

June 15th elegy sung for Mrs Dickson, who confessed the faith two days before death. (She was probably one of the Dickson family of gunsmiths who were prominent in the Edinburgh church. The firm continues, under different ownership.)

August 17th Elegy sung for Mr Thomas Vincent, elder in London.

October 8th Elegy sung for Mr Charles Leighton of London, and also for Mr George Barnard who confessed the faith upon his deathbed.

1893: October 8th: Elegy sung for Mr Waterston our Elder, and Mrs Paterson our deaconess.

1891: March: Robert Vincent called to the deacon's office in London.

March 29th: Elegy sung for Mrs Sime of Galashiels.

November 29th: Mrs Richardson received into the church at Dundee.

1892: January 17th: Mrs W. B. Sandeman made a deaconess, also Mrs James Young.

Bessie Lawson of America died.

December 24th John Duff, a stranger from Atherton near Manchester confessed the faith and was received into the Church.

1895: April, Jane Sandeman (an invalid) confessed the faith to the Elders.

June 23rd, Elegy sung for Jane Sandeman.

1896: June: The Church in Perth united with us in brotherly fellowship.

1897: June 13th: John Duff separated from the church.

1898: May 17th. Albert F Sandeman ordained an Elder, there being present to assist our Elders two Elders from Perth, Mr Fairweather and Mr Gardiner; one from Dundee, Dr Miller; and one from London, Mr F Blaikley.

May 19th: Mrs Ferguson (Katie Forrest) confessed her faith to the Elders on her sickbed and had her two children baptized.

After 1900 this extract ceases and there are only a few notes for the twentieth century.

1907; William Boswell Sandeman joined the church. He was made a deacon in 1919 and an Elder in 1920.

1914: William Ferguson joined the church. He was made an Elder on 12th June 1924.

1936: Gerard Lionel Sandeman joined the church. He was made a deacon in 1939 and an Elder in 1967.

1937: Norman Sandeman joined the church. He was made a deacon in 1956 and died in 1962.

1938: Patrick Sandeman, from London, was made a deacon in 1939 and died c.2000.

1939: Dennis Sandeman joined the church. He was made an Elder in 1947 and died in 1958.

These four men were the sons of William Boswell Sandeman. And one last rather wistful note was added:

18th September 1963, Eric Baxter spoke to the Elders.

I have been informed that he died as an Episcopalian at the end of last century.[6] On an early visit to the church I spoke to Mrs Baxter, presumably from the Dundee family, who told me that she attended a Baptist Church on occasional Sunday evenings.

The order of service for the ordaining Gerard Sandeman as an elder on Saturday 2 December 1967 has survived and is a good example of a Glasite liturgy which was unchanged over the years except as numbers grew fewer.

The Church met, fasting, at 9.00 a.m.

P. W. Sandeman (deacon) read Psalm 93 verses 1–5.

William Ferguson led the Lord's Prayer.

Psalm 51 verses 1–5 were sung.

George Punton led the prayer of confession, blessing and thanksgiving. 1–5.

Psalm 51 verses 6–10 were sung.

F. A. Fairweather (possibly an Elder, certainly from a Perth Glasite family) led a prayer of thanksgiving and praise.

Psalm 51 verses 11–14 were sung.

G. B. Williams (Elder from London) prayed for a blessing on the reading of the Word.

Verse 1 of Psalm 127 was sung.

In our fasting let us read the book of Isaiah 58 verses 3–12; Matthew 6 verses 6–18; Luke 12 verses 33–38; Ephesians 4 verses 4–16.

Then Psalm 51 verses 18–19 were sung.

6. Private information.

Then Mr Fairweather said; let us hear what was done in the first churches in setting apart for the Elder's office.

Acts 13 verses 1–3; 14 verses 21–23; Titus 1 verses 5–9; Acts 20 28–35; 1 Timothy 4 verses 13–16; 2 Timothy 2 verses 1–7, 15, 16, 19–26; 3 verses 1–4, 14–17; 4 verses 1–5.

Psalm 51 verses 18–19 were sung

Then the Elders 'moved down.'

William Ferguson prayed for 'God's blessing on our ordaining Gerard Sandeman to the Elder's office with the laying on of hands.'

They bring up the new Elder and receive him with the right hand of fellowship.

Psalm 68 verses 18–20 were sung.

George Punton announces the collection.

Then there is breakfast.

After breakfast the new Elder recited the Lord's Prayer[7] and the Church sang Psalm 145 verses 1–7.

Presumably this service included non-members, of whom there were a number, particularly relatives of members, who attended the services, as no hymns were sung nor was there the Lord's Supper. Letters to Gerard Sandeman from relatives in England connected with his ordination are a reminder that 'scattered brethren' living beyond reach of Sunday services, remained faithful to the church's ethos. His seventy-five-year-old aunt in Ware, Hertfordshire, wrote 'the Lord is bearing long with us, let us hope we may all be kept in the bundle, and that his coming may be soon.'[8]

We have seen earlier examples of the sequence of Sunday services. In the last years the worship still followed the old pattern with scripture readings of whole chapters. One Sunday, when the list of the dukes of Edom (Gen 36) was read out in its difficult to pronounce entirety, I asked why this was done and received the answer, 'every name is in the Lamb's Book of Life.'

The morning worship was held from 10.45 until 12.30, and four chapters of scripture were read: one chapter each from Genesis to the end of Judges; Ruth to Esther; Job to Song of Solomon; Daniel to Malachi; before the service the elders gathered in a corner of the Meeting House, called the Presbytery, to ensure that they knew which chapters were to be read and by whom. The magnificent three decker pulpit/platform enclosed the elders on the top deck, the deacons on the second while the third was used as the Communion Table. Eventually the whole Bible was read in public in around two years, not a verse being omitted. An exhortation largely in the words

7. It was the custom for the elder to recite the Lord's Prayer in every service.
8. Add. MSS Box 5.

of Scripture was given in both services by one of the elders. Although the Authorized Version was always used, the Glasites welcomed the Revised Version of 1885 and adapted their psalter to use its insights. Psalms in Robert Boswell's translation were sung unaccompanied with the note being given by pitch pipe. During prayers the worshippers stood with their hands facing upwards. In the afternoon, from 2.10 until 3.30, the elders read three chapters: Isaiah to Ezekiel; Matthew to Acts; and at the Love Feast Romans to Revelation, and then the communion was shared. An offering for the needs of the fellowship was collected from the members only using a box on the end of a long pole. There was a box to which all might contribute for the fabric at the door of the Meeting Room.

In the later days of the church the liturgy was necessarily shortened, simply because there were few brethren able to take part, and after William Ferguson died in 1985 the one remaining elder could not conduct the Lord's Supper, and the service consisted only of prayers, psalms, and Bible readings, with a short exhortation, sometimes original, sometimes read.

While the Sandemanians did not support joint Christian enterprises such as Bible societies they were generous to community causes. The Perth Church was credited with being the largest Church donor to the Infirmary at the end of the nineteenth century and liberality to civic causes remained a central part of church life. The Edinburgh Church made donations to such charities as St Columba's Hospice in its last years.[9]

The Love Feast was reserved to members, although I was offered lunch in a separate room when I first visited the church. On a later visit Gerard Sandeman let me watch him cut a slice from a large white loaf for communion and the rest, he told me, was destined for the Feast. Wine was ordered from the family firm of Sandeman. In 1947, when bread rationing was still in force, a letter was sent to the Divisional Food Officer explaining the meal served to members and the justification for it. The request for exemption was granted.

A glimpse of the support given to members is seen in a letter to Dennis Sandeman in 1947 from Emma Gorrie of Methven, daughter of John Gorrie, an elder of the now defunct Perth Church, complaining that she had not received the month's sum of one pound, which had been promised to her.[10]

Recently a collection of material from the Glasgow Glasite Church has been added to the Dundee Archive.[11] There is a *Diary* of an unnamed elder, (from internal evidence probably Archibald Sandeman) which runs from

9. Hospice receipt books (personal research).

10. Letter from Emma Gorrie, 1947 (uncatalogued).

11. MS 364/1/1.

1888 until 1900, and sheds light on the day to day life of that church. Glasgow was in fellowship with one of the London churches, Dundee, Newcastle, and a remnant in Aberdeen, and news and visitors frequently arrived in time for welcome and consideration at the Sabbath meetings. One problem of these quite small fellowships was the provision of two elders on a given Sabbath so that the Lord's Supper could take place, and quite a lot of careful planning is recorded. On Sabbath 24 November 1888 the diarist notes:

> A visit of a presbytery to Newcastle having been arranged to take place today, Mr Moir went from Dundee and John (Sandeman) from here. In order that the churches of Dundee and Glasgow might not both be without a Presbytery I went to Dundee and lodged with Dr Philips Jnr. and made some calls with him on Saturday afternoon to the sick and elderly. On Sabbath we met with the church as usual, happy in observing the ordinances and meeting the brethren- a good many not very well and unable to be out. . . Met a number of friends at tea at Mr Walter Baxter's. After tea his baby was baptized. I officiated, and the child is named Mary. Present were Mrs Moir, happy to be living in Dundee again, various Baxters, John Sandeman etc. John also returned from Newcastle. Miss Margaret Proctor had died on Saturday. Mr and Mrs Deacon and other friends much in their usual health. Mr Proctor able to be out all day.[12]

On Sabbath 4 May 1890 a more complicated arrangement was necessary to accede to a request from Mr Leighton in London to provide a presbytery for that church, and a letter was sent to Dundee to arrange the presbytery between the churches. On 25 May news came from the London church that Mrs Craig, the deaconess, Mr Vincent, and Mr Leighton had discussed her need to go to her daughters in Cambridge as one had been deserted by her husband and left with young children. The minds of some brethren were disturbed by this but 'no scripture would forbid her going.' On Thursday the diarist attended a social meeting, on the sabbath Walter Baxter from Dundee was present, and he stayed with Miss M. C. Barnard. Familiar Sandemanian surnames appear very frequently.

On Sabbath 31 August 1890 the diarist comments that meetings have been very thin for several sabbaths. 'Today many friends home from the country.'[13] This seems to have been a problem, at least in Glasgow and London. In a letter in a separate collection dated 20 July 1908 from Henry Young, elder in London, to John Sandeman, Bearsden, Glasgow,

---

12. MS 364/1/1, 2, 3.
13. MS 364/1/9.

he comments on the elderly Mr Loveday's concerns about members going away to the country for the sake of their health and their neglecting ordinances. He quotes Isa 58, and Isa 50:10–11 and Heb 10:23–25. He suggests that holidays should be taken near home, as 'our number is so reduced that the absence of a few is much felt.' The matter was brought to the Love Feast and an aged sister spoke of her daughter's position with young children and a husband not in the church. It was heartily conceded that she was not free to choose. 'With women who are free and with men it is different. They should not go to places from which they cannot return to be present at the ordinances every sabbath day.'[14]

Literature

While, as we have seen there was a great deal of material published when the movement was vigorous, some writing continued into the twentieth century. *Christian Songs* continued to be used, the 1872 edition in Perth and the 1875 edition in Edinburgh, with suitable verbal amendments from time to time. The paraphrase of Revelation, 'Thy worthiness,'[15] was sung every Sunday at Communion, and the psalms in Robert Boswell's version, revised in the light of the Revised Version of the Bible, were sung in public worship. Hymns were sung only at the Love Feast, as were, at least into the early twentieth century, elegies to mark the death of members.

Although James Allen of Gayle had been cut off in the late eighteenth century, and an attempt by the elders of the Kirkby Lonsdale church in the early nineteenth century to donate copies of his work *The Dangers of Philosophy* to the London Church had been turned down, in 1924 some of his writings were republished by Archibald Sandeman. *Notes on Mark, Luke and John* made up one volume which included a plea for the rediscovery of his *Notes on Matthew*, and a second volume covering the Acts of the Apostles and the Epistles of Paul followed. His *Treatise on Redemption* was reprinted in 1927. These books were printed by Young of Perth, not a Glasite firm. In 1893 George Waterston of Edinburgh published a pamphlet on the book of Revelation. He had also issued a compilation of *Notes on Our Lord's Law as to Offences arising in His Churches* in 1888.

William Ferguson seems to have been the only elder to have entered a Newspaper correspondence. In November 1950 there was a flurry of letters in the *Scotsman*, the main Edinburgh daily, on baptism. Mr Ferguson wrote on 13 November that he was in favor of infant baptism. He held that the

14. Add. MSS 11/9.

15. "Song 16," *Christian Songs*.

New Testament translators wisely use 'baptism' instead of 'immersion', and he regrets that Karl Barth had committed himself to Adult baptism. 'But' he wrote, 'they are blameworthy who foster what has become a superstitious practice—the christening of infants whether the parents believe or not and calling this baptism. For this reason, baptism is now lightly thought of.'

In a letter of 19 December 1947 to Mr (Archibald) Sandeman, Mr Ferguson gave his thoughts on a variety of Glasite doctrines and practices.

> In writing down these thoughts, I am assuming that I require to hear what the Scriptures say today (what the Spirit saith to the churches) and not what it said yesterday or the day before. I cannot ignore those who have gone before, but I must beware lest I lean on the tradition of the elders.

The Glasites would not belong to Provident Societies, and he raised questions about annuities, unemployment schemes, and voluntary insurance under the (then new) National Health Service. He touched on marriage services, the lot, the baptism of grown-up children of professing members, long prayers, separation from worship with other churches, and public and private prayer.

Games of chance were to be avoided because they were frivolous. He had seen a play where 'dice were thrown to decide whom to marry.' In matters of discipline letter writing should be eschewed, unless the offending person asks for something in writing. Scripture says, 'Go tell him face to face.' Marriage concerns not the church but the family, so a church ceremony is unscriptural, but there is no ground for refusing a private ceremony with prayer. Logically we should not mention marriage, health, or happiness in church but only spiritual concerns, but see Eph 6:1–3. On the vexed question of the interpretation of 'husband of one wife' he refers to 1 Tim 3:2, 1 Tim 5:9 and John 4:16–18.[16]

On the question of the assurance of hope, which had been the essence of the division with the Perth church in the late eighteenth century, he has quite a lot to say.

> I find that generally speaking brethren are: a. meticulous, b. careful and c. not so careful in their walk. If a brother delivered from the sin of self- righteousness was meticulous in his walk and declared 'I find comfort in my faith bearing its proper fruit and thus I am assured of life through Christ' I would be very cautious and enquire whether it was love of the Truth or a desire

16. It is worth noting that Gerard Sandeman was widowed and remarried. His first wife was the daughter of Professor Hugh Ross McIntosh of the chair of theology in New College, Edinburgh, a minister of the Church of Scotland.

again to do righteousness for its own sake that had made him meticulous in his walk. Cf Romans 7:19. Shifting the emphasis from Christ and His Resurrection to an assurance of hope through good works is dangerous, Hebrews 6:11, 12. Assurance must not lead to boasting, 2 Peter 1:10, 11. The careful and not so careful do not seem to be bothered with thoughts anent the assurance of hope.

So far as things strangled are concerned it is for the believer to be fully persuaded in his own mind about shot game and all flesh being cleaned from blood, Ezek 28:3, Eph 4:13. Uniformity of practice must be confirmed with unity of spirit. 'If I see a rabbit hung by the rear legs, then I know that the blood has been poured out. If I see a hare hanging by its forelegs, then I know the blood has been retained'. On the matter of the true church he writes, 'No man can judge a church true or false. It may be flattering to us to think we conform as we can to the pattern of the early churches, but it seems irrelevant to consider all deviations from this pattern as corruption and error'.[17]

Sometime during the 1920s a married daughter of a deceased elder of the Waterston family wished to join the church and the questions to be answered are carefully set out and presumably would not have varied much for many years.

1. What is leading you to seek to become a member of this church?

2. Who do you believe Jesus Christ to be?

3. What view have you of your character in the sight of God?

4. We are told that all there is in the world is lust of the flesh, lust of the eyes and the pride of life. Do you find yourself condemned in any of these?

5. What hope have you as a sinner before God?

6. What view have you of the Church?

7. What do you see as the marks of the true Church and how is it to be maintained? Matthew 18, vv. 15–17.

8. Have you counted the cost of taking part with our Lord's despised cause in the world and being subject to the teaching of the scriptures in all humility?

9. You were brought up in the Church and will understand all the practices and ordinances of the Church—the refraining from blood eating,

17. Add. MSS 11/22.

from covetousness, using the lot for entertainment or gain, avoiding life assurance, and also keeping separate in communion with other churches which are not of the same mind.

When she replied positively to these questions the elders discussed her answers, recommended her to the church, the roll was called, and each member voted. Unanimity was always required in all church matters. She was accepted with prayer and the laying on of hands.[18]

The matter of discipline continued to be taken very seriously. A short paper dated sometime in the middle of the twentieth century, and possibly written by Gerard Sandeman, illustrates the procedure. 'The discipline of a church of God is ever a very great trial to every one of us, the trial being whether we as individuals are to be guided by our way of looking at the grave matter or are we to be guided by our Master even the Head of the Church.' Several scriptures are then cited, including Eph 5:15 and 16, Matt 18:2–4, Matt 17:24–27, 2 Thess 3:6–7, 14–15, 1 Cor 5:2–8.

It continues:

> Our love to our brother who has disobeyed the Lord Jesus is to withdraw ourselves from him, to keep out of his company, and by so doing to remind him of his sin, so that we still count him a brother and not an enemy. I agree therefore that X be put away from among us, and by so doing we show our love to God.

Presumably there is a good hope of restoration, as happened to the future Elder George Punton, who was put away from the deacon's office on 10 December 1935, in a simple procedure without prayer. He was restored to the deacon's office in 1949, and he was ordained an elder on 12 November 1955.[19]

The pattern of the church was continued until the end, with occasional revision or updating when social mores or laws demanded a response.

18. Uncatalogued document.
19. Add. MS 409/6/32.

Conclusion

WERE THE GLASITES/SANDEMANIANS AN aberration in the story of Christendom, or do they have a voice worth listening to among the many varieties of the Christian faith? Part of the difficulty in answering this question is that they are hard to categorize. A small, diminishing group who usually kept very much to themselves, they are in danger of being considered a quaint bye-way, and the nickname often given to them of the 'Kail Kirk' would confirm this aspect of their practice and belief. But they were not the only church which served lunch between the services, although the fact that they made attendance at the meal compulsory was probably unique.[1]

In theological terms they were rational Calvinists. In no way did they challenge orthodox doctrinal statements. They were trinitarians, they studied the scriptures in great detail, and held a high view of inspiration. They also held the orthodox doctrine of the person and work of Christ, practiced the two ordinances of baptism and Communion, adhered to the common ethical code of the church, and were known for their benevolence within the fellowship and in the secular community.[2] Their defining doctrine of faith may seem stark, and certainly they made little if any room for emotion in religion. While Sandeman took his condemnation of the 'popular preachers' to a polemical extreme, his definition of faith as a purely intellectual act was not so far removed from the teaching of his younger contemporary, John Erskine of Carnock, minister of the Greyfriars Parish[3] in Edinburgh. Yeager says:

---

1. Horton Davies remarks, in *Worship and Theology in England*, 4:164, 'in more bizarre fashion, Glas had insisted on celebrating the love-feast or agape with broth.'

2. 'It was not indeed, by departing from the orthodox creed, on the subject of the Trinity, the person of Christ, the mode of acceptance by God, or the doctrine of salvation by grace that they differed from the original independents, for on all these points they were zealously Calvinistical' (Bennett and Bogue, *History of the Dissenters*, 4:107). The authors then give a very unfriendly review of the Sandemanians.

3. Successively of Old and New Greyfriars.

His view of faith came very close to that of John Glas and Robert Sandeman, who made faith strictly an intellectual exercise, but Erskine deviated from them by insisting that a person utilise the means of grace for conversion to Christianity, and that once enlightened by the Spirit, the mind actively developed knowledge of the Lord.[4]

Macleod remarks that

there was a somewhat similar doctrine of faith that was taught by John Erskine of Edinburgh . . . who sought to lay stress not on the likeness but on the unlikeness of their views. . . . He held that faith is radically belief of the truth and this is an exercise of the understanding by way of assent.[5]

But Erskine also spoke of the functioning of the emotions and will in a way that Sandeman did not. Yet Sandemanians believed that the outcome of faith as assent would be the labour of love and true charity, that marked the Christian life. They were sometimes accused of Antinomianism but that slander they refuted.

A nephew of John Erskine, the lay theologian Thomas Erskine of Lallathin, in his *Essay on Faith* writes 'to have faith in a thing, to believe a thing, and to understand a thing as a truth are expressions of the same import.' Needham points out that the intellectual view of faith is not in itself a serious departure from the mainstream Calvinistic position. He cites Augustine, who defined faith as 'to think with assent' and mentions Calvin, John Erskine, Thomas Chalmers, James Haldane, and others as understanding faith as mental assent.[6] Their doctrine of faith was not in itself a factor in separating Sandemanians from every other church. Rather it was their extreme emphasis on it, the acerbity of Sandeman's exposition of his position, and the insistence on what they believed to be primitive practice[7] in the order of the churches which isolated them.

Yet they considered themselves to be the only true church and forbade even attendance at the services of those 'who did not walk with them.' They practiced strict discipline and the church rolls have many instances of names firmly stroked out. Their adherence to their own interpretation of church

4. Yeager, *Enlightened Evangelicalism*, 102.

5. Macleod, *Scottish Theology*, 187.

6. Needham, *Thomas Erskine of Linlathen*, 82, 83.

7. It is interesting to note that the search for the primitive church embraced many varieties of Christianity. The Orthodox, as well as Anglo-Catholics, used the phrase, which was a watchword of Scotch Baptists such as William Jones, and of the followers of Alexander Campbell.

customs, such as abstinence from blood and the sacredness of the lot, not to speak of the holy kiss, marked them out from other churches. In some ways they resembled the 'London' Exclusive Brethren, but unlike them they did not have, at least after the death of John Glas, a definite leader, and most certainly they did not accept a progressive revelation of doctrine. All was set quite firmly in the early days of the movement, although occasionally an elder would question some teachings such as the necessity of more than one elder in the church before discipline and communion could take place.[8]

When the *Blackwell Dictionary of Evangelical Biography, 1730–1860* was being planned I was asked to contribute articles on Glas and Sandeman, and the question did arise, Were these men evangelicals in any accepted sense? The articles duly appeared and Geoffrey Cantor's article on Michael Faraday is in the *IVP Biographical Dictionary of Evangelicals*. Faraday's biography is also in the *Blackwell Dictionary*. Taking David Bebbington's quadrilateral template as a guide, how do they fare?

The four defining characteristics of Evangelicalism are largely, in recent writing, agreed to be conversionism, activism, biblicism, and crucicentricism.[9]

Conversionism

To become a member of a Glasite church the candidate was required to confess the faith and then the roll was called and unanimity, the agreement of every member, male and female, was necessary. Thereafter the candidate was greeted with the kiss of peace. As we have seen the questions that the elders asked were entirely cerebral and there was no reference to conversion, new birth or anything that could be described as emotional. We may trace the process in the life of Michael Faraday. He was probably baptised as an infant and would have accompanied his parents and his brother and sisters to the long and, to a child, presumably dull services. During the Love Feast he would have had his broth and sandwiches with the other children in the meeting house. Although Faraday's mother never became a member of the church she and the family continued to attend faithfully after the death of her husband in 1810. There was nothing like a Sunday School in any Sande-manian church, but Faraday does refer to a singing school. In 1818 Faraday, George Barnard, Thomas Deacon, all from leading families in London and beyond, joined with Edward Barnard Deeble, who was presumably a rela-tive of Sarah, and an untraced man, J. Corder, in a Study Circle where each

8. For example, Allen, *Letters*, 21.

9. Bebbington, *Evangelicalism in Modern Britain*, 3.

read a paper for the improvement of their minds and their literary style. This is at least an indication of mental activity among young London Sandemanians.[10] In 1821 Faraday married Sarah Barnard, great-niece of John Barnard, whose mother belonged to another prominent family, the Booseys, in the Church of St Faith-in-the-Virgin near St Paul's Cathedral. Not until 1837 were English Sandemanians able to celebrate marriage in a registry office. This was an important change as they did not believe that there was a scripture warrant for a church marriage service.

On 15 July 1821 Faraday made his confession of faith and commitment to the customs of the Church. Sarah had already become a member in 1819. He was elected deacon on 1 July 1832 and elder on 15 October 1840. Colin Russell, describing Faraday's faith, suggests that by 'listening to the reading and exposition of scripture as he grew up, Faraday gradually, perhaps imperceptibly, adopted their values as his own and identified in a deeper way with the community.'[11] Conversion was not a word used in the Sandemanian churches. 'Confessing the faith' is the usual phrase and promotion to office as deacon or elder was based on trust and the observation of the church. It is interesting that, especially in the latter years of the Church men and women are recorded as 'confessing the faith on their deathbed.' Does this suggest some form of urgency, or was there family pressure brought to bear on the dying? There was a definite line of division between members and 'the auditory' but the evangelical view of 'conversion' would have been alien to the churches.

There was also, arising particularly from Sandeman's condemnation of 'popular preachers,' an antipathy towards anything that was aggressively evangelical. In 1859, while revivals were breaking out in Britain and America, Faraday is quoted as saying

> The Revivals &c. cannot trouble the Christian who is taught of God (by His Word and the Holy Spirit) to trust in the promise of salvation through the work of Jesus Christ. He finds his guide in the Word of God and commits the keeping of his soul into the hands of God. He looks for no assurance beyond what the Word can give him, and if his mind is troubled by the cares and fears which may assail him, he can go nowhere but in prayer to the throne of grace and to Scripture. No outward manifestation, as of a revival &c. can give either instruction or assurance to him, nor can any outward opposition or trouble diminish his confidence in 'Christ crucified, to the Jews a stumbling block,

10. Jenkins, *Michael Faraday's Mental Exercises*, 10.
11. Russell, *Michael Faraday, Physics and Faith*, 44.

and to the Greeks foolishness; but to them who are called Christ the power of—God and the wisdom of God. . .'[12]

Faraday uses evangelical language but in a particular manner, and the emphasis on the Word of Scripture is clear. Gerard Sandeman remarked to me one Sunday, 'we have only the bare Word of God.' The doctrine of assurance, as we saw in the controversy centering on the Perth church, was always a difficult area for the churches. The fear of pride, of Pharisaism, was ever present, and the sense of continuing personal unworthiness made clear statements on assurance difficult. The Bereans made assurance part of faith. The Sandemanians were very wary of such claims. William Buchanan delivered an exhortation in Edinburgh on 7 June 1860, 'at a time of religious revival agitations.' He said:

> Warnings against false Christs etc. It is therefore to be con-
> sidered what is to be the conduct of His disciples in regard to
> these things, as these delusions fast increase around us. We
> find the Lord never meddling with the affairs of states or na-
> tions but paying tribute for Himself and Peter to avoid offence.
> In the present day many schemes are afloat for the prevention
> of immorality and the evils affecting society, but with these the
> disciples have nothing to do. They are told to study to be quiet
> and to do their own business, unlike the Pharasees [sic] blowing
> trumpets before giving alms and praying at street corners.'[13]

It must be noted that Buchanan was a distinguished Edinburgh lawyer.

Activism

Along with the rejection of revivalism there is a negative attitude to mission of any sort, which also set the churches apart from the mainstream of evangelicalism, which regarded active proclamation of the faith and the spreading of the Gospel to the whole world, especially after the eighteenth-century revivals, as an obvious duty. Alex Moir, a Glasgow elder, wrote to Miss A. Blaikley in London on 2 February 1857 answering a query. He says that 'our taking no hand in this movement [sc. missionary] is a thing which I find the religious world frequently reproaches us with.' They were accused of selfishness and illiberality

---

12. Quoted in Davie, *Gathered Church*, 70.
13. Buchanan, *Select Exhortations*, 70. MS 9/4/9.

but the main thing is whether the Missionary Movement is warranted by the divine word. The apostles were chosen to be witnesses of the Resurrection of Jesus Christ and of all that He did and said. Unto them was committed the completion of the New Testament Revelation. The commission was peculiarly theirs and they received it immediately from the Lord Himself-they only are his ambassadors and theirs only was the duty of going abroad preaching the Gospel. No one else except Paul was given this duty. There is no account of the apostles having transferred their commission to others. This, if it happened, would have been mentioned in the epistles. . . . No injunction is given to Elders to go about preaching in Timothy or Peter—Elders are among you.'

Moir goes on to claim that after the Reformation and the discovery of the art of printing the two witnesses of Rev 11 are the two Testaments.

Those who conduct the carrying abroad of the Scriptures are in this the hand of the Lord who makes all things work together for good. Their being employed in bringing about the Divine predictions is no evidence of their Christianity. Satan himself is transformed into an angel of light. It is no great thing if Satan's ministers be transformed as ministers of righteousness, even if they hold scripture lightly as if it were the Word of man. They are not to be supported as a corrupt tree cannot bear good fruit. But by the Scriptures themselves which are thus spread abroad, the Lord may take 'one of a city, and two of a family and bring them to Zion.'[14]

These latter thoughts seem to apply to Bible Societies and perhaps to the Apocrypha and other controversies in the early part of the nineteenth century. The sentiments are strongly expressed and represent the most exclusive aspect of Sandemanianism. Cooperation with other churches and even occasional attendance at their services were frowned upon and sometimes condemned. Sandemanians were generous to civic causes such as local hospitals and were willing to become involved to a certain extent in charitable endeavors, so long as they did not compromise their separatist stance.

When an apparent opening for mission arose, the response is interesting. In February 1839, answering queries from Robert Sandeman, a soldier in the East Indies, presumably India, the Perth Church wrote 'please intimate in our name to Markham Sherwill, George Salmon, Hugh Troup and Walter Sherwill as well as to your sister Letitia that we have received their

14. MSS 9/4/1, Moir, 182.

several addresses and that upon their several confessions made by each of their character in the sight of God, and of the ground of their hope, we cordially and with one mind acknowledge them as brethren, and companions in the kingdom and patience of Jesus Christ.' As they have little prospect of a settled life in India

> be moderate and gentle in a land where arbitrary power prevails, while leaving the conversion of the ignorant and benighted tribes among whom you sojourn to Him who says, 'I form the light and create darkness', remembering that the song of redeeming love shall be sung at last by a company gathered out of every nation, tribe, kindred and tongue.

I think the eschatological hope is worth noting.[15] The same note is struck in the *Christian Songs*, for example Song 69: 'The glorious myriads round the throne' and Song 70: 'Ten thousand thousands there shall raise their glad notes.' If no works can gain salvation, and bare faith is all that is necessary, so no means towards conversion may be used. But God has promised thousands and myriads of believers and it is the Christian's duty to leave the work to him.

I speculate that the Robert Sandeman in the letter became General Robert Turnbull Sandeman of the East India Company's army, who was born in Perth in 1804, and was the father of the well-known Sir Robert Sandeman, soldier, and author.[16]

Biblicism

There is no doubt that Sandemanians were Biblicists. We have already seen how Sandeman advised his followers to use the whole Bible to discover and reinforce their faith. The desire and design of the churches was to reproduce the teaching and practice of the primitive church, and such customs as plurality of elders, weekly communion, the Love Feast and the kiss of peace, abstinence from games of chance, the prohibition of the eating of blood, and loyalty to the duly appointed government were all based on scripture texts. Occasionally there is debate about a particular issue, and if no text

15. Letter in Dundee MSS 9/3/32, "Church at Perth to Robert Sandeman." See also McWhirter, "Kail Kirk": 'a curiosity regarding the Perth congregation was the fact that members who emigrated to the East Indies introduced business colleagues to the doctrine of the Glasites with the result that a number joined the Church. One or two of these men later settled in the Perth district, the last passing away early in the present century.'

16. ODNB, "Sir Robert Sandeman."

can be adduced then there is freedom of judgement, even if it led to contentious conclusions. In June 1780 some London Sandemanians joined armed associations of citizens because of the Gordon riots of that year. American brethren disapproved, but the London elders concluded

> that when suffering for the sake of the truth is out of the question, Christ has allowed his people the liberty of self-defence against violence done to their lives and consciences in common with other men and as members of worldly societies to associate with them for that purpose.[17]

They were cessationists, holding that the special gifts of the Spirit ceased with the death of the last apostle, so that a clear command, such as that in Jas 5 to call for the elders to anoint the sick, is held not to be applicable. James Allen sets this out clearly.

> In the days of the Apostles, while the working of miracles and the gifts of healing were continued, the Elders of the Church anointed the sick in the name of the Lord, and they were healed by the prayer of faith (Mark 6v13.) We have no warrant to imitate them in this ceremony, unless we are possessed of their faith. And since the completion of divine revelation, the miracle working faith is no more.'[18]

The reading of every word of Scripture in the Sunday services must have resulted in a wide knowledge of the Bible among the members, and the surviving exhortations, of which there are many, testify to the elders' knowledge of Scripture, and to their wish to let the Bible speak without the words of man interfering. The advent of the Revised Version of the Bible in 1885 was noted and accepted and the Psalter was slightly modified in its light.

Crucicentrism

There are many references in the literature to the Great Atonement and the shedding of Christ's blood on the cross. Despite their isolationism the churches maintained a witness to the power of the death of Christ and the facts of the cross and the resurrection were central to Sandemanian teaching. That they did not express their beliefs in conventional evangelical language did not imply that the cross and Jesus' death were not central to their beliefs.

---

17. *Winslow Family Memorial*, 158.
18. Allen, *Notes on the Acts and the Epistles*, 241.

Thus, we can place the Sandemanians on the edge of evangelicalism. Bebbington's well-supported claim that Evangelicalism was influenced by Romanticism makes clear another area in which the Sandemanians differed from the prevailing cultural milieu in the eighteenth and early nineteenth century. They were rational Calvinists, denying emotion any place in salvation and belief, and in a time when miracles of various kinds, spiritual healings, prophecies, and other phenomena were at least of interest to other Christians, the Sandemanians remained firmly grounded in their unemotional faith. In a letter of January 1769 Sandeman wrote from Danbury to Colburn Barrell:

> I am very well pleased with all your proceedings in regard to Adam and Townsend. I mean where you tell Adam that the manifestations he valued himself so much upon came not from the Father of lights but from the Prince of Darkness.[19]

We do not hear what these 'manifestations' were but this was the era of awakenings and revivals, for which Sandeman would have had little time.

Here is the view of Faraday, the preeminent scientist and deeply loyal Sandemanian. At his Friday lectures in the Royal Institution the latest scientific discoveries could be discussed in front of large audiences. When the public fascination with new discoveries included heterodox or alternative science as well as that propounded by Faraday and his colleagues at the Royal Institution, a fascination which embraced mesmerism, phrenology and the power of herbs, this was much to Faraday's disgust. In 1848 stories of messages from the beyond began to spread from New York State where two young sisters claimed to hear rappings which they interpreted as in some way supernatural. As Cantor remarks, 'Not only was America both socially and spiritually ready to latch on to the report of the Rochester rappings and turn them into a craze comparable in size with health foods or jogging in our day, but Britain was equally fertile ground.' Faraday was appalled, both on scientific and on Christian grounds. Having heard rumors that he sided with the spiritualists, rappers, and table-turners, he wrote to the *Times* in June 1843, and to the Athenaeum in July of the same year, describing experiments which he had conducted which proved to his satisfaction that table-turning was the result of involuntary muscular action, 'and not the presence of a natural force, such as gravitation or electricity, or even a supernatural one.' He was disturbed by the gullibility of the general public which he attributed to the lack of scientific grounding given in the existing educational system. He also condemned the new craze for contacting

---

19. Macintosh, *Letters in Correspondence*, 104.

the spirits of the dead as anti-Christian, citing such passages as Acts 8:7 where Philip cast out unclean spirits in Samaria. With Faraday experimental science and Scripture worked together to establish rationality. Here he 'discriminated not merely between truth and error but also between informed judgement and prejudice.'[20] Sandemanian faith lived in the daylight and any sort of mystic assertion, any cloudiness of alleged supernatural influence was excluded by the pure light of scripture.

Place Among The Churches

Where can we place the church among the denominations and sects that surrounded it? Despite all the criticisms levelled at its practices and its view of faith it cannot be classified as a heresy. We have seen how its beliefs are largely Calvinist. Members saw it as the continuation of the church of the New Testament, founded by Christ and rediscovered in the experience and teaching of John Glas and his friends. To be faithful to the testimony in every detail is the one thing needful and the gradual decline was accepted with sad equanimity. The Lord will not fail his church and will raise up another such as Glas in our time. William Ferguson standing beside a full-length portrait of John Glas in his living room, pointed to some volumes of Barth's *Church Dogmatics* on his bookshelves as evidence of this hope and belief.[21]

In his evaluation of the movement Hornsby criticizes the Glasites for their failure to evangelize, their excessive literalism in the interpretation of scriptural statements and injunctions, for the severity of their discipline, and for their defective psychology of faith.[22] How did such a circumscribed body along with its derivatives, the Scotch Baptists and the Old Scots Independents, have such an appeal at a particular time and in particular parts of one small country? Theology, individual conviction, practice and social conditions all conspired to produce one of the very few spiritual movements uniquely arising in lowland Scotland. Sects in the USA, Russia, England and the South Sea islands have been exhaustively analyzed and documented. Ancient and modern heresies, and new religious movements and cults and even hyper-real religions have been thoroughly investigated, and an attempt must be made to place the Scottish Independent movement socially and theologically. I have avoided the word 'sect' because of the pejorative use of the category, consigning sectarians to the fringes of society or of the church, yet the Glasite movement fits some of the criteria that sociologists such as

20. Cantor, *Faraday*, 148–49.
21. Personal reminiscence, ca. 1970.
22. Hornsby, "John Glas (1695–1773)," 226–49.

Bryan Wilson and David Martin have used, although it fits none exactly. Tentatively they may be placed in the category of revolutionist sects.[23] Despite their quietism, their hymns proclaim eschatological longings, where they see themselves as representatives of God in the new world he is going to bring in.

> He judgment unto victory shall bring, to put his foes to shame:
> His brethren then triumphantly shall sing the glories of his name'.

and,

> These are the times when Christians yet shall bliss unbounded share;
> Let all who for this mercy wait, to meet their God prepare.
> For lo! He comes! Loud anthems raise; be his great name ador'd:
> May our last theme be Jesus' praise, our song, 'Come quickly, Lord'.

John Glas's own hymn proclaims:

> When this world's course is run, and the judgment is begun;
> We shall have a joyful day, when the King of Kings comes.[24]

These hymns continued to be sung by the members at the Love Feasts until the churches closed.

Yet the Sandemanians were at home in the world as it was. They were criticized for seeing little harm in such diversions as routs, balls, and the theatre, and many were remarkably successful in business. London brethren especially were eminent in science, particularly in the Royal Institution, as artists and craftsmen, as publishers and booksellers.[25]

In Scotland, but not so much in London, economic factors were important in the early days. Stark's theory, that "men get together to form sectarian groupings if they are unhappy in and revolt against a social system in which their position . . . was humilific, for instance because their livelihood was insecure, their wages low, or their status unsatisfactory," has some relevance.[26] Many of the first converts were weavers, either, as in Dundee, working together in factories, or as in Paisley, working in their own households at their own pace and having time to hold discussions on radical politics and religion.[27] There are many examples of new religious movements taking place among weavers. Charles Wesley preached to weavers in Dublin

---

23. Wilson, *Religious Sects*, 93.

24. *Christian Songs*, 92.

25. Cantor, *Faraday*, appendix C.

26. Stark, *Sociology of Religion*, 2:6.

27. Gilmour, *Reminiscences of the Pen' Folk*.

and his brother John to stocking weavers in Nottingham.[28] Those towns in Scotland where the Glasites, and their close relatives the Scotch Baptists and the Old Scots Independents, gathered, were weaving centers, and on the East Coast were easily connected by sea. Montrose, Arbroath, Dundee, and Perth shared both industry and accessibility. To these economic factors could be added the use of the Press, and the powerful influence of Glas and Sandeman as teachers and preachers, although in the various controversies it is notable that protagonists did not consider themselves bound by the leaders and turned for guidance to the Scriptures.

John Glas certainly saw his followers as the rediscovered true, primitive church. In his writings on eschatology he notes the swift decline of the church from the fourth century onwards and the baleful influence of Constantine's acceptance of Christianity. In his *Grave Dialogues betwixt three Free-Thinkers* (1738)[29] he writes of the gradual re-appearance of the two witnesses of Rev 11, who were killed, but who returned to life. Glasites maintained that the witnesses were the Old and New Testaments, and Glas saw

> the revival of the ancient scripture-profession of Christianity, in the brethren of Bohemia, who, being animated by the spirit of the scriptures, wholly separated themselves from the Papists and from the Calixtines, and having chosen ministers of the church of their own company, without regard to human learning, or any other teaching, but what the spirit of God gave them by a translation of the scriptures, they set up congregations of their own, which, in the midst of various persecutions and manifold afflictions were preserved in Moravia, Bohemia, Poland and other places till the Reformation from Popery came to take place in the several Protestant nations. Thus the witnesses appeared alive again, and exalted above philosophy, tradition, and all dependence upon the authority of the church, or of Synods and councils.[30]

He then praises 'these bold fellows, the Waldenses,' with whom the Bohemians had differences. They were offended at the Waldensians for dissembling and attending the worship of the Roman church, and for heaping up wealth, rather than laying up treasure in heaven. The Bohemian brethren seemed to him a much better pattern for the true church.[31]

28. Stark, *Sociology of Religion*, 9.

29. Glas, *Works*, 4:296.

30. Glas, *Works*, 4:297.

31. Glas, *Works*, 4:298.

In 1889 James Rorie, the Dundee doctor who preserved much of the archive and who separated from the Dundee Church and identified with the fellowship in Edinburgh, wrote of the kinship he felt with the Waldensians and Wiclif [*sic*]. He saw the Reformers as daughters of the Church of Rome and claimed that it was through the Puritans and Independents that the truth was gradually clarified until in the eighteenth century Glas and Dale in Scotland, Ingham in England and Walker in Dublin were led to scriptural views.[32]

We have seen that the followers of Alexander Campbell acknowledge the influence of Glas and Sandeman, although they disagree about the importance of this. The churches of the Restoration, now the Disciples of Christ, the a capella Churches of Christ and the Independent Churches of Christ, numbering in the USA several million members, are the largest bodies who can trace at least some of their practices, such as weekly communion and, especially in the earliest days of the movement, an intellectualist view of faith, to the Glasite movement. Emphases vary among the Churches of Christ. Dr Lynn McMillon has written, in *Restoration Roots*,[33] a lucid account of the early history of the Sandemanian movement and pointed out that Alexander Campbell acknowledged the influence of Glas's *King of Martyrs* on his own concept of the strict separation of the church and the state. He also owed to the Sandemanians the practice of weekly communion and an intellectualist view of faith. McMillon visited the Edinburgh Meeting House and recorded his impressions in articles in the *Restoration Quarterly*. On the other hand, Allen and Hughes in *Discovering our Roots, the Ancestry of the Churches of Christ*, give quite a different account. They hold that Glas, Sandeman and Haldane were essentially eighteenth-century Puritans 'neither unique or unusual in Scotland or Ireland for that time.'[34]

From the Campbellites came in the mid-nineteenth century the Christadelphians, followers of the teachings of Dr John Thomas, who also show the influence of the movement, not least in the practice of private rather than public reading of the whole Bible on an annual scheme.[35] When, in the 1980s, the Edinburgh Christadelphian Ecclesia moved to new premises they held a historical exhibition of their story. I was invited and was delighted to see that the first exhibit was a large portrait of John Glas.

Hornsby clearly delineated the defects of the movement. There are some positives in the legacy of the Sandemanian/Glasite Church. They were the first protestant body to adopt weekly communion services, to use 'man-made'

32. Dundee MSS 9/4/1, "Letter from Dr Rorie to Mrs Baldwin."

33. McMillon, *Restoration Roots*, 87–90.

34. Allen and Hughes, *Discovering our Roots*, 47.

35. See Scotland, *Sectarian Religion in Contemporary Britain*, 36–58.

hymns in their worship, albeit in the private confines of the Love Feast. They were the first to repudiate the intimate linkage of magistracy and church which was so evident in early Presbyterianism, and their emphasis on a purely spiritual church of Christ has characterized the Voluntary movement in Scotland and elsewhere and the churches of the Congregationalist and Baptist tradition. They appear to have been the first in Scotland to honour elderly widows with ordination by the laying on of hands to the office of deaconess.[36] Their influence on the Brethren Movement is not so evident, although Embley has drawn attention to the parallels between Glas's *King of Martyrs* and J. N. Darby's early work.[37] Neil Dickson, in his *Brethren in Scotland, 1838–2000,* sees Glasite traits in early Brethren meetings, and claims the phrase, 'the Church should edify itself,' and lay presidency at communion as Glasite influences possibly mediated by Scotch Baptists.[38]

I hope that this collection of stories and doctrines may allow some sunshine to fall on the Sandemanians, who deserve to be remembered for their faithfulness and their undeviating loyalty to the 'One Thing Needful.'[39]

---

36. My thanks are due to Professor S. J. Brown for pointing this out to me. The Baptists in Bristol set aside elderly widows as deaconesses in the mid seventeenth century; Hayden, *Records of a Church of Christ in Bristol, 1640–687,* 117.

37. Embley, in Wilson, *Patterns of Sectarianism,* 215n3. Embley points out that Darby's early tract, *Considerations addressed to the Archbishop of Dublin and the clergy who signed the petition to the House of Commons for protection,* shows that he had the same point of departure from the Established Church as Glas had in his *Testimony of the King of Martyrs.*

38. Dickson, *Brethren in Scotland,* 47.

39. See Betjeman's poem "Sandemanian Meeting House," *Collected Poems.* Mentioned in the introduction.

Bibliography

Adams, James. *The Independent Ghost Conjur'd*. Edinburgh: 1728.

Ahnert, Thomas. *The Moral Culture of the Scottish Enlightenment*. Newhaven and London: Yale University Press, 2014.

Allen, C. Leonard, and Richard T. Hughes. *Discovering our Roots*. Abilene: Abilene Christian University Press, 1988.

Allen, James. *Letters*. Acc. M. 409/5/11.

———. *Notes on the Acts and the Epistles*. Repr. ed. Edinburgh: Robert Forrest, 1924.

———. *Notes on the Gospels*. Repr. ed. Edinburgh: Robert Forrest, 1924.

———. *A Treatise of Redemption*. Repr. ed. Edinburgh: Robert Forrest, 1927.

Anderson, James R., ed. *The Burgesses and Guild Brethren of Glasgow, 1573–1750*. Scottish Record Society. Edinburgh: 1925.

Anon. "A Historical Sketch of Independency in Scotland." *London Christian Instructor* March 1819.

Anon. "The Sandemanians." *Eclectic Review*. London, 1838.

Anon. *A Short but Exact Account of the Rise and Progress of the Difference and Awful Division that took place at Perth among those who are called in common Glassites which ended in their separation, (and a few in Arbroath) who took part with them from their sister Churches in Scotland and England*. Repr. ed. Perth: 1833.

Anon. *Statement of the Differences which unhappily subsist between the Congregational Churches of Perth and Arbroath and those with whom they were formerly connected*. Perth: 1799.

Archer, Charles. *William Archer, Life, Works and Friendships*. London: George Allen and Unwin, 1931.

Backus, Isaac. *True Faith Will Produce Good Works*. Boston: D Kneeland, 1767.

Baker, William R., ed. *Evangelicalism and the Stone-Campbell Movement*. Abilene: Abilene Christian University Press, 2006.

Barbour, Margaret Fraser. *Memoir of Mrs. Stewart Sandeman by Her Daughter*. London: 1922.

Barnard, John. *The Nature and Government of the Christian Church*. London: 1761.

Baron, Carol K. "Efforts on Behalf of Democracy by Charles Ives and His Family: Their Religious Contexts." *Musical Quarterly* 87/1 (Spring 2004) 6–43.

Bebbington, David W. *Evangelicalism in Modern Britain*. London: Routledge, 1989.

Bennett, James, and David Bogue. *The History of the Dissenters*. 4 vols. 2nd ed. London: Frederick Westley and H. A. Davies, 1833.

Betjeman, John. *Collected Poems*. London: John Murray, 2006.

Binfield, Clyde. "The Coats Family and Paisley Baptists." *BQ* 36 (1995) vol. 1: 29–42, vol. 2: 80–95.

Bishop, Nathaniel. *Diary*. Acc. MS 409/5/2. Copied by his great-granddaughter, Mary Meeker Brister, 1890.

———. *Letter on Baptism*. MS 364/4/3.

Boston, Thomas. *The whole works of the late Reverend Thomas Boston, of Ettrick: now first collected and reprinted without abridgement; including his memoirs, written by himself*. Aberdeen: G. and R. King, 1848.

Brine, John. *Animadversions upon the Letters on Theron and Aspasio. Addressed to that Ingenious Author*. London: Ward, 1758.

Brown, Callum G. *Religion and Society in Scotland since 1707*. Edinburgh: Edinburgh University Press, 1997.

Brown, J. *Religious Denominations of Glasgow*. Glasgow: 1865.

Buchanan, William. *Select Exhortations Addressed to the Churches of Christ*. Dundee, 1910.

Cameron, Archibald Cowie. *The History of Fettercairn*. Edinburgh: J. and R. Parlane, 1899.

Campbell. R. L. *James Hervey, Theron and Aspasio, and the controversy aroused by it*. Edinburgh University, 1954. Unpublished thesis.

Campbell, John. "The Berean Church, Especially in Edinburgh." RSCHS 6.2 (1937).

Cantor, Geoffrey. "Dissent and Radicalism? The Case of the Sandemanians." *Enlightenment and Dissent* 10 (1991) 3–20.

———. *Michael Faraday, Sandemanian and Scientist. A Study of Science and Religion in the Nineteenth Century*. Basingstoke: Palgrave Macmillan, 1991.

———. "Reading the Book of Nature." In *Faraday Rediscovered*, edited by David Gooding and Frank A. J. L. James, 69–82. Basingstoke: Palgrave Macmillan, 1989.

———. "Why Was Faraday Excluded from the Sandemanians in 1844?" *British Journal for the History of Science* 22/4 (1989) 433–37.

Chambers, Robert. *Domestic annals of Scotland, from the reformation to the revolution 1858–1861*. Edinburgh, London: W. & R. Chambers, n.d.

Christian Songs. Latest editions, Perth, 1872. Edinburgh: 1875.

Cole, Richard C,. ed. *General Correspondence of James Boswell*. Edinburgh: Edinburgh University Press, 1997.

Conolly, Matthew F. *Biographical Dictionary of Eminent Men of Fife*. Cupar: 1866.

Cruft, Kitty, et al. *The Buildings of Scotland, Borders*. Yale: Yale University Press, 2006.

Currie, Robert, et al. *Churches and Churchgoers. Patterns of Church Growth in the British Isles since 1700*. Oxford: Clarendon, 1977.

Davie, Donald. *A Gathered Church. The Literature of the English Dissenting Interest, 1700–1930*. London: Routledge, 1978.

Davies, C. Maurice. *Unorthodox London: Or, Phases of Religious Life in the Church of England*. London: Forgotten, 2018.

Davies, Horton. *Worship and Theology in England*. Vol. 4. Grand Rapids: Eerdmans, 1996.

Dawson, Jane. *John Knox*. Yale: Yale University Press, 2015.

Dickinson, W. Croft., and Gordon Donaldson, eds. *A Source Book of Scottish History*. Vol. 3. Edinburgh: Thomas Nelson, 1954.

Dickson, Neil. *Brethren in Scotland, 1838–2000*. Carlisle: Paternoster, 2002.

Drummond, Andrew L., and James Bulloch, eds. *The Church in Late Victorian Scotland, 1874–1900*. Edinburgh: Saint Andrew, 1978.

————. *The Church in Victorian Scotland, 1843–1874.* Edinburgh: Saint Andrew, 1975.

————. *The Scottish Church, 1688–1843.* Edinburgh: Saint Andrew, 1973.

Dundas, John. *State of the processes depending against Mr. John Simson Professor of Divinity in the University of Glasgow* [. . .]. Edinburgh: Davidson and Fleming, 1728.

Dunlop, Annie I., et al. *Miscellany of the Scottish History Society 6.* Scottish History Society 3, vol. 33. Edinburgh: T. & A. Constable, 1939.

Escott, Harry. *A History of Scottish Congregationalism.* Aberdeen: Congregational Union of Scotland, 1960.

Eves, H. "Meeting Places of the Sandemanians in Boston." *Transactions of the Colonial Society of Massachusetts, 1899–1900* (1900) 109–30.

Faithfull, Pamela. "An Evaluation of an Eccentric. Matthew Allen, M.D., 1783–1845." Unpublished PhD diss. Sheffield University, 2001.

Fallow, H. F. "Two Johns, Wesley and Glas." *Proceedings of the Wesley Historical Society* 20/4 (Dec 1935) 86.

Faraday, Michael. *The Correspondence of Michael Faraday.* Edited by Frank A. J. L. James. 6 vols. London: Institute of Engineering and Technology, 1991.

Fasti Ecclesiae Scoticanae, The Succession of Ministers in the Church of Scotland from the Reformation. 8 vols. Edinburgh.

Fawcett, Arthur. *The Cambuslang Revival, Scottish Evangelical Revival of the Eighteenth Century.* Edinburgh: Banner of Truth Trust, 1971.

Ferguson, William. *Scotland, 1689 to the Present.* Edinburgh: Mercat, 1968.

Fergusson, James. *Balloon Tytler.* London: Faber and Faber, 1972.

Fernandez-Armesto, Felipe, and Derek Wilson. *Reformation: Christianity and the World, 1500–2000.* London: Bantam, 1996.

A Few Sandemanian Fragments, Letters etc. Lithographed. Perth: 1877.

Finn, Nathan A. *Introduction to Andrew Fuller, Apologetic Works.* Vol 5, *Strictures on Sandemanianism, Complete Works of Andrew Fuller.* Berlin: De Gruyter, 2016.

Fleisher, D. *William Godwin; A Study in Liberalism.* New York: A. M. Kelly, 1951.

Fuller, Andrew. *Strictures on Sandemanianism.* London: T Williams and Son, 1812.

Gadsby, William. *The Works of the Late William Gadsby.* London: Groombridge and Sons, 1851.

Gammie, Alexander. *Churches of Aberdeen.* Aberdeen: Aberdeen Daily Journal Office, 1909.

Gauldie, Enid, ed. *The Dundee Textile Industry.* Scottish History Society 4, vol. 6. Edinburgh: T. & A. Constable, 1969.

Gay, David. *The Secret Stifler, Incipient Sandemanianism and Preaching the Gospel to Sinners.* Biggleswade: CreateSpace, 2016.

Gibson, William. *Enlightenment Prelate—Benjamin Hoadly, 1676–1761.* Cambridge: James Clarke, 2004.

Gifford, John, et al., eds. *The Buildings of Scotland, Edinburgh.* Edinburgh: Harmondsworth, 1984.

Gilley, Sheridan. *Newman and His Age.* London: Darton, Longmann and Todd, 1990.

Gilmour, David. *Reminiscences of the Pen' Folk, Paisley Weavers of Other Days.* Paisley: Alex Gardner, 1873.

Glas, John. *A Narrative of the Rise and Progress of the Controversy about the National Covenants, 2nd edition with Continuation and Further Continuation.* Dundee: 1828.

————. *The Testimony of the King of Martyrs concerning His Kingdom Explained and Illustrated in Scripture Light.* Preface by Robert Ferrier. Edinburgh: Lyson, 1729.

————. *The Works of Mr John Glas, Second edition.* 5 vols. Perth: R. Morison and Son, 1782.

Gooding David, and Frank A. J. L. James. *Faraday Rediscovered.* Basingstoke: Palgrave Macmillan, 1989.

Gordon, Charlotte. *Romantic Outlaws: The Extraordinary Lives of Mary Wollstonecraft and Mary Shelley.* London: Windmill, 2016.

Graham, Henry Grey. *The Social Life of Scotland in the Eighteenth Century.* London: Adam and Charles Black, 1937.

Gray, James. *The Naked Truth.* 1729.

Haldane, Alexander. *The Lives of Robert and James Haldane.* Repr. ed. Edinburgh: Banner of Truth Trust, 1990.

Hall, James. *Travels in Scotland, by an Unusual Route.* Vol. 2. London: J. Johnson, 1807.

Hamilton, James. *Michael Faraday.* London: HarperCollins, 2002.

Hankins, Jean E. "A Different Kind of Loyalist: The Sandemanians of New England during the Revolutionary War." *New England Quarterly* 60/2 (1987) 223–49.

Hastings, James. *Encyclopaedia of Religion and Ethics.* Edinburgh: T. & T. Clark, 1908.

Hayden, Roger, ed. *The Records of a Church of Christ in Bristol, 1640–1687.* Bristol Record Society 27. Bristol: Bristol Record Society, 1974.

Henderson, G. D. *Religious Life in Seventeenth-Century Scotland.* Cambridge: Cambridge University Press, 2011.

Hindmarsh, D. Bruce. *The Spirit of Early Evangelicalism. True Religion in a Modern World.* Oxford: Oxford University Press, 2018.

Horn, Barbara. L. H., ed. *Letters of John Ramsay of Ochtertyre.* Scottish History Society series 4, vol. 3. Edinburgh: T. & A. Constable, 1966.

Hornsby, J. T. "The Case of Mr John Glas." RSCHS 6 (1937). Pages unknown

————. "John Glas (1695–1773): A Study of the Original Development and Influence Of Glasite Movement." Unpublished diss. Edinburgh University, 1936.

————. "John Glas, His Later Life and Work." RSCHS 7 (1940) 94–113.

Jenkins, Alice, ed. *Michael Faraday's Mental Exercises.* Liverpool: Liverpool University Press, 2008.

Jones, William, ed. *Sandeman-Cudworth Correspondence.* In *New Evangelical Magazine* 9. London (1823). Pages unknown.

Kemp, Daniel W., ed. *Bishop Pococke's Tours in Scotland 1747–1760.* Edinburgh: Scottish History Society, 1887.

Langdon, Samuel. *An Impartial Examination of Robert Sandeman's Letters.* Portsmouth, New Hampshire: 1765.

Larsen, Timothy, and M. Ledger-Lomas, eds. *Oxford History of Protestant Dissenting Traditions.* Oxford: Oxford University Press, 2017.

Latourette, Kenneth S. *A History of the Expansion of Christianity* 4. New York: Harper and Brothers, 1941.

Lloyd-Jones, D. Martyn. *Sandemanianism.* In *The Puritans, their Origin and Successors.* Edinburgh: Banner of Truth Trust, 1987.

Lumsden, Christine. *A Rich Inheritance, Sir William Sinclair and the Keiss Baptist Church.* Didcot: Baptist Historical Society, 2013.

Macintosh, Daniel, ed. *Letters in Correspondence by Robert Sandeman, John Glas and their contemporaries, with discourses.* Dundee: Hill and Alexander, 1851.

Mackelvie, William, et al. *Annals and Statistics of the United Presbyterian Church.* Edinburgh: Oliphant and A. Elliot, 1873.

Mackenzie, Eneas. *Historical Account of Newcastle-Upon-Tyne Including the Borough of Gateshead.* Newcastle-upon-Tyne: Mackenzie and Dent, 1827.

MacLaren, A. Allan. *Religion and Social Class; Disruption Years in Aberdeen.* London: Routledge, 1974.

MacLean, Coline, and Kenneth Veitch, eds. *Scottish Life and Society.* Vol. 12, *Religion.* Edinburgh: John Donald, 2006.

Macleod, John. *Scottish Theology.* Edinburgh: Free Church of Scotland, 1943.

Marshall, James S. *The Life and Times of Leith.* Edinburgh: John Donald, 1986.

Martin, C. P. *Recollections of the Walkerite or so-called Separatist Meeting in Dublin.* CBRF (May 1971) 2–10.

Mather, Samuel. *A modest account concerning the salutations and kissing in ancient times in a letter to a friend requesting the same, wherein Mr Sandeman's attempt to revive the holy and charitable kiss and the love feast is countered.* Boston: 1768.

McBain, James M. *Eminent Arbroathians: Being sketches historical, genealogical, and biographical, 1178–1894.* Arbroath: Brodie and Salmond, 1897.

McClendon, James. Wm. Jr. *Biography as Theology; How Life Stories Can Remake Today's Theology.* Nashville: Abingdon, 1974.

McGavin, James, et al., eds. *Historical sketches of the rise of the Scots Old Independent and the Inghamite churches: with the correspondence which led to their union.* Colne: Earnshaw, 1814.

McLean, Archibald, and William Jones. *The Works of Archibald McLean.* Montana: Kessinger, 2009.

McMillon, Lynn A. "The Quest for the Apostolic Church: A Study of the Scottish Origins of American Restorationism." Unpublished diss. Baylor University, 1972.

———. *Restoration Roots.* Dallas: Gospel Teachers, 1983.

McNaughton, William D. *Early Congregational Independency in Lowland Scotland.* Vol. 1. Glasgow: United Reformed Church Senate of Scotland, 2005.

McWhirter, Archibald. "The Kail Kirk." *Perthshire Advertiser,* Feb 9, 1949.

Middleton Murry, John. *Heaven—and Earth.* London: Jonathan Cape, 1938.

Milne, Hugh M. *Boswell's Edinburgh Journals, 1767–1786.* Edinburgh: Mercat, 2001.

Morison, J., ed. *Supplementary Volume of Letters and other documents by John Glas, Robert Sandeman and their contemporaries.* Perth: 1865.

Muirhead, Andrew. *Reformation, Dissent and Diversity.* London: Bloomsbury, 2015.

Mullan, David G. "The Early Career of John Glas." *Journal of the United Reformed Church History Society* 6/4 (1999) 233–61.

Murray, Derek B. "Baptists in Scotland before 1869." *BQ* 23/6 (1970) 251–65.

———. "An Eighteenth Century Baptismal Controversy in Scotland." In *Baptism, the New Testament and the Church, Historical and Contemporary Studies in Honour of R. E. O. White,* edited by Stanley Porter and Anthony Cross, 419–29. Sheffield: Sheffield Academic, 1999.

———. *The First Hundred Years.* Glasgow: Baptist Union of Scotland, 1969.

———. "Henry David Inglis." *BQ* 40 (2004) 310–17.

———. "The Influence of John Glas." *RSCHS* 22 (1984) 45–56.

———. "The Scotch Baptist Tradition in Britain." *BQ* 33/4 (1989) 186–98.

———. "The Social and Religious Origins of Scottish Non-Presbyterian Dissent, from 1730–1800." Unpublished diss. Saint Andrews University, 1976.

Needham, Nicholas. *Thomas Erskine of Linlathen.* Edinburgh: Rutherford House, 1990.

Nockles, Peter B. *The Oxford Movement in Context; Anglican High Churchmanship, 1760–857.* Cambridge: Cambridge University Press, 1994.

Paul, James Balfour. *Diary of George Ridpath, Minister of Stichel, 1755–1761.* Scottish History Society series 3, vol. 2. Edinburgh: T. & A. Constable, 1922.

Philip, Adam. *The Evangel in Gowrie.* Edinburgh: Oliphant Anderson and Ferrier, 1911.

Pickles, H. M. *Benjamin Ingham, Preacher amongst the Dales of Yorkshire, the Forests of Lancashire and the Fells of Cumbria.* Coventry: H. M. Pickles, 1995.

Pike, Samuel, ed. *An Epistolary Correspondence between S. P. and R. S.* London: 1764.

———. *Philosophia sacra: or, The principles of natural philosophy. Extracted from divine revelation.* 1753.

———. *A Plain and Full Account of the Christian Practices Observed by the Church Assembling in St. Martin's le Grand.* London: 1766.

———. *Some important cases of conscience answered, at the casuistical exercise, on Wednesday evenings, in Little St. Helen's, Bishopsgate-Street.* Glasgow: Robert Smith, 1762.

Pirie, Alexander. *Dissertation on Hebrew Roots.* Edinburgh: James Morrison, 1807.

Pottle, Frederick A., and Charles McWeiss. *Boswell in Extremes.* London: Heinemann, 1971.

Rack, Henry D. *Reasonable Enthusiast.* London: Methodist Publishing, 1989.

Raffe, A. "John Glas and the Development of Religious Pluralism in Scotland." *JEH* 70/3 (Apr 2019) 527–45.

Reid, Robert [Senex]. *Old Glasgow and Its Environs: Historical and Topographical.* Glasgow: D. Robertson, 1864.

Report by the Commissioners of Religious Instruction, Scotland. 12 vols. Edinburgh: Johnston, 1819–1838.

Riley, James F. *The Hammer and the Anvil, A background to Michael Faraday.* Clapham: Dalesman, 1954.

Rippon, John. *The Baptist annual register, for 1794, 1795, 1796–1797, including sketches of the state of religion among different denominations of good men at home and abroad.* London: 1797.

Rivers, Isabel. *Shaftesburian Enthusiasm and the Evangelical Revival.* In *Revival and Religion since 1700; Essays for John Walsh,* edited by Jane Garnett and Colin Matthew, 21–40. London: Hambledon Continuum, 1993.

Rorie, J. *Notes on the New Testament.* MS 318/4/1.

———. *On the Sinfulness of Eating Blood.* MS 318/4/3.

Ross, James. *A History of Congregational Independency in Scotland.* Glasgow: Hay Nisbet, 1900.

Russell, Colin A. *Michael Faraday, Physics and Faith.* Oxford Portraits in Science. Oxford: Oxford University Press, 2000.

Sampson, Fiona. *In Search of Mary Shelley: The Girl Who Wrote Frankenstein.* London: Profile, 2018.

Sandeman, Archibald. *Diary.* MS 364/1/1.

Sandeman-Barrell Papers. Boston: Massachusetts Historical Society.

Sandeman, George. *The Second Coming of the Son of Man—Is It Nigh?* N.p., 1894.

Sandeman, John Glas. *The Sandeman Genealogy.* Edinburgh: George Waterston and Sons, 1950.

Sandeman, Robert. *An Essay on Preaching.* Edinburgh: 1763.

————. "Letter from Palemon to His Father." *Dundee Chronicle Office*, 1835.

————. *Letters on Theron and Aspasio*. Edinburgh: 1757. Repr. ed., New York: John Taylor, 1838.

Sanderson, Elizabeth. *Women and Work in Eighteenth Century Edinburgh*. Basingstoke: Palgrave Macmillan, 1996.

Saumarez Smith, John, ed. *A Spy In The Bookshop: Letters Between Heywood Hill and John Saumerez Smith 1965–74*. London: Frances Lincoln, 2006.

Scotland, Nigel. *Sectarian Religion in Contemporary Britain*. Carlisle: Send the Light, 2000.

Scott, James. *Notebook*. Unpublished scrapbook, Dundee University Archives.

Scott, Walter. *Guy Mannering*. London: Penguin Classics, 2003.

Sefton, Henry. "Revolution to Disruption." In *Studies in the History of Worship in Scotland*, edited by Duncan Forrester and Douglas M. Murray, 65–78. Edinburgh: T. & T. Clark, 1984.

————. "Rev Robert Wallace, an Early Moderate." RSCHS (1968) 1–22.

Sell, Alan P. F. "John Chater: From Independent Minister to Sandemanian Author." *BQ* 31.3 (July 1985) 100–117.

Seymour, Miranda. *Mary Shelley*. London: Grove, 2000.

Sharp, L. W. *Early Letters of Robert Wodrow, 1698–1709*. Scottish History Society series 3, vol. 24. Edinburgh: T. & A. Constable, 1937.

Shaw, Duncan, ed. *Reformation and Revolution; Essays Presented to the Very Reverend Hugh Watt, D.D.* Edinburgh: Saint Andrew, 1967.

Shelley, Mary. *Frankenstein: Or the Modern Prometheus*. London: Penguin, 2003.

Shenton, Tim. *An Iron Pillar, Life and Times of William Romaine*. Darlington: Evangelical Press, 2004.

Short, L. B. "William Christie and the First Unitarian Church in Scotland." *Transactions of the Unitarian Historical Society* 14 (1967). Pages unknown.

Simplex [John Young, W. S.]. *The Church of God*. In *Christian Advocate and Scotch Baptist Repository*. Beverley (August 1850).

Simpson, Edmund K. "Independency and Its Eclipse." *Evangelical Quarterly* 5.4 (1933) 365–78.

Sinclair, John, ed. *The New Statistical Account of Scotland*. 15 vols. Edinburgh: Blackwood, 1845.

————. *The Statistical Account of Scotland 1791–1799*. Wakefield: EP, 1973–83.

Small, R. *History of the Congregations of the United Presbyterian Church 1733–1900*. Edinburgh: David M. Small, 1904.

Smith, David C. *The Historians of Perth*. Perth: John Christie, 1906.

Smith, John H. *The Perfect Rule of the Christian Religion; A History of Sandemanianism in the Eighteenth Century*. Albany, NY: State University of New York Press, 2008.

————. "'Sober Dissent' and 'Spirited Conduct' The Sandemanians and the American Revolution, 1765–1783." *Historical Journal of Massachusetts* 28 (2000) 142–65.

Smout, T. C. *A History of the Scottish People 1560–1830*. London: HarperCollins, 1969.

Spurlock, R. Scott. *Cromwell and Scotland; Conquest and Religion, 1650–660*. Edinburgh: John Donald, 2007.

Stanley, F. "The Glassite-Sandemanian Movement in the Eighteenth Century British Atlantic World." Unpublished diss. Oxford University, 2004.

Starkie, Andrew. *The Church of England and the Bangorian Controversy, 1716–1721*. Woodbridge: Boydell, 2007.

Stark, Werner. *The Sociology of Religion.* Vol. 2, *Sectarian Religion.* London: Routledge and Keegan Paul, 1967.

Stayner, C. "The Sandemanian Loyalists." *Collections of the Nova Scotia Historical Society* 29 (1951) 62–123.

Thompson, David M. *Let Sects and Parties Fall.* Birmingham: Berean, 1980.

Thompson, Edward P. *The Making of the English Working Class.* London: Penguin, 1969.

Thomson, D. P., and Daniel Patterson, eds. *The Scottish Churches' Handbook.* Dunfermline: Lassodie, 1933.

Torrance, Thomas F. *Scottish Theology; From John Knox to John McLeod Campbell.* Edinburgh: T. & T. Clark International, 1996.

————. *Thomas Ayton's The Original Constitution of the Christian Church.* In *Reformation and Revolution; Essays Presented to the Very Reverend Hugh Watt, D.D.,* edited by Duncan Shaw. Edinburgh: Saint Andrew, 1967. Pages unknown.

Walker, Ralph, ed. *Private Papers of James Boswell.* London: William Heinemann, 1952.

Walker, Williston. *The Sandemanians of New England.* American Historical Association Annual Report for 1901, Washington, DC, 1902.

Warren, Austen. *The Elder Henry James.* New York: Macmillan, 1934.

Waterston, Charles. *Perth Entrepreneurs: The Sandemans of Springland.* Perth: Libraries and Lifelong Learning, 2008.

Waterston, George. *Notes on the Book of Revelation.* Edinburgh: 1893.

Watson, Nigel. *Seal of Success; the story of a Scottish family business George Waterston & Sons Ltd 1752–2002.* Edinburgh: George Waterston and Sons, 2002.

Watt, Douglas. *The Price of Scotland; Darien, Union and the Wealth of Nations.* Edinburgh: Luath, 2007.

Watters, A. C. *History of the British Churches of Christ.* Birmingham: Berean, 1948.

Watts, Michael. *The Dissenters.* Vol. 1. Oxford: Clarendon, 1978.

Wesley, John. *A Sufficient Answer to the Letters the Author of Letters on Theron and Aspasio in a Letter to the Author.* London: 1760.

Whitebrook, Peter. *William Archer, A Biography.* London: Methuen, 1993.

Whitley, Laurence. *A Great Grievance; Ecclesiastical Lay Patronage in Scotland Until 1750.* Eugene, OR: Wipf and Stock, 2013.

Whyte, Ian D. *Scotland before the Industrial Revolution: An Economic and Social History c. 1050–c. 1750.* London: Longman, 1995.

Wilson, Bryan, ed. *Patterns of Sectarianism; Organisation and Ideology in Social and Religious Movement.* London: Heinemann, 1967.

————. *Religious Sects; A Sociological Study.* London: Liberex, 1970.

Wilson, Walter. *History and Antiquities of the Dissenting Churches and Meetings-Houses of London.* Vol. 3. London: Button, 1808.

White, Gavin. "Hutchinsonianism in Eighteenth Century Scotland." *RSCHS* 21 (1982) 157–69.

Wodrow, Robert. *Correspondence.* 3 vols. Edinburgh: 1842.

Yeager, Jonathan M. *Enlightened Evangelicalism; The Life and Thought of John Erskine.* Oxford: Oxford University Press, 2011.

Yuille, George. *History of the Baptists in Scotland.* Glasgow: Baptist Union of Scotland, 1926.

Subject Index

Author Index